DON'T BE A DUMMY BEHIND THE WHEEL

by

Mihai Noaje

Self-published by the author

Buffalo, New York

First Edition
Self-published by the author
Buffalo, New York
www.notadummy.com

ISBN (Paperback): 979-8-9993485-0-0
ISBN (eBook): 979-8-9993485-1-7
Library of Congress Control Number (Paperback): 2025913490

Some illustrations in this book were generated or enhanced using artificial
intelligence tools and further edited by the author. Final text editing and refinement
were also assisted by artificial intelligence and further polished by the author.

Printed in the United States of America

DEDICATION

For everyone who's ever asked, *"Am I doing this right?"*
Keep learning and stay safe—one mile at a time.

CONTENTS

DISCLAIMER

Oh, hey—here's the fine print:

1. **This Isn't Driver's Ed (Officially)**
   This book isn't a substitute for a certified driving course, test prep, or whatever your local DMV requires to hand over that shiny license. Think of it as the unofficial guide—the sidekick to your state manual. Use it to boost your skills, not replace the legal stuff.

2. **U.S. Roads, U.S. Rules (Mostly)**
   This book was written with American roads, signs, and driving laws in mind. If you're reading from outside the U.S., some tips might not apply—or might even get you honked at. Always double-check your local rules before trying anything from these pages abroad.

3. **Unique Drivers, Unique Situations**
   Due to the nature of driving, the opinions and advice in this book might not apply perfectly to your road reality. Everyone's vehicle, reflexes, and environment are different, so trust your best judgment (and local laws!).

4. **Totally Fictional, 100% Imaginary**
   If anything in this book sounds like a stunt, it's been performed by fictional professional drivers on fictional closed tracks—do not try them at home (or anywhere else).

5. **Translation: Don't Do Stupid Stuff**
   Always obey the law, exercise preventive driving, and maintain control of your car. If your gut says it's a bad idea, spoiler alert—it probably is.

6. **Stay Safe & Keep It Fun**
   This book aims to help you steer clear of trouble, not steer you into it. Stay alert, stay responsible, and enjoy the ride!

Props for actually reading the fine print! Now get out there, buckle up, and keep driving— just skip the big-screen stunts, all right?

Safe travels!

NO, SERIOUSLY...
WHY DID I WRITE THIS?

A Coffee-Spill Epiphany

Around 7:30 a.m., on a drizzly Tuesday. I'm getting on the freeway, my thumb over my phone to pick what I want to hear next. One tap, eyes off the road for half a breath, then bam! The SUV ahead jams its brakes. I stomp mine, and the phone cartwheels into the footwell. As it does, my heart starts banging harder than the music. When the panic fog lifts, I realize: 1) my bumper is maybe three inches from theirs, 2) my cup of coffee made a perfect spin before spraying across the dash, and 3) I should have listened to my better judgment and not acted like a dummy behind the wheel.

Cue facepalm. If spilling the coffee felt messy, imagine explaining a fender-bender to insurance—or worse. That close encounter is just a glimpse of the many split-second happenings on U.S. roads that upend families' lives. According to the U.S. Department of Transportation, more than 3,300 people die in crashes caused by distracted driving, and approximately 289,000 people are injured. Think about it, that is about 900 injuries per day!

At that moment, I recalled the many times I'd watched drivers make sloppy mistakes, completely skip over the basics everyone's supposed to know, and turn everyday roads into danger zones. You know, those rules that seem so obvious to follow but somehow innocently go over everyone's head. What if there was a guide that helped out in more ways than one? That helped you not only ace the driving test but also helped you deal with the real-world "uh-ohs" that the DMV booklet ignores. Right then, the idea smacked me in the face harder than a double espresso! What we really need, I thought, is a driver's ed guide with some zest—one that gives rookie drivers the know-how to handle those "yikes, now what?" curveballs real traffic throws. This book? Yep, that's the guide!

Why Your Uncle's "Back in My Day" Advice Isn't Enough

- **Roads Evolve Faster Than Memes**: Roundabouts, diverging-diamond interchanges, e-scooters zooming at 20 mph—none of that was on the test in 1985.
- **Teen Drivers Are *Still* Double-Risky**: Novice drivers are **twice as likely as adults** to land in a fatal crash.

- **Driving-School Time Crunch**: State courses race through rules like a Netflix skip intro; plenty of real-world situations never make the syllabus.

What This Book *Is*

- A **non-judgmental guide** that talks to you like a savvy older sibling.
- A **glove-box companion**—grab a quick tip while your fries cool.
- A **one-stop reference** covering situations your driving instructor never had time for (hydroplaning, ramp meters, deer dodging, etc.).
- A **bad-habit detox** for rolling stops, cell-phone drifts, and blinker amnesia.
- A **reboot** for lapsed drivers who last touched a steering wheel in the times when people were still buying DVD's.

And What It *Isn't*

- A lecture from a traffic-court judge.
- A 400-page DMV manual that doubles as a doorstop.
- A replacement for local laws—always peek at your state's quirks.
- A magic shield—practice still matters.
- A judgment zone—no finger-wagging here.

What You'll Get from This Book

- Basics of how cars work
- Essentials of driving
- Real-life driving skills
- Secrets to becoming an experienced driver
- And more!

My Promise to You

This book will be your co-pilot, glovebox pal, and mentor on the road.

This book is the experienced driving instructor you turn to when you need a little reminder or confidence booster to tackle an unknown or tricky driving scenario. Everything you need, all in one place—and all laid out in simple, logical steps.

My goal? To help you make smart decisions that will keep you and others safe on the road.

Driving is as an adventure, not a chore—stay curious and keep learning!

Who Is This Book For?

- **This book is designed to help new drivers** prepare for the *real* world of driving.

- **This book is also a great pit stop for those who already have a license** but feel a little rusty or unsure behind the wheel.

- **This book will teach you how to become a safer driver—** whether you're a total newbie, have held your license for a while, or fall somewhere in between.

Have fun and enjoy the ride!

HOW TO GET THE MOST
OUT OF THIS BOOK

Content Breakdown – 5 Parts

- Essentials of driving
- Real-life driving skills
- Secrets to becoming an experienced driver
- Exploring defensive driving and other safety aspects
- Staying safe when you're not driving

Short Chapters, Real Skills

Each chapter is like a mini-lesson you can read in five minutes. Seriously. They're designed to stand alone, so you can tackle exactly what you need—when you need it. Need help parallel parking? Flip to that chapter. Merging stresses you out? There's a chapter for that, too.

How to Use This Book

- If you're just starting out: read from the beginning to build your foundation.
- If you've got your license and want to level up: skip around and read what you need.
- Bookmark the chapters you know you'll come back to (hello, roundabouts).

Pro Tips & Common Mistakes

These callouts throughout the book aren't just filler—they're golden!
- **Pro Tips** are here to give you shortcuts, insider advice, and real-world driving wisdom that makes things easier.
- **Common Mistakes** are like gentle nudges to help you dodge those all-too-common blunders that most rookies (and even seasoned drivers) make.

Expect a little sarcasm, a few bad jokes, and a lot of metaphors. Why? Because learning is easier when it's fun. You'll laugh, you'll nod, and you might even cringe at that one story—but you'll remember it all.

PART I:

HERE ARE THE BASICS

1. WHY GETTING A DRIVER'S LICENSE?

Have you ever waited for a friend to take you home? Found yourself missing the last train? Just wanted to get home and get into your sweats? Welcome to the life of not having a car, where you rely on someone else's wheels or a Sunday bus. Absolutely, rideshare apps fill a gap, and a bike or scooter can handle short commutes, but nothing says independence like having your own license.

In this chapter, we'll discover why a little piece of plastic that says you can drive still has value for people, even as many preach the good word about public transit, carpooling, or digital workplaces.

THE FREEDOM FACTOR

Independence & Convenience
- **Errands on Your Timeline**: No more borrowing cars or juggling bus schedules. Need groceries at 10 p.m.? Go. Feel like a spontaneous midnight milkshake run? No problem! License and keys in hand, you're set.
- **Beyond Boundaries**: A license opens up distant friends' houses, job interviews in the next town, or those scenic overlooks you can't reach via subway.

Just Try a Road Trip
- **Spontaneous Getaways**: Nothing beats packing the trunk, blasting tunes, and hitting the open road without pre-booking tickets or waiting for someone else's schedule.
- **Stop Where You Want**: See an interesting roadside diner? Pull over. Spot a scenic vista? Park and snap selfies. You're the captain of this voyage.

Pro Tip: Celebrate Freedom
That tiny plastic card is your ticket to on-the-spot adventures. Use it and enjoy the extra wiggle room in life!

Common Mistake: Taking Freedom for Granted
Once you've got the license, don't forget the responsibility that comes with it. There's a reason it's considered an "adulting" milestone.

OPPORTUNITIES & ACCESS

More Job Options
- **Commute Flexibility**: Many workplaces are far from bus routes or require early/late hours. Driving there can be easier than juggling sporadic buses or hoping for an affordable rideshare.
- **Company Requirements**: Some gigs (delivery, sales calls, event set-up) need a valid license. Without it, you might miss out on roles that involve travel or on-site visits.

Broader Reach
- **Better-Paying Gigs**: Sometimes, higher wages or cooler opportunities lie outside your public transport zone. With a license, you can chase them.
- **Educational & Social Events**: Attending workshops, clubs, or out-of-town seminars becomes smoother—no hassling a friend for a lift.

Pro Tip: Think Long-Term
Even if you live in a walkable city now, life changes: career shifts, moving into the suburbs, or having kids. A license stays useful no matter where you end up.

LIFE SKILLS & GROWTH

Responsibility 101
- **Car Care & Budgeting**: Owning or even borrowing a car means tracking fuel costs, scheduling maintenance, and planning repairs—soft skills that boost adulting confidence.
- **Road Etiquette & Safety**: Understanding traffic rules fosters courtesy, empathy for other road users (including cyclists and pedestrians), and a sense of mutual respect on the streets.

Personal Development
- **Problem-Solving**: Flat tires, engine troubles, or tricky parking spots teach resourcefulness.
- **Confidence Builder**: Conquering that first solo highway merge or parallel parking on a busy street can make you feel on top of the world.

Common Mistake: Ignoring The Learning Curve
A few hours in the driver's seat rarely means mastery. Embrace practice sessions—safe driving is a skill that matures over time.

LIFE ON THE ROAD TODAY

Public Transport vs. Private Car
- **Urban Exceptions**: If subways and buses are top-tier where you live, a car might be less critical, until you want to haul heavy groceries or travel off the grid.
- **Ridesharing & Apps**: Handy, yes, but surge pricing or service downtime can sting. Plus, you rely on someone else to show up.

Shift in Driver Demographics
- **Younger Drivers**: Studies show fewer teens get licensed right at 16 these days—citing costs, eco-concerns, or the ease of online shopping.
- **Still a Vital Skill**: Nonetheless, each year millions of new drivers find that a license is essential for big reasons: jobs, freedom, and personal plans.

Pro Tip: Keep Options Open
Even if you prefer cycling or carpooling daily, a license acts like a safety net for emergencies, unexpected errands, or nighttime rides.

WHY BOTHER WITH THE TEST?

"But I Can Just Ride, or Use an App"
- **Scheduling Stress**: Late buses, missed connections, or a rideshare driver canceling last-minute can ruin your day.
- **Group Road Trips**: When you can drive, you're not left out if your friend group decides to rent a car and do a long trek.

Summed-Up Perks
- **Independence**: Go where you want, whenever.
- **Opportunity**: Unlock job interviews, weekend adventures, and far-flung family visits.
- **Skill for Life**: Even if you switch to e-bikes or scooters, that license remains an asset in your back pocket.

Common Mistake: Delay, Delay, Delay
Putting off learning to drive may seem fine now, but if an unplanned opportunity demands it (like a spontaneous out-of-town job), lack of a license can block your path.

Getting your driver's license might not be rocket science, but it's undoubtedly an essential piece in the adulting puzzle. Whether you dream of **late-night store runs**, **spontaneous road trips**, or simply **not missing out on a better job** across town, a driver's license is the pocket-sized symbol of freedom, independence, and all the places you can go.

Whether you're already flipping through the driver's manual or still deciding if you even want a car, the fact that you're reading this book means you're looking to learn and grow. That curiosity and sense of responsibility will guide you well on the road ahead—because being a "good driver" means more than completing the test.

2. HOW TO GET A DRIVER'S LICENSE?

Alright, alright, alright... so, you've decided you *do* want to sit behind the wheel—great! Now, let's talk about **how to become a licensed driver**. Don't worry—this process might sound intimidating, but we will go through it **step-by-step**.

STEP 1: BOOKMARK YOUR LOCAL DMV

Yes, the DMV—home of legendary queues and questionable vending machines. Luckily, this is the digital age, so your smartphone or laptop is your best friend. A quick search for "[Your State] DMV" should take you straight to:

- **Forms & Manuals:** Download your state's official driving manual, which outlines local laws, road signs, and test procedures. It's usually short and sweet, but don't toss this book aside for that one! Think of their manual as the appetizer and *this* book as the main course.
- **Appointment Scheduling:** Many DMVs now let you book a time slot online, saving you from standing in line all day.

STEP 2: GET YOUR LEARNER'S PERMIT

In most places, you'll need to pass a **written test** to earn a learner's permit. This involves:

- **Registration & Fees**: Bring your ID, proof of residency, and money for the permit fee.
- **Vision Test**: Yes, you actually need to see where you're going.
- **Written Exam**: Covers traffic laws, signs, and safe-driving basics. Some states waive this requirement if you've taken an approved driver's ed course—check local rules.

Common Mistake: Overlooking Permit Restrictions
Once you get your permit, you can drive with a licensed adult. But watch those restrictions: many states limit your driving at night or how many passengers you can have. Violations are no joke—DMVs crack down extra hard on learner's permit holders.

STEP 3: PRACTICE, PRACTICE, PRACTICE

You've got the learner's permit—now it's time to rack up some serious behind-the-wheel hours. Most states require a certain number of supervised hours (and some specifically at night or in bad weather) before you can take your road test. Here's where you can really shine:

- **Friends & Family**: Great for free tips, but be cautious. Like a young baseball player learning a swing, if you pick up bad habits early, they're tough to unlearn.
- **Professional Driving Lessons**: Think of these as coaching sessions with a pro. They'll teach you proper posture, steering techniques, and everything you need to feel confident.

We're raising a virtual glass of a non-alcoholic beverage to your success—because, trust me, your future self will thank you for laying a solid foundation now.

STEP 4: SCHEDULE & TAKE THE ROAD TEST

Once you've met all the requirements, it's showtime:

- **Prove Your Skills**: Starting, stopping, signaling, turning, parking, reversing—you name it.
- **Show Safe Habits**: Adjusting mirrors, checking blind spots, obeying signs, and not panicking when a squirrel darts out (seriously, it happens).
- **Stay Calm**: Nerves are normal, so take a deep breath. The examiner isn't out to get you—they just want to make sure you're road-ready.

Nail this test, and you'll walk (or rather, *drive*) away with your brand-new license, complete with that ear-to-ear grin in your photo.

STEP 5: CELEBRATE YOUR SHINY NEW LICENSE

Yes, you did it! You're officially a licensed driver. This is just the beginning of your journey, though—every hour behind the wheel helps build your "muscle memory," turning conscious skills into reflexes.

- **Nerd Fact**: According to Malcolm Gladwell's *Outliers*, you need about 10,000 hours to become an expert at something.
- **Fun Fact**: The AAA Foundation for Traffic Safety says the average American drives around 17,600 minutes every year (about 300 hours). At that rate, it might take 34 years to become a "driving expert". Talk about a long-haul project!

But hey, don't let the big numbers scare you! Every minute you drive more mindfully, you improve. Whether you're merging onto a busy highway or parallel parking on a crowded street, keep practicing, stay open to learning, and always aim to be better—and safer—than you were the day before.

Pro Tip: Be a Long-Term Learner
Even a "perfect" driver can improve. Conditions change, technology evolves, and your reflexes sharpen with every mile.

QUICK TIPS & TAKEAWAYS

1. **Know Your DMV**: Their website is your go-to for rules, forms, and scheduling.
2. **Study the Basics**: The written test is easier if you truly *understand* the laws, not just memorize them.
3. **Practice with Purpose**: Learn from a pro if possible, and drive in varied conditions (nighttime, rain, quiet back roads, etc.).
4. **Stay Calm, Drive On**: The road test isn't a pop quiz. You have prepared, so be confident!
5. **Keep Improving**: A license isn't the end; it's your ticket to a lifelong journey of learning behind the wheel.

Are you ready to leave those unreliable public bus schedules and crazy Uber rides behind you? At first, each step may seem challenging, but with patience and determination, you'll have the license before you know it.

Buckle up—this adventure is only getting started!

3. I GOT IT!... NOW WHAT?

A.K.A. "Welcome to Your Next Level of Adulting!"

Congratulations! You've just acquired a new "superpower," and with great power comes great responsibility. (Yes, that's a nod to Spider-Man—but it applies perfectly to driving, too.) Now that you hold a license, it's easy to feel like an expert driver. The truth? Every time you get behind the wheel, you share the road with countless others whose safety depends on *your* actions. That's pretty big stuff.

So, let's talk about what comes next—and how to keep that shiny new license from inflating your ego or getting you into trouble.

INSURANCE AND CAR REGISTRATION ESSENTIALS

Now that you have your license, you also need the official paperwork that keeps you—and your car—legit on the road:

INSURANCE

- **Required Coverage**: In most places, driving without insurance is illegal. This usually includes liability coverage to protect you (and others) in case of an accident.
- **Cost Factors**: Age, driving history, and even your ZIP code can affect your premium. New drivers often pay more, so shop around or consider being added to a family plan.

Pro Tip: Discounts Galore
Ask about good student discounts or defensive-driving class discounts. Insurance companies love safe drivers—and your wallet will, too.

CAR REGISTRATION

- **Vehicle Title & Registration**: You need a valid registration to legally drive. Check your state's DMV website for forms and fees, and don't forget to renew on time—no one likes surprise penalties!
- **Keep Paperwork Handy**: Keep proof of registration and insurance in your glove box (and maybe a scanned copy on your phone for quick reference).

Basically, you can't just drive off in a shiny set of wheels without handling these grown-up details. The steps above might feel tedious, but once they're done, you'll climb into the driver's seat feeling much more legit.

THE MAKE-IT-OR-BREAK-IT PHASE

Your early days as a licensed driver are prime time for building muscle memory and locking in good habits. Everything you do—checking mirrors, using blinkers, staying aware of speed limits—becomes second nature.

Don't skimp on these basics:
- **Shoulder Checks**: A quick look over your shoulder can prevent a costly collision.
- **Blinkers, Blinkers, Blinkers**: Other drivers aren't mind readers. Signal your intentions, always.
- **Watch Your Speed**: Driving too slowly can be as hazardous as speeding, so practice matching the traffic flow without losing caution.

Common Mistake: Overconfidence
Feeling invincible behind the wheel can lead to sloppy habits. Stay humble and keep refining those basics you learned in driver's ed.

ROOKIE DRIVER REALITIES

Keep in mind that nobody on the road knows you're a newbie. Sometimes you'll inch below the speed limit (maybe unfamiliar roads or nasty weather), and impatient drivers may tailgate or honk. Don't panic or stomp the gas in fear. Instead:
- **Stay Cool**: Remember, they were new once, too.
- **Right Lane, Right Choice**: If you're on the highway and not in a hurry, stick to the far-right lane.
- **Pull Over (When Safe)**: If you're on a single-lane road and cars are stacking up behind you, finding a safe spot to pull over can ease the tension.

Pro Tip: Drive at Your Own Pace
Remember, every driver out there was a beginner once—just keep your cool and let impatient drivers pass you. You'll be surprised how much more relaxed you feel when you're not looking in the rearview mirror every five seconds, worried about the speed demons behind you.

PRACTICING ON DIFFERENT ROADS & CONDITIONS

Don't limit yourself to the same short route every day. Vary your driving experiences:

- **City Streets vs. Highways**: Learn to handle both stop-and-go traffic and high-speed merges.
- **Different Speeds**: Master city limits, rural roads, and freeways.
- **Weather Smorgasbord**: Rain, fog, snow—experience them all (safely!) to gain confidence.
- **Nighttime Driving**: Roads look totally different after dark; it's a whole new skill set.

Pro Tip: Level Up Your Driving Game
Think of every new driving experience—rainy roads, nighttime drives, busy intersections—as unlocking a new skill. The more challenges you face, the stronger and more confident you become behind the wheel.

SHARING THE ROAD

No, you're not alone out there. Motorcycles, bicycles, pedestrians, and fellow drivers are all in this together:

- **Look Out for Others:** Cyclists and pedestrians can be harder to spot, especially in bad weather or low light.
- **Stay Defensive:** Assume the unexpected. If that car ahead brakes suddenly, you're prepared to react smoothly.
- **Politeness Counts:** A quick wave to let someone merge or cross doesn't cost a thing and keeps the roads friendlier.

That license in your wallet is **just the start**. The more you drive, the more natural it becomes. Soon enough, **you'll spot rookie mistakes** from a mile away. And guess what? As you get more experienced, **others might label *you* the pro**—but don't let it get to your head!

Stay curious, stay humble, and remember that every mile you log is another step in mastering your new superpower. Enjoy the ride, and welcome to your next level of adulting!

4. TALK LIKE A DRIVER:
DEFINITIONS YOU ACTUALLY NEED TO KNOW

Ever found yourself nodding along when a friend casually mentions "superelevation" or "carpool lanes," while secretly thinking, "Uh, what language is that?" Fear not—this chapter is your personal decoder ring for all the weird, wacky, and downright confusing terms you'll encounter on your driving adventures.

In addition to car parts and basic driving concepts, we'll also tackle road construction lingo and common driving strategies, so you're never left scratching your head when someone says "median strip" or "hairpin curve." We'll keep it fun, straightforward, and maybe even a little sassy—because learning doesn't have to be boring.

Below, you'll find an **alphabetical glossary** of terms that pop up frequently in manuals, traffic reports, or everyday car talk. Some entries include fun facts, examples, or jokes—because, well, that's just how we roll.

A

ABS (Anti-Lock Braking System): A safety system that prevents your wheels from locking when you brake hard. Instead of skidding like a cartoon character, you maintain steering control (and dignity).

Fun Note: Feeling a pulsation in the brake pedal when ABS activates? Totally normal—don't freak out!

Acceleration: When you press the gas and feel that forward surge. Whether you leave other cars behind or they leave you behind depends on what's under your hood.

Acceleration Lane: An extra lane on a highway entrance ramp where you can speed up (within reason) to match the main traffic flow. Think of it as your runway to merge onto the highway stage.

Apex (in Cornering): The innermost point of a curve on the road (or racetrack) that drivers aim to "clip" for the smoothest, most efficient path. On public roads, please corner safely—no racecar heroics.

Asphalt: A common road surface material made from gravel and bitumen, often called "blacktop." Fresh asphalt can be blissfully smooth, but beware of tar lines on hot days—they can turn into slippery surprises.

B

Blind Spot: That sneaky area around your car that side and rear-view mirrors can't capture. A well-timed shoulder check is your secret weapon against collision surprises.

Blinker/Turn Signal: The flashing light that says, "I'm turning or changing lanes." If only everyone used them, telepathy wouldn't be a required skill on the road.

Brake Pads: The parts that press against brake discs to slow your car. They wear down over time—like sneakers, except far more vital to your survival.

C

Car Registration: Official documentation showing that your car is legally recognized and up-to-date with local authorities. Renew it on time, or risk late fees (and potential facepalms).

Carpool Lane (a.k.a. High-Occupancy Vehicle Lane/HOV Lane): A restricted lane (often during peak times) for vehicles with a driver and at least one passenger. Great if you're traveling with friends—less great if you're the solo type.

Catalytic Converter: A device in your exhaust system that reduces harmful emissions. Think of it as the bouncer at the tailpipe club, turning away nasty pollutants before they party in the atmosphere.

Clutch (Manual Transmission): The pedal that disconnects the engine from the wheels so you can change gears. Master it, and you're a driving wizard; fail, and you might stall out in awkward places.

Collision Coverage: Insurance that helps pay to repair or replace your own car if it's damaged in an accident. It's often optional, but if you'd rather not empty your wallet after a fender-bender, it's worth considering.

Comprehensive Insurance: Optional coverage for non-collision incidents (vandalism, hail, theft). Not mandatory everywhere, but highly recommended if you like sleeping well at night.

Concrete: Another common road surface material, often used for highways and bridges. It can be more durable than asphalt, but sometimes a bit noisier to drive on.

Construction Signs: Temporary traffic signs (usually orange with black symbols) that warn of road work zones. They come in various shapes, so pay close attention if you value your tires and suspension.

Corner: A sharp turn in a road, often with limited visibility due to buildings, parked cars, or other structures. Approach carefully; you never know what's around the bend.

Crossroad (a.k.a. Intersection): Where two or more roads cross each other at the same level. Could be a four-way stop, traffic light, roundabout, or an exciting free-for-all if signage is unclear.

Curve: A bend in the road that provides a gradual change of direction. A mild arc is usually easy to navigate, but still requires your full attention—no daydreaming allowed.

D

Dedicated Turning Lane: A lane reserved for vehicles turning left or right. It gives turning cars a place to queue without slowing down through-traffic—everyone wins.

Defensive Driving: A driving strategy of actively scanning the road, anticipating hazards, and avoiding other people's mistakes. Think of it as "Jedi mode" for the highway.

Dipstick: That metal rod in your engine's oil reservoir used to check oil levels. Also, a euphemism for a reckless driver, but we'll stay polite.

Divider (Median): A barrier (concrete, grass, guardrail, etc.) separating opposite lanes of traffic. Keeps you from playing chicken with oncoming cars—always a plus.

DMV (Department of Motor Vehicles): The place you love to hate—where you snag your driver's license, vehicle registration, and maybe a mild tension headache. Thankfully, many DMVs now let you do things online, so you can avoid those legendary lines.

Drivetrain: All the parts that deliver power from the engine to the wheels (transmission, driveshaft, axles, etc.). Without it, your car is just an expensive noise machine.

E

Engine: Your car's heart, converting fuel into motion. Treat it well with regular check-ups, and it will usually return the favor by not leaving you stranded at 2 A.M.

Expressway: Controlled-access highway—fewer stoplights, designated on-ramps, and typically higher speed limits. A cousin of the highway, but sometimes with different signage or usage rules.

Exit Lane (a.k.a. Off-Ramp Lane): A short, dedicated lane allowing traffic to safely slow down and leave a major road without clogging up through-traffic.

F

Fast Lane (a.k.a. Passing Lane): The lane closest to the center of a multi-lane road, intended for faster-moving vehicles or those actively passing. If you're dawdling, shift over and let speed demons pass.

Fork Road: A place where one thoroughfare splits into two. Picture a big "Y" in the road—choose wisely to avoid an accidental detour.

Four-Wheel Drive (4WD): Power delivered to all four wheels simultaneously, usually found on trucks and SUVs for off-roading or tackling tricky weather. Perfect for that muddy backroad challenge.

Front-Wheel Drive (FWD): A setup where the engine powers only the front wheels. Good for everyday driving, decent traction in wet conditions—not exactly rally-car material, but it does the job.

Fuel Injection: A system spraying fuel directly into the engine intake for better efficiency and performance, much like a skilled barista adding just the right amount of espresso.

Fog Lights: Special front lights aimed low to help you see in fog, mist, or heavy rain—without the glare of regular high beams bouncing back at you. Use them wisely; in clear weather, they'll just blind other drivers.

G

GPS (Global Positioning System): Your digital map guide. Usually helpful, but can occasionally lead you astray ("Turn right into this lake!"). A good dose of common sense is still required.

Governor (Speed Governor): A device or software that limits your vehicle's max speed. Parents of teenagers might wish for a super-aggressive version.

Guardrail: A metal or concrete barrier to keep cars from veering off the road or into oncoming traffic. Like a safety net for those "oops" moments.

H

Hairpin Curve: A very sharp U-shaped curve, often seen in mountainous areas or rally stages. Approach with caution—you don't want to meet oncoming traffic at speed!

Hazard Lights: When all four turn signals flash to warn others you're moving slow, pulled over, or in distress. Not to be used as a "parking spot saver," please.

HAWK Beacon (High-intensity Activated crossWalK): A special traffic signal activated by pedestrians or emergency vehicles. It goes through flashing yellow, solid yellow, and then red to stop traffic, letting folks cross safely. Don't freak if you've never seen one—just follow the lights as you would at any signal.

High-Occupancy Lane: See **Carpool Lane**.

Highway: A high-speed, high-capacity thoroughfare with multiple lanes in each direction, no stoplights, and designated inlets/outlets. Opposing directions are separated by barriers or wide medians. Cyclists and pedestrians? Typically forbidden.

Horsepower: A unit of engine power—1 HP = the ability to move 550 lbs one foot in one second. More HP often means more "vroom," but it won't fix bad driving habits.

Hydroplaning: That heart-stopping moment when your tires lose contact with the road surface due to water, causing you to "float." Slowing down in wet conditions and having decent tire tread drastically reduces your chances of doing an accidental Olympic ice-skating routine on the highway.

I

Idle: When your engine's running but the car's not moving—like waiting at a red light, pondering what's for dinner.

Ignition: The system that starts your car. Could be a key turn or push-button. Without it, you're not going anywhere—like forgetting your Netflix password on a Friday night.

Interchange: A grade-separated junction (using overpasses, under-passes, ramps) where at least one road can pass without crossing the traffic streams of another. Think of it like a multi-level highway puzzle that keeps traffic flowing.

J

Jack: A device for lifting your car off the ground so you can change a tire or investigate that rattling noise underneath. Use with caution—gravity is unforgiving.

Junction: A point where two roads join together. Could be a T-junction, Y-junction, or some other shape, but the idea is the same: roads converge, traffic decisions ensue.

Jump-Start: Reviving a dead battery using a healthy one and some jumper cables. Like a jolt of coffee for your car.

K

Key Fob: The remote that locks/unlocks your car and may even start it. When its battery dies, you'll be reminded cars used to have purely mechanical keys—old-school style!

L

Lane Discipline: Keeping to your lane, signaling when changing lanes, and avoiding meandering over lines. Sloppy lane discipline is a top cause of side-swipes and headaches.

Lane Splitting: When motorcycles ride between lanes of cars. Legal in some places, illegal in others. Either way, watch for them before you switch lanes.

Learner's Permit: That magical slip of paper (or card) allowing you to legally drive under certain conditions—usually with a licensed adult present. It's your warm-up phase for real-world driving before the big road test.

Liability Insurance: Covers damage you cause to others in a crash. It's usually the legal minimum—like wearing shoes in a restaurant: a courtesy to everyone else.

M

Median Strip: A line or area separating opposing lanes of traffic. Could be paint markings, a wide grass strip, a field, or a concrete barrier. Prevents head-on collisions—and sometimes looks nice with flowers.

Merging Lane (a.k.a. On-Ramp Lane): A short lane allowing vehicles to accelerate before joining main traffic, reducing the speed gap and easing conflict. Use it to get up to speed and blend in smoothly.

MPG (Miles Per Gallon): How far you can travel on one gallon of gas. Higher MPG = fewer stops at the pump and more money for road-trip snacks.

Merging: The act of smoothly joining a lane of moving traffic. Eye contact and courtesy help—plus using your blinker like it's your job.

N

Neutral: A gear position where the engine doesn't power the wheels. Useful for towing or that moment you realize you're about to stall and want a quick fix.

O

Oil Filter: The part that cleans contaminants from your engine oil. Change it regularly, or your engine might go on strike.

Overpass: A bridge that carries one road (or railway) over another. Often narrower than the main road, meaning shoulders may be minimal— careful if you need to pull over.

Oversteer/Understeer

- **Oversteer:** Rear wheels lose grip, and your car's back end swings out. Fun on a racetrack, scary on a public road.
- **Understeer:** Front wheels lose grip, causing the car to go straight instead of turning.

P

Passing Lane: See **Fast Lane**. It's intended for overtaking slower vehicles, not for daydreaming (unless you enjoy dirty looks).

Pillars (A-Pillar, B-Pillar, C-Pillar, etc.): Vertical support columns along your car's body that hold up the roof and frame your windows. They're labeled alphabetically from front to back—A-pillars at the windshield, B-pillars in the middle, C-pillars by the rear seats, etc. Their shape and size play a big role in determining the extent of your blind spots.

Power Steering: A system that uses hydraulic or electric assistance to make turning the steering wheel easier than arm-wrestling your car's front tires. If it fails, you'll get an unplanned arm workout—and a jolt of adrenaline.

Public Road: Any road, street, boulevard, expressway, highway, or thoroughfare open to the public for travel or transportation. If everyone can use it, it's a public road.

Q

Quarter Panel: A body panel on the side of your car, usually behind the rear door. You'll learn its name quickly if it gets dinged.

R

Residential Area: A region primarily occupied by private homes. Typically has lower speed limits and more pedestrians, so slow down and watch out for kids, pets, and rogue basketballs.

Road Markings: Painted lines, arrows, and symbols guiding traffic flow. Follow these to avoid angry honks and unexpected chats with the local traffic enforcer.

Road Rage: Overblown anger behind the wheel. Better left at home—this isn't an action movie, folks.

Road Test: The grand finale of your learner's journey. An examiner checks if you can actually handle real-world traffic, not just fill in bubbles on a written exam. Pass, and you get that sweet plastic card making you an official driver!

Roadway: The part of a thoroughfare actually used by vehicles. Usually marked by painted lines, it's what your tires cling to while driving.

Roundabout (a.k.a. Rotary or Traffic Circle): A circular intersection where traffic flows in one direction around a central island. Vehicles in the circle have the right-of-way—so yield before entering, or prepare for honks.

Rumble Strips: Raised or grooved sections on the road edge that vibrate your car if you stray. Like an alarm clock for distracted or sleepy drivers.

S

Scanning: A key defensive driving strategy: constantly shifting your gaze to mirrors, road signs, traffic ahead, etc. Stay aware, stay alive!

Seatbelt: The unsung superhero of car safety. Strap it across your body to keep yourself from flying around the cabin like a deranged pinball during a collision. "Click It or Ticket" is more than a slogan—it's a life-saver.

Serpentine (a.k.a. Twist Road): A winding or turning road with multiple hairpin curves allowing traffic to climb steep elevations. You'll see these in mountainous regions—cue scenic views!

Shared Center Lane (a.k.a. Turning Lane): A middle lane on a two-way street for turning left from either direction or entering from a side road. Not to be confused with a dedicated turning lane for an intersection—it's more like a "neutral zone" for left turns only.

Shock Absorbers: Hydraulic devices that reduce or dampen the bouncing of your suspension. Without these, you'd feel every pebble, pothole, and speed bump like a rollercoaster gone wild.

Shoulder: The emergency stopping lane next to the outermost traffic lane on a motorway. Also handy if you get a flat tire or need a quick breather.

Skid: When your tires lose grip on the road and start sliding uncontrollably—like a surprise ice rink under your wheels. Could be caused by rain, snow, or over-enthusiastic braking. Keep calm and steer gently toward your intended path.

Slow Lane: The outermost lane on a multi-lane motorway, typically for slower-moving vehicles. On uphill stretches, an extra slow lane may appear for heavy trucks—use it so speedier traffic can pass.

Speed Bump (a.k.a. Speed Breaker): A raised hump in the road designed to slow traffic, especially in residential areas or parking lots. Hit it too fast and your suspension will protest... loudly.

Superelevation (a.k.a. Cross Slope or Banked Turn): The engineering term for how the outer edge of a curved roadway is higher than the inner edge, allowing for higher-speed turns with less skidding. You'll see it on highways with sweeping curves or racetracks.

Suspension: Those springs, control arms, and linkages that keep your tires in contact with the road (and keep you from bouncing around like popcorn). A well-tuned suspension = better handling and a comfier ride.

Swaybar (a.k.a. Anti-Roll Bar): A metal rod linking opposite wheels to reduce body roll in turns. Think of it as your car's built-in stabilizer, keeping it from leaning through curves like a wobbly, off-balance giraffe.

T

Tailgating: Following another vehicle too closely. Also a fun party before a football game, but let's stick to safe driving distances on the road.

Traffic Conflict: A transportation engineering term for an event where two or more vehicles' paths intersect such that a collision is likely unless at least one vehicle takes evasive action.

Traffic Lane: A designated part of a thoroughfare for a single line of vehicles. Proper lane usage reduces collisions and keeps traffic flowing smoothly.

Traffic Signs: Signs (often reflective) providing rules, warnings, directions, or points of interest.

- **Regulation Signs**: White rectangles with black letters/symbols stating legal rules (e.g. speed limits).
- **Warning Signs**: Yellow diamonds (or fluorescent yellow-green) that alert you to hazards or special conditions. The STOP sign (red octagon) is also a warning/regulatory hybrid.
- **Destination Signs**: Green rectangles pointing you to exits, towns, or highways.
- **Service Signs**: Blue rectangles showing services like rest areas or gas stations.

- **Attraction Signs**: Brown rectangles indicating parks, historical sites, or recreational points.
- **Construction Signs**: Orange signs for work zones—stay alert.

Traffic Signals: Red, yellow, green, or orange lights controlling movement at intersections or pedestrian crossings. "Green means go"—but always look both ways in case someone else missed the memo.

Tunnel: An enclosed underground (or under-mountain) passage, usually with a limited width and no shoulders. Headlights on—especially if it's poorly lit.

U

U-Turn: A 180-degree turn to go back in the direction you came from. Legal in some places, illegal in others—look for signs, or you might get an expensive lesson.

V

VIN (Vehicle Identification Number): Your car's unique "fingerprint," often found on the dashboard near the windshield. You'll need it for registration, insurance, and proving it's *your* car.

Vulnerable Road Users: Pedestrians, cyclists, and motorcyclists who lack a car's protective shell. Give them space and be extra alert—they're counting on it.

W

Wheel Alignment: Adjusting the angles of the wheels to match manufacturer specs. If your car pulls to one side like a wayward shopping cart, it's alignment time.

Wiper Fluid: That magical liquid clearing off bug splatter, bird gifts, or dust from your windshield. Keep it topped off, or you'll be squinting through grime.

Warning Signs: See **Traffic Signs**.

X

Xenon Headlights (HID): Bright white-blue headlights using xenon gas. Excellent visibility—just don't blind oncoming traffic with poorly aimed high beams.

Y

Yaw: Refers to a car's rotation around its vertical axis. If the rear end suddenly slides around on wet roads, that's yaw in action—brace yourself.

Yield: Giving right-of-way to other vehicles or pedestrians. If that triangular sign says "YIELD," it's telling you to pause and let others go first.

Z

Zero-Emission Vehicle (ZEV): A ride with no tailpipe pollutants, like electric or hydrogen fuel-cell cars.

Zipper Merge: Merging strategy where drivers in two parallel lanes alternate like the teeth of a zipper. It's efficient and polite—if everyone cooperates.

TAKEAWAY

- **Stay Curious**: If a new term crops up, look it up—being in the know makes you a safer, savvier driver.
- **Practice & Apply**: Knowing terms is one thing; using them on real roads is where it counts.
- **Road & Car Savvy**: Understanding both vehicle parts *and* roadway lingo makes you a well-rounded driver who can handle (almost) anything.

With these definitions—covering everything from catalytic converters to hairpin curves—you're well-equipped to navigate your car's inner workings, decipher road signs and lane markings, and understand how modern thoroughfares are designed. Keep this glossary handy so that when someone mentions a "shared center lane" or "zipper merge," you'll nod wisely instead of muttering, "The zip-what-now?"

Time to put on your thinking cap (or driving cap, if you prefer) and show off those fresh vocabulary skills! Think of this quiz like a pit stop on your road to becoming a driving know-it-all—quick, painless, and guaranteed to rev up your confidence. Ready, set… quiz!

QUICK QUIZ: TEST YOUR GLOSSARY KNOWLEDGE

1. Which lane on a multi-lane roadway is generally intended for faster vehicles or overtaking?
A) Shoulder
B) Fast Lane (Passing Lane)
C) Merging Lane
D) Slow Lane

2. What do we call the middle lane on a two-way street designated solely for left turns from either direction?
A) Dedicated Turning Lane
B) Shared Center Lane
C) Carpool Lane
D) Expressway

3. If you see an orange sign with black letters/symbols, what kind of traffic sign is it?
A) Attraction Sign
B) Warning Sign
C) Construction Sign
D) Service Sign

4. Which term refers to a sudden or likely collision scenario that requires an emergency maneuver to avoid impact?
A) Traffic Conflict
B) Road Rage
C) Defensive Driving
D) Liabilities

5. On highways, what is the purpose of an *exit lane* (off-ramp lane)?
A) To help vehicles accelerate up to highway speeds
B) To allow vehicles to decelerate before leaving the main roadway
C) To serve as a carpool lane during rush hour
D) To provide a storage lane for broken-down vehicles

6. Which statement best describes a *hairpin curve?*
A) A slight bend requiring minimal steering input
B) A U-shaped turn typically found in mountainous areas
C) A circular intersection with a central island
D) A sharp uphill incline on the highway

7. In a **superelevated** curve, which edge of the roadway is higher?
A) The inner edge
B) The left shoulder only
C) The outer edge
D) Both edges are level

8. FWD (Front-Wheel Drive) means:
A) Only the rear wheels receive power from the engine
B) All four wheels receive power
C) The engine powers only the front wheels
D) It's an old term for manual transmissions

9. Defensive Driving involves:
A) Driving as fast as you can
B) Constantly scanning and anticipating potential hazards
C) Using hazard lights to hold a parking spot
D) Avoiding highways at all costs

10. Zipper Merge refers to:
A) A lane where everyone lines up single-file with no merging
B) Stopping at a crossroad and waiting until lanes are empty
C) Two parallel lanes where drivers alternate like teeth in a zipper when merging
D) A forbidden maneuver in most countries

QUIZ ANSWERS

1. **B** - Fast Lane (Passing Lane)
2. **B** - Shared Center Lane
3. **C** - Construction Sign
4. **A** - Traffic Conflict
5. **B** - To allow vehicles to decelerate before leaving the main roadway
6. **B** - A U-shaped turn typically found in mountainous areas
7. **C** - The outer edge
8. **C** - The engine powers only the front wheels
9. **B** - Constantly scanning and anticipating potential hazards
10. **C** - Two parallel lanes where drivers alternate like teeth in a zipper when merging

5. CHOOSE YOUR PATH: ROAD TYPES AND WHAT THEY MEAN FOR YOU

Ever noticed how you can drive for just ten minutes and suddenly feel like you've entered a whole new world of road rules? One minute, you're on a quiet street where a cat sunbathing in the middle of the road is your biggest obstacle, and the next, you're merging onto a highway where everyone's driving like they're auditioning for the next Fast & Furious movie. Different roads, different vibes—and we're here to break it all down.

In this chapter, we'll classify roads based on three significant factors—**capacity**, **location**, and **construction type**—all while exploring how each category affects your driving experience. So, buckle up because it's time to put your brand-new license to the test!

CLASSIFYING BY CAPACITY

LOW-CAPACITY ROADS

Residential Streets
- **What They're Like**: Picture mailboxes, kids on bikes, and speed limits hovering around 25 mph (or even lower). Speed bumps are likely, and a neighbor strolling right down the middle isn't uncommon.
- **Driving Tips**: Watch for sudden stops, oblivious pets, and neighbors who think the street is their personal walking path. Speed bumps and "No Outlet" signs often make guest appearances here, so slow is the way to go.

Pro Tip: Be Ready for Anything
Keep your speed in check, scan well ahead, and assume every bend might hide a wandering pet or a child chasing a ball.

Rural Lanes and Local Roads
- **What They're Like**: Often narrow, sometimes barely wide enough for two cars to squeeze past. Lighting can be minimal at night, and sharp bends or hills can conceal oncoming traffic.
- **Driving Tips**: Use high beams in dark areas, but dim them for oncoming vehicles. Watch for wildlife, farm equipment, and anything else that goes bump in the night.

MODERATE-CAPACITY ROADS

Arterials and Collectors
- **What They're Like**: These routes connect neighborhoods to business areas. Speeds can range from 30–45 mph in urban spots up to 50+ mph in rural stretches. Expect traffic lights, stop signs, and plenty of mid-block driveways.
- **Driving Tips**: Stay alert for cars turning in and out of side roads, gas stations, or shopping centers. This is the transitional zone between quiet backstreets and full-blown highways.

HIGH-CAPACITY ROADS

Freeways, Highways, and Expressways
- **What They're Like**: Multi-lane, higher speeds (55–70 mph or above, depending on local laws), and no stoplights—just ramps for entering and exiting. It can feel like Grand Central Station on wheels during rush hour.
- **Driving Tips**: Master the art of merging. Signal your moves well ahead and keep an eye on your blind spots. Another thing to remember: the left lane is generally for passing, not for daydream cruising.

CLASSIFYING BY LOCATION

URBAN ROADS

City Streets
- **What They're Like**: Stoplights galore, tight grid layouts, and pedestrians at every corner. Delivery trucks might double-park, forcing you to squeeze by.
- **Driving Tips**: Stay patient. Frequent stops and starts are normal. Keep your foot close to the brake and watch for people or bicycles darting out between parked cars.

Suburban Avenues
- **What They're Like**: Wider lanes than downtown, but still prone to congestion. Speeds increase, turning lanes multiply, and you might see dedicated bike or bus lanes.
- **Driving Tips**: Pay attention to lane markings, especially if you need to make left turns. Merge carefully and watch for cyclists when shifting lanes.

RURAL ROADS

Farm-to-Market & Country Roads
- **What They're Like**: Scenic and often less crowded (may tempt you into daydreaming)—until you're stuck behind a slow-moving tractor. Surfaces can be gravel, dirt, or plain old cracked pavement.
- **Driving Tips**: Take it easy on speed—conditions like gravel, dirt, or potholes can trip even experienced drivers up. Curves or hidden driveways can appear suddenly, and night driving demands extra caution (and properly aimed high beams).

SPECIALIZED CORRIDORS

Industrial Roads
- **What They're Like**: Warehouses, factories, and plenty of heavy trucks. The pavement can be rough from constant freight traffic.
- **Driving Tips**: Anticipate wide loads and slower vehicles. Keep a safe following distance—loose cargo can be a real hazard if it falls off a truck. Stay alert for tractor-trailers, give them plenty of room for wide turns, and steer clear of their blind spots.

Tourist or Scenic Routes
- **What They're Like**: Winding roads with jaw-dropping views. Speed limits can fluctuate. Watch out for sudden stops from sightseers snapping photos.
- **Driving Strategies**: Expect frequent pull-offs or rest areas. Watch for cars ahead that may brake unexpectedly. Stay alert if the scenery is too gorgeous—the temptation to stare at mountains instead of the road is real.

CLASSIFYING BY CONSTRUCTION TYPE

PAVED ROADS

Asphalt (Blacktop)
- **Pros**: Smooth, easy to maintain.
- **Cons**: Potholes form if maintenance lags. Tar lines get slippery in high heat or heavy rain.

Concrete
- **Pros**: Often used for major highways, durable.
- **Cons**: Can be louder and produce that rhythmic "thump-thump" over expansion joints or a "bouncy" ride if the slabs are curled.

UNPAVED ROADS

Gravel or Dirt
- **Pros**: Low-cost, rural charm.
- **Cons**: Dust clouds in dry weather, mud in wet weather, lower traction overall. Slow down and keep your steering steady to avoid fishtailing. Left neglected, dirt roads can become cratered enough to resemble the lunar surface.

Chip Seal (Tar-and-Chip)
- **Pros**: A budget-friendly hybrid surface.
- **Cons**: Rougher texture—think "light off-roading". Keep a safe distance from the vehicles ahead and watch for loose stones that can cause chips in your paint (or windshield).

SPECIALIZED SURFACES

Cobblestone or Brick
- **What They're Like**: Historic and charming, but bumpy and slippery when wet.
- **Driving Tips**: Go slow. Bouncing over old stones at high speed is no fun for your suspension (or passengers).

Metal Bridges or Grates
- **What They're Like**: Might feel like the car is "floating" a bit due to reduced tire grip.
- **Driving Tips**: Keep a steady wheel and avoid sudden moves. Slick conditions can amplify that skating-on-ice sensation.

DRIVING TIPS & CONSIDERATIONS

Speed Management
- Lower-capacity roads might tempt you to speed if empty, but hidden intersections or sharp curves can sneak up.
- On high-capacity roads, practice lane discipline and use your signals. If you're not passing, consider moving right.

Weather & Lighting
- Paved city streets might handle rain well, but rural gravel roads can turn into mudslides.
- Dark rural roads demand high beams (and quick reflexes if you see wildlife).

Sharing the Road
- In residential areas: watch for kids, cyclists, and occasional street basketball games.
- On rural roads: be prepared to slow down for a farmer's tractor or wandering livestock.
- Highways with multiple lanes: check blind spots religiously, especially around big trucks.

Know the Signage
- Residential: Kids at play, speed bumps, or "No Outlet" signs.
- Rural: Cattle crossing, narrow bridge, or no-passing zones.
- Highway: Exit markers, milepost signs, and carpool lane indicators.

HIGHWAY NERD CORNER:

The massive U.S. interstate network—now spanning more than 48,000 miles and still growing—originated with the Federal Aid Highway Act of 1956, which President Dwight D. Eisenhower authored.

Ever notice how some Interstates, like I-95, run north–south while others, like I-10, go east–west? That's no coincidence. The American Association of State Highway and Transportation Officials (AASHTO) created a numbering system where **odd numbers** run north–south (increasing from west to east), and **even numbers** run east–west (increasing from south to north). So next time you're cruising down I-95, feel free to impress your passengers with a bit of highway trivia.

6. READ THE ROAD: HOW TO UNDERSTAND SIGNS, SIGNALS, AND MARKINGS

Ever felt like the road is speaking a secret language you're only partly fluent in? You see solid lines, dashed lines, arrows, diamond-shaped signs—some even show deer or twisting arrows—and you're supposed to know how to respond instantly? These markings, signs, and signals may seem like colorful doodles at first glance, but they form a system designed to keep everyone safe and moving in harmony. Mastering them is your ticket to confident, hassle-free driving, so let's decode them together!

ROAD MARKINGS — THE PAVEMENT'S VISUAL CODE

Lines & Their Meanings
- **Single Yellow Line**: Separates traffic moving in opposite directions. If dashed, passing can be allowed, only when it's safe.
- **Double Yellow Line**: Solid means do not pass; treat it like a bright divider that keeps you away from head-on collisions. If your side has a dashed line, passing is permitted—just make sure conditions are safe.
- **White Lines**: Split lanes going in the same direction. Solid white lines discourage crossing, dashed ones allow merging or passing.
- **Edge Lines**: Mark the outer boundary of drivable pavement. Crossing over one usually means you're off the road (hello, shoulder!).

Pro Tip: Nighttime Vision
Headlights make painted lines reflect better, but slow down in poor weather or if the lines are faded. Rely on caution as much as reflection.

Arrows & Painted Words
- **Turn Arrows**: They clarify if a lane is purely for turning or shared with through traffic. Accidentally cruising into a left-turn lane when you want to go straight can create major confusion.
- **High-Occupancy Vehicle (HOV) / Carpool Lanes**: Restricted traffic lanes reserved for the exclusive use of vehicles with a driver and at least one passenger – commonly marked by a diamond ($\Diamond$).
- **Bike Lanes**: Bike symbols mark—you guessed it—bike lanes; stay alert for bicyclists who might make unexpected turns.

Crosswalks

- Where pedestrians have the legal right-of-way, marked by two parallel lines or a set of bold "zebra" stripes across the road. Remember to stop *before* entering the crosswalk—blocking it forces people to detour into traffic. These markings often appear at intersections but can also pop up mid-block near schools, parks, or bus stops. Stay alert and yield to anyone on foot, because once they step inside that painted zone, they're counting on your cooperation.

Common Mistake: Crosswalk Whoops

Stopping *past* the wide "stop line" or rolling onto crosswalks endangers pedestrians and risks a ticket. Stop *before* the line, even if you're in a hurry.

TRAFFIC SIGNS—SHAPES, COLORS, AND ALL THAT JAZZ

Regulatory Signs

- **Stop (Octagon)**: The big, red, and unavoidable. Come to a complete stop—no rolling.
- **Yield (Triangle)**: Let others go first if they're in or near the intersection; do not come to a full stop unless there's actual traffic requiring you to yield (the car behind you will know you're a pro!).
- **Speed Limit (Rectangle)**: The law, not a suggestion—resist the lead foot!
- **No Parking / One Way / Lane Use**: Typically rectangular; read them carefully to avoid headaches (and fines).

Warning Signs

- **Yellow Diamonds**: "Road curves ahead," "Steep hill," or "Animal crossing"—these are your forewarnings.
- **Fluorescent Yellow-Green**: Often for school or pedestrian zones—definitely slow down and pay attention.
- **Pennant (Sideways Triangle)**: Marks the start of a "No Passing Zone." It's placed on the left side of the road, so if you see this pointy sign, it's time to stay put and not overtake.

Guide & Informational Signs

- **Green**: Directions, highway exits, mileage markers.
- **Blue**: Services like gas, food, and hospitals.
- **Brown**: Recreational or cultural points of interest—parks, historical sites, scenic overlooks.

Pro Tip: Construction Zone Orange

Orange signs and cones = "Slow down and pay extra attention." Fines can double in work zones, so keep your wallet happy by maintaining low speeds.

TRAFFIC SIGNALS—LIGHTS THAT RULE THE ROAD

Standard Colors

- **Red**: Stop. You might turn right on red if it's legal, but check for oncoming traffic or "No Turn on Red" signs first.
- **Yellow**: Caution—prepare to stop if you can do so safely. Don't floor it just to beat the light.
- **Green**: Go, but scan the intersection. Some joker might run the red in the cross-traffic.

Arrows & Special Signals

- **Green Arrow**: Protected turn—oncoming traffic should be stopped.
- **Flashing Yellow Arrow**: You may turn left if it's clear, but oncoming traffic has right-of-way.
- **Flashing Red**: Treat it like a stop sign—full stop, then proceed.
- **Flashing Yellow**: It means "proceed with caution." You don't have to stop, but slow down, check traffic, and only continue when it's safe to do so.

Common Mistake: Yellow-Light Racing

Hitting the gas at yellow to sneak through an intersection often leads to collisions. If you're far enough away to stop safely, do it. Also watch out for trailing vehicles that might expect you to go and could end up rear-ending you.

PEDESTRIAN & EMERGENCY-VEHICLE HYBRID BEACONS (ALSO KNOWN AS HAWK BEACONS)

Dark or Off

- **Keep Driving**: The beacon stays unlit until a pedestrian (or emergency vehicle) activates it. You can go, but stay alert for sudden changes.

Flashing Yellow

- **Warning phase**: Someone is requesting to cross. Slow down and be ready to stop if needed.

Solid Yellow
- **Prepare to Stop**: The beacon is about to turn solid red for crossing pedestrians or emergency vehicles (such as fire trucks exiting the station with lights and sirens on, responding to a call).

Solid Red
- **Stop completely**: Pedestrians or authorized vehicles now have the right to cross.

Flashing Red
- **Treat** it like a stop sign—come to a full stop, then proceed only if the crossing is clear.

Pro Tip: Read the Signs!
HAWK beacons can look unfamiliar, but they're usually paired with helpful signage that explains precisely what to do—like when to stop and when it's okay to proceed. Don't panic if you haven't seen one before—just follow the instructions.

OTHER SPECIAL-USE SIGNALS

- **Pedestrian Countdown Timers**: If you see them ticking down, expect a light change soon. Stay alert for pedestrians who might dash across in those final seconds.
- **Railroad Crossing Lights**: If they're flashing, or a gate is lowering, do not attempt your best action-movie stunt—trains always win.

COMMON MISTAKES & MISINTERPRETATIONS

Rolling Through Stop Signs
- Slowing down but never entirely stopping can land you in trouble, especially if there's a hidden cop or a clueless pedestrian.

Stopping At Yield Signs with No Traffic to Yield to
- Coming to a complete stop is unnecessary and can disrupt traffic flow by forcing drivers behind you to brake unexpectedly. This creates confusion and even the potential for minor collisions.

Ignoring / Overlooking Speed Limit Drops
- School zones, construction sites, or residential areas often have strict speed limits. Doubling the speed can double your ticket cost!

Misreading Turn Lanes
- Accidental turning from a through-lane or vice versa can mean side-swipes or fender-benders. Watch for big painted arrows or overhead signs.

Tunnel Vision
- Focusing only on the car ahead leads to missed signs. Keep your eyes moving—far ahead, to the sides, and on your mirrors.

Cultural Differences & Local Quirks
- Traveling abroad? Familiarize yourself with different shapes, colors, or metric vs. imperial speed signs. If unsure, your best bet is to slow down and observe.

Road markings, signs and signals aren't suggestions—they're the cheat codes to driving trouble-free. Respect them, and you'll stay safe. Ignore them, and the road has a way of reminding you who's really in charge.

SIGN SHAPES & COLORS

Octagon
(red)

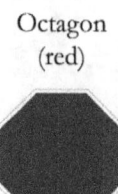

Stop sign

Triangle
(red)

Yield sign

Circle
(yellow)

Railroad crossing
warning signs

Crossbuck
(white)

Railroad grade
crossing signs

Diamond
(yellow)

Warning signs
(permanent)

Diamond
(orange or hi-vis pink)

Warning signs
(TTC Zones)
Temporary Traffic Control Zones

Rectangle
(white)

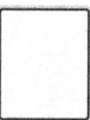

Regulatory signs

Pennant
(yellow or orange)

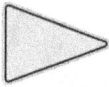

No passing zone
(permanent or TTCZ)

Rectangle or Square
(blue)

Service signs

Rectangle
(green)

Highway
directions

Rectangle or Square
(brown)

Recreational,
cultural, historical

Various Shapes
(yellow or hi-vis green)

School zones

7. KNOW YOUR RIDE: CAR COMPONENTS EXPLAINED IN PLAIN ENGLISH

Your car isn't just a glorified metal box with wheels—it's a complex machine with countless parts working in harmony to get you from point A to point B. Knowing what each component does and why it's important can make you a smarter, safer driver. Plus, when something goes wrong, you'll have a better idea of what might need fixing. Let's dive under the hood and explore the essential parts that make your car tick!

DRIVER'S SEAT & SEATBELTS

Driver's Seat
- **What It Does**: Supports your body while you drive, providing comfort and proper posture.
- **Importance**: A well-functioning seat ensures you can reach all controls easily and reduces the risk of fatigue on long drives.

Seatbelt
- **What It Does**: Secures you in place during a collision, preventing ejection and reducing injury.
- **Importance**: The most critical safety feature in your car. Always wear it—it can save your life.

MIRRORS (REARVIEW & SIDE)

Rearview Mirror
- **What It Does**: Provides a view of the traffic directly behind you.
- **Importance**: Essential for safe lane changes and monitoring overall traffic flow.

Side Mirrors
- **What They Do**: Offer a view of the lanes adjacent to you, minimizing blind spots.
- **Importance**: Critical for avoiding collisions when merging, changing lanes, or backing out of parking spots.

Common Mistake: No Shoulder Checks
Relying solely on mirrors without performing shoulder checks can leave you vulnerable to unexpected vehicles in your blind spots.

STEERING WHEEL

Steering Wheel
- **What It Does**: Controls the direction of your vehicle.
- **Importance**: Central to maneuvering your car safely and accurately. A responsive steering system ensures you can navigate tight turns and avoid obstacles effectively.

Pro Tip: Power Steering

When your car is turned off, the power steering system disengages, making the steering wheel much harder to turn. Always keep the engine running when making sharp or emergency maneuvers to ensure full steering control. Avoid letting your car roll down a slope in neutral with the engine off—you could end up facing a dangerous situation!

PEDALS & FOOT CONTROLS

Gas Pedal (Right)
- **What It Does**: Controls the engine's power output, accelerating the vehicle.
- **Importance**: Smooth acceleration ensures better fuel efficiency and safer driving, especially in traffic or tight spaces.

Brake Pedal (Left)
- **What It Does**: Slows down or stops the vehicle by applying brake force to the wheels.
- **Importance**: Reliable brakes are crucial for avoiding collisions and controlling your speed in various driving conditions.

Clutch (Left of the Brake Pedal, only for Manual Transmission)
- **What It Does**: Engages and disengages the engine from the transmission, allowing gear changes.
- **Importance**: Essential for smooth shifting and maintaining control over the vehicle's power delivery.

Common Mistake: Improper Brake Pedal Control

Slamming the brake pedal instead of gradually applying pressure can cause skidding or loss of control, especially on slippery roads.

GEAR SHIFT & TRANSMISSION

Automatic Transmission
- **What It Does**: Automatically changes gears based on speed and engine load.
- **Importance**: Simplifies driving by handling gear shifts for you, allowing you to focus more on the road.

Manual Transmission
- **What It Does**: Requires the driver to manually select gears using a stick shift and clutch pedal.
- **Importance**: Offers greater control over the vehicle's power and can enhance driving enjoyment, but requires more skill and coordination.

Electronic or Dial Shifters
- **What They Do**: Replace traditional stick shifts with electronic controls or dial mechanisms.
- **Importance**: Modernizes the driving experience and can offer additional features like sport modes or easy gear selection.

DASHBOARD & INSTRUMENT PANEL

Speedometer
- **What It Does**: Displays your current speed.
- **Importance**: Helps you stay within speed limits and avoid speeding tickets.

Tachometer
- **What It Does**: Shows engine RPM (revolutions per minute).
- **Importance**: Useful for monitoring engine performance and preventing over-revving in manual transmissions.

Fuel Gauge
- **What It Does**: Indicates the amount of fuel remaining in the tank.
- **Importance**: Prevents running out of gas unexpectedly, which can leave you stranded or force you to drive inefficiently.

Pro Tip: Understand the Symbols
The tiny triangle next to the fuel pump pictogram indicates which side of your car the fuel door is on. This handy symbol can save you time and frustration—no more circling the car wondering where to open the tank!

Warning Lights
- **What They Do**: Alert you to various issues (e.g., check engine, oil pressure, battery).
- **Importance**: Early warnings allow you to address problems before they become serious and expensive.

Common Mistake: Warning Lights

Ignoring warning lights can lead to severe engine damage or breakdowns, making timely responses essential for your vehicle's health.

HVAC & COMFORT CONTROLS

Heating, Ventilation, Air Conditioning (HVAC)
- **What It Does**: Controls the interior temperature and airflow.
- **Importance**: Ensures a comfortable driving environment, which can reduce driver fatigue and improve focus.

Pro Tip: Using the AC to Dehumidify the Air

Although it might seem unusual, turning on the AC in humid or cold weather is the quickest way to eliminate window condensation. The AC removes moisture from the air inside your car, keeping your windows clear and your visibility sharp.

Defrost & Rear Defogger
- **What They Do**: Clear mist, frost, or ice from the windshield and rear window.
- **Importance**: Maintains clear visibility in cold or humid conditions, essential for safe driving.

Pro Tip: Keep it Fresh

Have you ever noticed a musty odor when you turn on the AC after months of not using it? That smell comes from mold growing in your air filter. Replace the cabin air filter regularly to improve the air quality inside your car and keep it smelling fresh.

LIGHTS & WIPERS

Headlights
- **What They Do**: Illuminate the road ahead for visibility during low-light conditions.
- **Importance**: Essential for night driving, inclement weather, and early morning or late evening commutes.

Pro Tip: Mind Your Beams

If the blue "high beam" indicator lights up on your dashboard while you're following closely or encountering oncoming traffic, it means your high beams may be blinding other drivers. Switch to low beams to ensure everyone's visibility remains clear and safe.

Fog Lights
- **What They Do**: Provide additional lighting in foggy or misty conditions.
- **Importance**: Enhances visibility without causing excessive glare, making it easier to see the road and other vehicles.

Pro Tip: Fog Light Savvy

Fog lights cast a horizontal beam to help you see in low-visibility conditions like fog, rain, or snow. However, using them in clear weather can blind oncoming drivers and the car in front of you. Only turn on your fog lights when visibility is poor and switch back to low beams only once conditions improve.

Windshield Wipers & Washer
- **What They Do**: Clear rain, snow, debris, and insects from the windshield.
- **Importance**: Maintains a clear view, crucial for safe driving in bad weather or dirty conditions.

HORN & OTHER HANDY BUTTONS

Horn
- **What It Does**: Emits a sound to alert other drivers or pedestrians.
- **Importance**: Useful for preventing accidents by signaling your presence, but should be used sparingly to avoid unnecessary honking. In other words, use it only to handle urgent and dangerous situations, not to indicate that you're rushing.

Hazard Lights
- **What They Do**: Flash all turn signals simultaneously to indicate a hazard or emergency.
- **Importance**: Alerts other drivers that you're experiencing an issue, like a breakdown or accident, and need to slow down or stay clear.

Pro Tip: Quick Alert & Safe Following

If traffic comes to a sudden stop in front of you, manually activate your hazard lights to signal drivers behind you to slow down. Additionally, always maintain ample space between your car and the vehicle ahead. This extra buffer not only gives you more time to react but also compensates for drivers behind you who may not be paying full attention, providing them room to brake safely and helping to prevent rear-end collisions.

Other Handy Buttons
- **Heated Seats & Steering Wheel**: Provide extra comfort in cold weather.
- **Cruise Control**: Maintains a steady speed without keeping your foot on the gas pedal.
- **Infotainment Controls**: Manage navigation, music, and phone connectivity—use responsibly to minimize distractions.

Pro Tip: Read the Manual
Familiarize yourself with all buttons and controls before driving to avoid fumbling while on the road. Safety first!

UNDER THE HOOD (A BRIEF OVERVIEW)

Engine & Battery
- **Engine**: The powerhouse that converts fuel into motion.
- **Battery**: Provides electrical power for starting the engine and running electronics.
- **Importance**: Regular maintenance ensures reliable performance and prevents unexpected breakdowns.

Fluids
- **Engine Oil**: Lubricates engine parts to reduce friction and wear.
- **Coolant**: Regulates engine temperature to prevent overheating.
- **Brake Fluid**: Transfers force from the brake pedal to the brake pads.
- **Windshield Washer Fluid**: Cleans the windshield for better visibility.
- **Importance**: Keeping these fluids at proper levels is crucial for vehicle functionality and longevity.

Fuses & Air Filters
- **Fuses**: Protect electrical circuits from overloads.
- **Air Filters**: Clean the air entering the engine, improving performance and fuel efficiency.
- **Importance**: Regular checks and replacements keep your car running smoothly and prevent damage to key components.

Common Mistake: Neglecting Your Car's Health

Neglecting to change air filters and fluids can reduce engine efficiency and increase fuel consumption. Follow your car's maintenance schedule and make it a habit to replace them as recommended.

STORAGE & CARGO

Trunk / Hatch
- **What It Does**: Provides space for carrying luggage, groceries, and other items.
- **Importance**: Properly loading the trunk ensures balanced weight distribution, which affects handling and braking.

In-Car Storage
- **Glove Box, Center Console**: Ideal spots for keeping important documents, such as registration and insurance, as well as emergency items.
- **Importance**: Organized storage helps prevent distractions and keeps essential items within easy reach.

Pro Tip: Keep It Clean

Avoid overloading storage compartments to maintain easy access to necessary items and ensure they don't become projectiles in a sudden stop.

WHEELS & TIRES

Wheels
- **What They Do:** Wheels are the circular components that the tires are mounted on.
- **Importance:** Wheels support the weight of your vehicle and ensure smooth rotation. Properly balanced wheels prevent vibrations and uneven tire wear, while avoiding bends or damage is crucial for maintaining optimal handling and stability. Bent wheels can lead to poor alignment, making your car harder to control and increasing the risk of accidents.

Tires
- **What They Do**: Tires are the rubber components that make contact with the road, providing traction, absorbing shocks, and enabling steering and braking.
- **Importance**: Properly maintained tires are essential for safe driving, effective braking, fuel efficiency, and optimal vehicle performance.

Pro Tip: Tread Smart
Regularly check your tire pressure and tread depth. Properly inflated and well-treaded tires improve safety, handling, and fuel efficiency, while preventing blowouts and skidding.

SUSPENSION & SHOCK ABSORBERS

Suspension
- **What It Does**: Connects your car to its wheels, soaking up bumps and jolts from the road.
- **Importance**: A smooth suspension system ensures a comfortable ride, responsive handling, and enhanced safety by keeping your tires firmly planted on the road.

Shock Absorbers
- **What They Do**: Control the up-and-down movement of the suspension, providing stability and a cushy ride.
- **Importance**: Proper shock absorbers prevent excessive bouncing, maintain tire contact, and improve overall vehicle control, especially on uneven surfaces.

Pro Tip: Bounce Back
Listen to your car's vibes. If it starts bouncing excessively or swaying side to side, your suspension or shocks might need a check-up. A balanced suspension keeps your ride smooth and steady, no matter the terrain!

Swaybar / Anti-roll Bar
- **What It Does**: Connects opposite wheels to reduce body roll in corners.
- **Importance**: Less wobble = more confidence in turns.

Nerd Tip: The Science Behind Swaybars
A swaybar, also known as an anti-roll bar, links the left and right suspension components. When your car enters a turn, the swaybar twists to counteract the roll caused by weight transfer. This twisting action distributes some of the load to the opposite side, keeping your vehicle more stable and improving handling.

Understanding your car's physical components isn't just for mechanics—it's for you, the driver. Each part plays a vital role in ensuring your vehicle runs safely and efficiently. By knowing what these components do and why they matter, you can better maintain your car, recognize when something's wrong, and communicate effectively when repairs are needed.

8. LET'S BOOGIE: CAR DYNAMICS EXPLAINED

Ever feel like your car has its own dance routine—sometimes light on its feet on smooth highways, other times slipping and sliding in the rain? That's **Car Dynamics**: the science (and art) behind how your vehicle moves, steers, and brakes in various conditions. If you master these basics, you'll transform from a cautious beginner into a confident driver who can handle whatever the road throws at you.

BASIC CAR DYNAMICS

Weight Distribution
- **What It Is**: How your car's weight is split between the front and rear.
- **Why It Matters**: Balance is key—front-heavy cars risk understeering in corners, and rear-heavy cars might oversteer if you gas it too hard. Not sure what understeer and oversteer mean? Head over to the glossary and brush up on those terms.

Traction (FWD, RWD, AWD, 4WD)
- **FWD**: Power to front wheels—great for daily commutes and mild snow.
- **RWD**: Power to rear wheels—popular in sporty cars for better handling in dry conditions.
- **AWD**: Power can go to all four wheels automatically based on input from sensors—ideal for unpredictable weather or light off-road.
- **4WD**: The driver manually engages/disengages all four wheels—top choice for rugged trails or deep snow.

Pro Tip: Right System, Right Job
City life? FWD or AWD probably do the trick. Off-road adventures? 4WD is your buddy. Choose wisely for your regular driving scenarios!

Friction
- **Key Idea**: It's the "grip" between your tires and the road.
- **Why It Matters**: Strong friction = better control. Worn tires or slippery roads reduce friction, making it easier to skid.

Pro Tip: Tire TLC
Regularly check tire tread and pressure. Good tires = better grip, safer cornering, and a smoother ride.

HANDLING & CONTROL

Cornering & Trajectory
- **What It Is**: How your car manages turns, from gentle curves to tight corners.
- **Why It Matters**: Going too fast or jerking the wheel can cause understeer (the car won't turn enough) or oversteer (the car whips around too much).

Pro Tip: Ease Into the Turn
Slow down *before* the corner, then smoothly guide your car through the turn.

ADVANCED SYSTEMS

Traction Control (TCS) & Stability Control
- **TCS**: Stops the wheels from spinning too fast (especially on wet or icy roads).
- **Stability Control**: Helps prevent skids or rollovers by adjusting brakes or engine power.
- **Key Reminder**: These systems aid your driving, but they're not magical. Keep your speed in check and your eyes on the road.

ABS (Anti-Lock Braking System)
- **What It Does**: Stops your wheels from locking up when you slam the brakes, letting you steer while braking hard.
- **Don't**: Pump the brakes if ABS activates—push firmly, and let the system do its thing.

Common Mistake: Relying Solely on Tech
While TCS, stability control, and ABS are lifesavers, they can't fix reckless driving. Smooth inputs and sensible speeds still rule!

VEHICLE GEOMETRY

Center of Gravity (High vs. Low)
- **High CG**: More top-heavy, prone to rolling or rocking around corners.
- **Low CG**: Stays planted in turns, improves cornering stability.
- **Quick Example**: SUVs (higher CG) vs. sports cars (lower CG).

Wheelbase
- **Definition**: The distance between the front and rear axles.
  - o **Long** = smoother ride, stable at high speeds.
  - o **Short** = nimble, but can be bumpier.

Pro Tip: Wheelbase Wisdom
A longer wheelbase offers comfort, while a shorter one gives quicker steering. Pick what suits your drive!

Track Width
- **What It Is**: The distance between the left and right wheels on the same axle.
- **Impact on Stability**: Wider track width improves cornering stability and reduces body roll.

ENVIRONMENTAL IMPACTS

Terrain & Weather
- **Smooth Highways vs. Rough Roads**: Highways let your car glide; gravel needs slower speeds and sharper focus.
- **Rain, Snow, Ice**: Lower friction = longer braking distances. Go easy on gas and brakes.
- **Strong Winds**: They can push you sideways. Grip that wheel firmly and adjust your steering gently.

Seasons & Elevation
- **Summer Heat**: Tires can overinflate, engines can overheat—check pressures and coolant.
- **Winter Chill**: Icy roads mean slower speeds, gentler braking, and winter tires if possible.
- **High Altitude**: Thinner air reduces engine power; drive calmly uphill and watch your brakes downhill.

Common Mistake: Riding The Brakes On Hills
Use lower gears or engine braking to avoid overheating your brakes, especially on long downhill stretches.

Car dynamics may sound super technical, but it's really about understanding how your ride behaves in different scenarios. By mastering basic weight distribution, traction concepts, and vehicle geometry, plus how advanced systems step in to help, you'll navigate corners, tackle tricky roads, and stay cool under changing conditions. Keep these tips in mind, and let your car's moves feel as natural as jamming to your favorite tune!

9. PICK THE RIGHT SIZE: BIG VS. SMALL CARS

If variety is the spice of life, then cars come with their own hot sauce labels—small, medium, large, and super-sized. From zippy subcompacts to hulking SUVs, size affects everything from how easily you can parallel park to how much it costs to gas up. In this chapter, we'll help you navigate the big vs. small car debate with a dash of humor and a whole lotta practicality. Let's find out which ride fits your lifestyle best!

TURNING & MANEUVERABILITY

Small Cars: The Swift Movers
- **Tight Turns**: With a smaller turning radius, you'll zip around corners like a roller skater in a rink.
- **Parking**: Slide into snug spots with ease—perfect for crowded city streets and jam-packed mall lots.
- **Watch Out**: Their light weight and compact frame can make them twitchy at high speeds or on bumpy roads.

Big Cars: The Gentle Giants
- **Wider Turns**: Need a bit more elbow room to maneuver— imagine a waltz instead of a cha-cha.
- **Parking**: You may circle around the lot seeking roomy spaces, and parallel parking might feel like an Olympic event.
- **Upside**: Solid presence on highways can add stability and help you feel more planted at speed.

Pro Tip: Spin With Confidence
If tight corners or petite parking spaces stress you out, a smaller car might be your choice. If your comfort zone is roomy highways and suburban roads, a bigger vehicle can serve you better.

BLIND SPOTS & VISIBILITY

Little Rides, Wide Views
- **Fewer Blind Spots**: Shorter, lower bodies often mean you can see more of what's happening around you—no major pillars blocking the show.
- **Rear Views**: Backing up is easier when the trunk ends just past your shoulder blades.

Larger Rides, Taller Perch
- **Commanding View**: A higher driving position grants a king-of-the-road feel, spotting traffic up ahead.
- **Blind-Spot Caveat**: Bulkier frames and longer bodies can create bigger blind spots—time to lean on mirrors, backup cameras, and a bit of caution.

Common Mistake: Mirror Neglect
Whether big or small, always adjust mirrors properly. Even a compact car has blind zones. Shoulder checks are not optional—no matter your ride's size!

WEIGHT, BRAKING & HANDLING

Heavy vs. Light
- **Big Cars**: More mass = momentum. This gives a solid, planted feel at speed, but watch out for longer braking distances.
- **Small Cars**: Lightweight means quicker stopping (in theory), but if the tires or brakes are subpar, you could still slide around.

Body Roll & Grip
- **Big Cars**: Might lean more in tight corners but can feel steady on straight roads.
- **Small Cars**: Nimble in corners but can get unsettled by rough patches or gusty winds.

Pro Tip: Feel The Beat
Test-drive your prospective car on the highway and on side roads. You'll quickly sense if the handling suits your style.

ACCELERATION & FUEL ECONOMY

Power & Pickup
- **Small Cars**: Less weight to haul around often means zippier acceleration, though engine size matters a lot.
- **Big Cars**: Larger mass might accelerate slower unless there's a beastly engine under the hood. That extra horsepower can guzzle fuel, though.

MPG & Your Wallet
- **Small Cars**: Typically sip gas, great for saving money on daily commutes.

- **Big Cars**: Tend to gulp more fuel, but some modern SUVs and crossovers come with efficient engines or hybrid setups.

Common Mistake: Ignoring Your Commute

It's easy to be smitten by a huge SUV's allure—until your daily city commute racks up hefty fuel bills. Weigh your need for cargo space against your tolerance for frequent gas station stops!

HIGH WINDS & STABILITY

Lightweights in the Wind
- **Small Cars**: Can feel like leaves blowing in a breeze during strong gusts—keep both hands on the wheel.
- **Key Tip**: Slowing down and staying alert helps you handle those pushy wind gusts.

Larger Vehicles & Crosswinds
- **Added Stability**: Extra weight might anchor you better.
- **Sail Effect**: Large, flat side panels can catch wind, causing sudden lane shifts if you're not prepared.

Pro Tip: Steady On The Breezes

In stormy conditions, reduce speed, leave extra following distance, and be ready to correct gently if winds nudge your ride off course—big or small.

SPACE & COMFORT

Big Car Comfort
- **Cabin Room**: Plenty of legroom for passengers, spacious cargo area, and often smoother rides over bumpy roads.
- **Hauling Master**: Ideal for big families, road trips with the crew, or stashing large gear.

Small Car Practicality
- **Cozy Interior**: Perfect for couples, singles, or city dwellers with minimal cargo needs.
- **Urban Bliss**: Maneuver cramped parking garages and narrow alleyways without breaking a sweat.

Common Mistake: Overestimating Your Space Needs

Don't buy a massive SUV if you rarely haul more than groceries. Gas, maintenance, and parking stress might outweigh those few times you'd really need the extra room.

LIFESTYLE & TIPS FOR DAILY USE

Urban vs. Rural
- **City Dwellers**: Compact cars handle tight spots, busy traffic, and limited parking.
- **Country Living**: More space for gear, bigger cargo capacity, and stable rides on long highways or rough county roads.

Hobbies & Hauls
- **Weekend Warriors**: Larger vehicles tow boats or campers, great for off-road excursions.
- **Commuter Heroes**: Small cars are wallet-friendly, especially if your drive is mostly city miles.

Pro Tip: Lifestyle Check
Think of your weekly routine—errands, commutes, trips. If 95% of your driving is in busy streets, a small car is a dream. If you're always loading sports equipment or towing a trailer, bigger might be better.

Size absolutely matters—but it's about matching your car's dimensions to your real-life needs. Love a lively city scene with tight parking? A small ride could be your best friend. Need to cart the family and gear on weekend getaways? A bigger vehicle is calling your name.

In the showdown of big vs. small cars, there's no one-size-fits-all winner—just the perfect match for *you*. By focusing on your environment, budget, and comfort, you'll find a car that glides into your life like a puzzle piece snapping perfectly into place.

Pro Tip: Test For Your Lifestyle
If you can, borrow a friend's car or rent one to see how it fits your daily routine. There's nothing like real-world practice to confirm your choice.

Common Mistake: Falling For Looks
A giant SUV may look impressive, but if you're tearing your hair out every time you try to park, it's not worth the stress. Prioritize function over flash!

10. POP THE HOOD: A PEEK INSIDE YOUR CAR'S POWERHOUSE

Engines are more than metal blocks—they're the heartbeat of your car. Whether you're into a gasoline growl, a torquey diesel, or a silent electric hum, each type has unique strengths and quirks. In this chapter, we'll breeze through cylinder layouts, displacement, forced induction, timing setups, and fuel options (including alternative and electric). By the end, you'll have a clearer sense of which engine best aligns with your driving style and lifestyle. Ready to lift the hood? Let's dive in!

CYLINDER CONFIGURATIONS & DISPLACEMENT

Cylinder Configurations
- **Inline (I4, I6, etc.)**: Cylinders in a row—common for simplicity and efficiency, they offer decent power in a compact size.
- **V-Configuration (V6, V8, V10, etc.)**: Two angled banks, saving space and often packing more power (V8 muscle cars, anyone?).
- **W-Configuration (W8, W12, W16)**: A rarer design combining multiple cylinder banks in a "W" shape. Used mostly in high-end performance or luxury vehicles (such as Bentley and Bugatti). Provides massive power and torque in a relatively compact package, but is more complex and costly to produce.
- **Boxer (Flat)**: Cylinders lying flat for a low center of gravity and better handling (e.g., Subaru, Porsche); however, trickier to service.

Displacement
- **What It Is**: The total volume of an engine's cylinders (in liters or cc).
- **Why It Matters**: Higher displacement usually means more torque (pulling power), but also more fuel consumption.
- **Bigger Displacement = More Air/Fuel**: Potential for bigger torque numbers—think of each cylinder as a bigger "cup" to fill with energy.

Pro Tip: Finding The Sweet Spot
If you love off-the-line punch, focus on torque. If you crave high-speed thrills, horsepower might be your priority. Most daily drivers need a balance of both.

FORCED INDUCTION VS. NATURALLY ASPIRATED

Naturally Aspirated (NA)
- **What It Is**: Engine breathes air at atmospheric pressure—no turbo or supercharger.
- **Pros/Cons**: Simpler, linear power delivery but limited by engine size for big power.

Forced Induction
- **Turbocharger**: Exhaust spins a turbine, forcing extra air into cylinders (delayed boost while exhaust pressure ramps up).
- **Supercharger**: Belt-driven, immediate boost response (no lag).
- **Pros**: Smaller engines can produce higher power.
- **Cons**: Added complexity. Turbo lag can affect driving feel.

Common Mistake: Boost Blindness
Don't assume a turbo will always save fuel—it depends on your driving habits. Heavy-footed drivers can negate the efficiency gains.

FUEL OPTIONS

Gasoline
- **Staple Fuel:** Everywhere, suits most small-to-medium cars.
- **Pros:** Readily available, wide range of engine sizes.
- **Cons:** Emissions, fluctuating pump prices.

Diesel
- **Torque Champion:** High compression ignites fuel, producing strong low-end power.
- **Pros:** Great highway mileage, ideal for towing.
- **Cons:** Fuel sometimes pricier, complex emissions systems.

LPG (Liquefied Petroleum Gas)
- **What It Is:** Pressurized propane/butane mix.
- **Pros:** Burns cleaner, cheaper in some regions.
- **Cons:** Fewer refill stations, reduced trunk space due to LPG tank.

ELECTRIC MOTORS & ALTERNATIVE ENGINES

Electric Motors
- **No Fuel Tank, No Exhaust**: Battery power, near-silent operation.

- **Pros**: Zero tailpipe emissions, quiet ride, instant torque for quick acceleration.
- **Cons**: Range anxiety, charging infrastructure, higher upfront cost.
- **Key Terms**:
  - **Range**: How far you can go on one charge.
  - **Regenerative Braking**: Recovers energy, slightly extending range.

Hydrogen Fuel Cells
- **What It Is**: Uses hydrogen to create electricity—emissions mostly water vapor.
- **Why It's Niche**: Limited hydrogen stations, higher costs, specialized maintenance.
- **Cool Factor**: Zero tailpipe emissions, quick refuels.

Rotary / Wankel Engines (Gasoline only)
- **What It Is**: Rotating rotor instead of pistons (think Mazda RX series).
- **Pros**: Compact, smooth, high-rev performance.
- **Cons**: Lower fuel efficiency, higher emissions, specialized servicing.

THE MAGIC OF TIMING & DETONATION CYCLE

The 4-Stroke Process
- **Intake:** Piston moves down, drawing air-fuel mixture (or air alone in diesel, since fuel is injected during compression).
- **Compression:** Piston rises, compressing the mix.
- **Power (Combustion):** Spark (gas) or high compression (diesel) ignites, forcing piston down.
- **Exhaust:** Piston moves up, expelling spent gases.

Pistons, Valves & Shafts
- **Crankshaft:** Turns piston motion into rotation (wheels eventually spin).
- **Camshaft:** Times the valve openings so each stroke occurs at the perfect moment.
- **Valves:** Inhale fuel-air, exhale exhaust.

Timing
- **Why It Matters:** Perfect timing ensures smooth, efficient power without piston-valve collisions. Mistiming = engine chaos (and $$).

HORSEPOWER, TORQUE, SPEED & ACCELERATION

Horsepower (HP)
- **What It Is**: The rate of work the engine can sustain—most noticeable at higher RPMs. Think top speed and passing power. (For a detailed definition of *horsepower*, head to the glossary)
- **Impact**: Great for highway merging, top-end excitement, or spirited driving.

Torque
- **What It Is**: The twisting force—felt when accelerating from a stop or towing.
- **Impact**: Heavier loads or steeper inclines demand strong torque. A torquey engine feels punchy at lower RPMs.

Speed & Acceleration
- **Number of Cylinders:** More cylinders can mean a smoother engine (each cylinder fires in overlapping sequences). High RPM + multiple cylinders often yields higher HP and, by extension, better top-end speed.
- **Displacement & Torque:** Bigger cylinders = more torque. Strong low-end torque = peppier acceleration from stops.
- **Small But Mighty**: Turbos on small engines can boost HP & torque without huge displacement (e.g., many modern compacts).

Pro Tip: Lifestyle Angle
If you do lots of stop-and-go, torque matters. Love highways? Higher RPM power might be your friend.

WHICH ENGINE TYPE SUITS YOU?

Commuter & City Dweller
- **Hybrid or EV**: Saves on gas, perfect for short trips, potential incentives.
- **Small Gas Engine**: Cheaper upfront, ubiquitous gas stations— simple fueling.

Adventurer & Long-Distance Driver
- **Diesel**: Great highway fuel efficiency, ideal for towing.
- **Gas SUV/Truck**: Robust variety, good for road trips, flexible hauling options.

Tech Enthusiast

- **EV or Hydrogen**: Cutting-edge, near-silent, minimal tailpipe emissions.
- **Performance Car**: Turbo or supercharged gas for thrilling acceleration if speed is your jam.

Pro Tip: Match Your Lifestyle

Ask yourself: "Do I tow trailers, commute long distances, or live near charging stations?" The right engine choice fits your routine—not just your dreams.

LIFESTYLE & DRIVING EXPERIENCE IMPACT

Cost & Maintenance

- **EVs/Hybrids**: Fewer moving parts but battery health matters.
- **Gas/Diesel**: Widely known, but oil changes, filters, and belts remain key.
- **Alternative**: Hydrogen refills or rotary upkeep can be specialized or costlier.

Driving Feel

- **Instant Torque of EV**: Swift, smooth acceleration; watch for charging on road trips.
- **Grunty Diesel**: Great for towing or off-road; be mindful of the emissions system requirements, such as diesel exhaust fluid (DEF).
- **High-Rev NA Gas**: Enjoy the rev-happy soundtrack—less torque at low revs though.
- **Turbocharged Fun**: Punchy acceleration when boost kicks in, but be aware of potential lag.

Common Mistake: Need v. Want

Don't overbuy on horsepower or torque if you rarely push your car's limits. Know your roads, budget, and patience for fueling or charging stops.

From classic gas engines to whisper-quiet electrics—and even the futuristic hydrogen or niche rotary—the range of "beasts under the hood" is vast. Each engine type shapes everything from daily comfort to how often you refuel (or recharge) and how you handle a loaded trunk or trailer. By understanding cylinder layouts, displacement, induction, and timing intricacies, you'll be able to pick the engine (or motor!) that suits your life, budget, and driving vibes best. The coolest part? Whichever path you choose—gas station, charger, or hydrogen pump—you'll be armed with the knowledge to make it truly work for you.

11. DIFFERENT DIETS FOR DIFFERENT CARS: FUEL TYPES MADE SIMPLE

Fuel is the lifeblood of your ride—whether that's the familiar roar of a gasoline engine, the torque-heavy hum of a diesel, or the near-silent swoosh of an electric motor.

In the **previous chapter**, we skimmed over various fuel types (LPG, hydrogen, etc.). Now, let's take a deeper look at the three you're most likely to encounter: **gasoline**, **diesel**, and **electric**. We'll also clarify what octane really means, why ethanol gets tossed into the gas mix, the basics of DEF for diesel, and how EV charging levels can impact battery life.

GASOLINE

Spark Ignition vs. Compression Ignition Refresher
- **Gas vs. Diesel**:
    - **Gasoline Engines**: Use spark plugs to ignite the air-fuel mixture.
    - **Diesel Engines**: Compress air until it's hot enough to ignite the fuel without a spark.
- **Why It Matters**: Spark ignition (gas) typically means smoother high-RPM power, while diesel's compression ignition yields strong low-RPM torque.

What Is Octane & Why It Matters
- **Octane Rating (e.g., 87, 91, 93)**: A measure of how resistant fuel is to **knock** (pre-ignition).
- **Knock Explained**:
    - Occurs when the air-fuel mixture ignites too early, causing pinging or knocking sounds.
    - Can damage engine parts like pistons if severe or ongoing.
- **High-Octane Fuel**:
    - **Turbo/High-Compression Engines** need it to avoid knock when working hard.
    - **Regular Engines** rarely see benefits from premium fuel if not designed for it—save your money unless your owner's manual recommends otherwise.

Ethanol in Gasoline
- **Why Add Ethanol?**
  - o **Boost Octane**: Ethanol helps raise the overall octane, reducing knock.
  - o **Renewable Content**: Produced from corn or sugarcane, partially offsets fossil fuel usage.
- **Pros & Cons:**
  - o **Lower Emissions** than pure gas in some respects.
  - o **Reduced MPG** because ethanol has lower energy density.
- **Ethanol-Free Gas:**
  - o Some older engines or small equipment prefer it to avoid fuel system issues or corrosion. Check your manual for compatibility.

Real-World Fuel Economy & Price Factors
- **Ethanol Blends** (E10, E15): Slight MPG drop vs. pure gasoline.
- **Seasonal Blends & Taxes**: Regional rules, refining complexities, and local taxes can make prices swing.
- **Driving Style**: Hard acceleration or high-speed cruising can diminish the MPG advantage of lower-octane or ethanol-blended fuels.

DIESEL

Diesel Basics & Why It's Different
- **Compression Ignition**: Air alone is compressed until it's hot enough to ignite injected diesel—no spark plugs needed.
- **Torque Lover**: Known for robust low-end torque, ideal for towing or heavier vehicles.

Seasonal & Cetane Variations
- **Summer vs. Winter Diesel:**
  - o **Winter Diesel**: Formulated to avoid gelling in cold temps; might alter engine performance slightly but ensures reliable starts in freezing weather.
- **Cetane Number**: Diesel's counterpart to octane, measuring ignition quality. Higher cetane usually means smoother, easier combustion.

Fuel Economy & Production Costs
- **Highway Hero**: Diesel engines often excel at steady-speed efficiency, meaning fewer fill-ups for long commutes.

- **Refining & Price**: Diesel is distilled at a higher temperature range from crude oil, which can make it pricier than gas—though improved MPG may offset cost differences for frequent travelers.

DEF (Diesel Exhaust Fluid)
- **What It Is**: A urea-based fluid (often called AdBlue) injected into the exhaust stream.
- **Why You Need It**: Converts harmful NOx emissions into harmless nitrogen and water, keeping diesels cleaner.
- **Driver Impact**: Must refill DEF tank periodically—running low triggers engine warnings or power reduction.

ELECTRIC MOTORS

No Fuel Tank, No Exhaust
- **Battery Power**: Energy is stored in lithium-ion (or similar) batteries, driving an electric motor.
- **Instant Torque**: Hit the pedal, feel the immediate surge—perfect for city stoplights or quick merges.

Charging Levels & Approximate Times
1. **Level 1 (120V)**:
   - **Charging Speed**: approx. 3–5 miles of range per hour.
   - **Use Case**: Overnight top-ups for short commutes.
2. **Level 2 (240V)**:
   - **Charging Speed**: approx. 15–30 miles of range per hour (varies by vehicle).
   - **Use Case**: Home or public chargers—full charge in a few hours, ideal for daily use.
3. **Level 3 (DC Fast Charging)**:
   - **Charging Speed**: 0–80% in approx. 20–40 minutes.
   - **Consideration**: Frequent fast charging can slightly degrade battery life over time.

Battery Health & Lifestyle
- **Battery Degradation**: Repeated fast-charging or exposure to extreme temperatures can reduce battery capacity over time.
- **Cost**: Electricity is often cheaper than gas or diesel per mile, plus near-silent operation means a calmer cabin. However, you must plan around available chargers and consider at-home installation costs.

LIFESTYLE & DRIVING EXPERIENCE

Commuter & City Dweller
- **Gas**: Simple to fill, wide availability, short distances won't kill MPG.
- **Diesel**: Might be overkill if you only drive a few miles daily, but still possible.
- **Electric**: Perfect for short trips; charge overnight at home or work. Low noise, minimal maintenance.

Adventurer & Long-Distance Driver
- **Gas**: Ubiquitous fueling stations, flexible range of vehicles.
- **Diesel**: Highway mileage champ, great for towing or off-road (just remember to keep the DEF topped up).
- **Electric**: Road trips require plotting chargers. Fast charging helps, but repeated Level 3 usage can affect battery longevity.

Performance Enthusiast
- **Gas**: Turbocharged or high-octane for peak power, just watch out for knock in forced-induction engines if you use low-grade fuel.
- **Diesel**: Punchy torque for spirited towing or hauling.
- **Electric**: Instant acceleration off the line—some EVs rival sports cars in 0–60 times.

Pro Tip: Match Your Routine
Are you a highway warrior, city commuter, or weekend adventurer? The right fuel (or electric) should fit your daily drives, fueling/charging infrastructure, and desired performance level.

From gasoline's octane-driven performance to diesel's torque-rich highway efficiency to the quiet punch of an electric motor—your choice shapes how often you stop for fuel (or a charge), how much you pay at the pump (or on your utility bill), and how your car performs day in, day out.

By grasping how octane rating fights knock, why ethanol is added, how DEF cleans diesel emissions, and the ins-and-outs of EV charging, you'll keep your vehicle happy, healthy, and ready for every mile ahead!

12. REFUELING WITHOUT LOOKING CLUELESS

Refueling might seem routine, but small details—from the pump you pick to how you handle the nozzle—can mean the difference between a breezy fill-up and a messy one. In this chapter, we'll focus on the **practical steps** of "feeding" your car—be that with gas, diesel, or electrons—so you can keep your ride running strong and avoid headaches at the station (or charger).

REFUELING 101 (GASOLINE OR DIESEL)

Identifying Your Fuel Type & Pump
- **Check the Label**: Inside your fuel door or on the gas cap, you'll usually see "Unleaded Only" or "Diesel." Never assume—especially if you're borrowing a friend's car.
- **Color Clues**: Many stations use different-colored nozzles for diesel (often green or yellow) vs. gasoline (black or another color). Always read the pump label before squeezing that trigger.
- **Nozzle Size**: Diesel pump nozzles are often slightly larger in diameter than gasoline nozzles—this helps prevent accidentally inserting a diesel nozzle into a gasoline-only vehicle, but always double-check before you fill!

Steps at the Pump
- **Engine Off**: Safety first—always switch off.
- **Static Discharge**: Touch metal on your car to avoid sparks when handling the nozzle.
- **Select Fuel Grade**: Use the octane recommended by your car's manual (or the right diesel pump). Over-octaning can be a waste, and misfueling can be a nightmare.
- **Watch the Flow**: Don't wander off while pumping. If the auto-click fails, you could end up with a big, smelly puddle at your feet.
- **No Overfill**: Once the pump clicks off, resist the urge to top up. It can damage your car's vapor system and waste money.

Pro Tip: Mind Your Fuel Door Location
Some cars have the fuel door on the left, others on the right. Look for the little arrow on your fuel gauge—it points to the side your fuel door is on, saving you awkward pump positioning.

DIESEL-SPECIFIC POINTERS

Things to Consider
- **Foaming Factor**: Diesel can foam up, causing early pump shutoff. Pump slowly near the end to avoid spillage.
- **Separate Lanes**: Some stations have dedicated diesel or truck lanes—helpful for bigger vehicles, but read the signs carefully.

What About DEF?
- **Diesel Exhaust Fluid (DEF)**: A separate fluid that helps reduce emissions. Has its own fill port (typically blue cap)—**do not** add it to your fuel tank.
- **Topping Up**: Your dash should warn you when DEF is low. Failing to refill can limit performance or trigger warnings.

Common Mistake: Gas In a Diesel (or vice versa)
Always double-check the pump. A moment of distraction can lead to an engine repair bill bigger than your vacation fund!

REFUELING YOUR EV

Finding a Charger
- **Maps & Apps**: Use mobile apps or built-in navigation. Not every station has EV chargers, and some chargers require specific memberships or cards.
- **Charger Levels**: Recall from the previous chapter
  - **Level 1**: Standard home outlet (slow); approx. 3–5 miles of range per hour.
  - **Level 2**: Faster 240V for home or public (approx. 15–30 miles of range per hour).
  - **DC Fast Charging**: Rapid top-ups (approx. 20–40 minutes to 80%), but repeated fast charges can slightly reduce battery health over time.

Plugging In & Etiquette
- **Know Your Port**: CCS, CHAdeMO, Tesla Supercharger, etc.— don't show up to the wrong station.
- **Move When Done**: Once you're juiced up, free the spot for the next EV driver. No "charging squatters," please!

Pro Tip: Battery TLC
For longer battery life, avoid letting your charge drop too low or parking at 100% for extended periods. Aim for a comfy "middle range" day-to-day.

FUELING SAFETY & ETIQUETTE

General Tips
- **No Flames or Smoking**: Gas vapors ignite easily—be mindful.
- **Phone Use**: Some places advise against using phones at the pump to reduce static or distraction risk.

Watch Your Surroundings
- **Pay & Go**: If your station requires pre-pay, do so to keep the line moving. If you pay after pumping, be quick—others might be waiting.
- **Clean Up Spills**: If you dribble diesel or gasoline, let the attendant know. A slippery fueling area is no fun for anyone.

Common Mistake: Adding a "Few Extra Cents"
Stubbornly topping off after the pump clicks can cause spills and harm your car's vapor system. Let the pump decide when you're done!

FUEL ECONOMY & THRIFTY TIPS

Light Driving Adjustments
- **Smooth Acceleration**: Hard launches gobble more fuel (or battery for EV's).
- **Route Planning**: Combine errands to reduce multiple cold starts—engines run more efficiently once warm.

Seasonal Considerations
- **Winter vs. Summer Fuel**: Gas often changes volatility in different seasons; diesel might have a winter blend. Adjust your expectations for MPG and performance in extreme weather.
- **Battery in Cold**: EV range can drop significantly in freezing conditions—plan more frequent charges or use battery preconditioning if available.

TROUBLESHOOTING REFUELING ISSUES

Gas-Pump Failures
- **Card Not Accepted:** Might be station limits or your bank's alert. Try another pump or method of payment.
- **Pump Clicking Repeatedly:** Could be a bent filler neck or a sensitive pump. Adjust the nozzle angle.

Diesel Foam Overflow
- **Slow the Flow:** Diesel can foam up, triggering the pump to click off early—try pumping at a gentler speed.
- **Spill Cleanup:** Diesel spills can be slippery; inform staff if it's more than a few drops.

EV Charger Issues
- **Charger Offline:** Apps usually show station status. If it's offline, find the next nearest station.
- **Cable Latch Stuck:** Some chargers or car ports require you to end the session in-app or in-car before unplugging.

Pro Tip: Plan Ahead

Going on a long trip? Map out diesel stations (if you're towing) or high-speed chargers (if driving an EV). Fewer surprises mean a more relaxed journey.

Common Mistake: Forgetting to Close the Fuel Cap

A loose or missing cap can trigger engine warning lights and compromise your car's evaporative emissions system. Always double-check it's tight before driving off.

Refueling (or recharging) isn't just about pumping liquids or electrons—it's about doing so safely and efficiently. A bit of foresight—knowing which pump to use, how your EV charger works, or how not to top off—keeps your wallet and your vehicle happy. By mastering these simple tips, you'll handle every pit stop like a pro!

13. STRETCH EVERY GALLON: TRICKS FOR MAXIMIZING FUEL EFFICIENCY

Fuel efficiency often boils down to a series of little habits—like "grazing" rather than "gorging." Instead of stomping on the gas pedal (or battery) every chance you get, consistent and mindful driving keeps your wallet fuller and your carbon footprint smaller. Whether you're running on dinosaur juice or electrons, the goal is the same: get more out of every drop (or charge). Let's dive into how you can drive farther while spending less.

UNDERSTANDING FUEL EFFICIENCY

The Basics
- **MPG (Miles Per Gallon)**: Common in the U.S. (and to an extent, UK with Imperial gallons). The higher the number, the further you travel on one gallon.
- **Liters per 100 km (L/100 km)**: Popular in Canada, Europe, and elsewhere. The lower the number, the better—it means you use fewer liters of fuel to travel 100 kilometers.
- **Why It Matters**: People often talk about "good" or "bad" mileage differently across countries. Recognizing both helps you compare efficiently if you read foreign car reviews or travel internationally.

Electric Vehicles
- **Miles per kWh (mi/kWh)**: This tells you how many miles the EV can travel on one kilowatt-hour of electricity.
- **MPGe (Miles Per Gallon Equivalent)**: 1 gallon of gasoline = 33.7 kWh of energy. So, if an EV travels 100 miles using 33.7 kWh, it's rated at 100 MPGe.

Pro Tip: Track Your Gains
Keep a small record of your fill-ups or EV usage to see how changes in your driving style improve efficiency over time.

HYPERMILING & DRIVING HABITS

Hypermiling is a driving strategy focused on squeezing every last mile (or kilometer) out of your fuel or battery. It involves techniques like smooth acceleration, early coasting toward stops, maintaining moderate speeds, and minimizing idle time.

The payoff? By adopting these habits, you can significantly boost your car's MPG, meaning fewer trips to the pump, a fatter wallet, and a surprisingly chill drive!

Smooth Acceleration & Braking
- **Easy Does It**: Hard launches and slamming the brakes waste energy. If you see a red light up ahead, ease off the gas and let momentum carry you—like grazing on energy instead of feasting.

Pulse-and-Glide
- **What It Is**: Accelerate to a set speed (the "pulse"), then coast (the "glide") until you slow somewhat. Repeat as road conditions allow.
- **Why It Works**: Minimal acceleration plus frequent coasting can boost economy significantly—just do it safely, watching traffic behind you.

Cruise Control vs. Terrain
- **Why It Matters**: On flat highways, cruise control smooths out speed fluctuations. But on hilly terrain, it may overcompensate— turn it off if your car hunts gears too often.

Common Mistake: Over-Focusing
Excessive hypermiling (constantly checking your instant MPG, creeping up to lights) can distract you from the road. Balance safety with your fuel-saving goals.

MAINTENANCE & AERODYNAMICS

Tires & Alignment
- **Proper Inflation**: Underinflated tires increase rolling resistance, tanking your MPG.
- **Wheel Alignment**: Misaligned wheels drag your car sideways, wearing tires unevenly and burning extra fuel.

Engine & Oil
- **Regular Oil Changes**: Fresh oil reduces internal friction. Use the recommended grade—thicker or thinner oils can impede efficiency (remember, oil viscosity can also change with ambient temperature.).
- **Air Filters**: A clogged filter starves the engine of air, forcing it to guzzle more fuel.

Less Drag, Please
- **Ditch Roof Racks**: If you don't need that cargo box, take it off. It's like wearing a parachute on your car.
- **Windows vs. AC**: At higher speeds, open windows create drag, so sometimes mild AC is more fuel-efficient than flapping windows.

WEATHER & TERRAIN CONSIDERATIONS

Seasonal Fuel Blends & Temp Swings
- **Gasoline "Winter" or "Summer" Mix**: Seasonal changes affect volatility, so your efficiency can shift with the weather.
- **Diesel & Winter**: Special anti-gelling additives help in cold climates. Don't be surprised if your mileage changes a bit.

Hills & Altitude
- **Climbing**: Uphill sections demand more power—moderate your speed.
- **Coasting Down**: Use your car's momentum; if you drive an EV or hybrid, regenerative braking can regain some lost energy.

Pro Tip: Driving Downhill
Shift to lower gears (a.k.a. engine braking) on long downhill descents to prevent brake fade—more on that in a later chapter. For now, remember that brake fade means your brakes lose some ability to slow or stop effectively.

ROUTE & BEHAVIORAL STRATEGIES

Trip Planning
- **Combine Errands**: Each "cold start" uses extra fuel until the engine warms up. Group tasks into one trip to reduce repeated warm-ups.
- **Avoid Rush Hour**: Constant stop-and-go crushes your fuel efficiency. If possible, shift your schedule slightly to avoid the heaviest jams.

Carpool & Load Management
- **Carpool**: Splitting fuel or commute expenses helps everyone.
- **Lighten the Load**: Check the trunk for clutter—extra weight drags your mileage (or range) down.

EV Drivers
- **Eco-Modes**: Many EVs have an "Eco" setting, limiting acceleration and optimizing regenerative braking.
- **Charge Strategy**: Finishing your charge near departure time helps manage battery temperatures and range.

TROUBLESHOOTING ISSUES

If Mileage Drops Suddenly
- **Check Tire Pressure**: A small leak or underinflation can erode MPG drastically.
- **Monitor Dash Lights**: A warning or check engine light could signal a misfire or an emission component failure.
- **Excessive Idling**: New commute patterns or more AC usage can explain a drop too.

Track Your MPG Regularly
- **Simple Math**: Track total miles since last fill-up, then divide by gallons used. If you notice a big dip, investigate.

Pro Tip: Keep It Realistic
Aiming for huge MPG or L/100 km gains overnight can be frustrating. Celebrate small improvements—an extra mile per gallon or a slight drop in liters per 100 km is still a win.

Fuel efficiency isn't just for eco-warriors or penny-pinchers; it's for anyone who hates wasting time and money. No matter if your dash reads miles or kilometers, or whether your car sips gas, gulps diesel, or surfs on electrons, efficient habits let you "graze" on fuel rather than wolfing it down. Over time, those little changes lead to big payoffs—fewer stops at the pump (or charger), lower costs, and a more relaxed ride. The kick? Smooth, efficient driving often feels calmer and more satisfying than speeding from red light to red light!

14. TIRE TALK: EVERYTHING YOU SHOULD KNOW ABOUT TIRES

Imagine wearing hiking boots to a ballroom dance, or slippers on a muddy trail: the wrong shoes can lead to slips, stumbles, and discomfort. The same principle applies to your car's "footwear"— putting on the wrong tires (or wheels) can ruin your handling, reduce comfort, and even mess with your speedometer. In this chapter, we'll explore **the different types of tires**, how each is sized, and why wheel choice and "unsprung weight" matter.

TIRE BASICS: DECODING THE NUMBERS

Tire Size Nomenclature
- **Example**: 205/55R16 91V
    - **205**: Tread width in millimeters.
    - **55**: Aspect ratio (sidewall height is 55% of the width).
    - **R16**: Radial construction, fits a 16-inch wheel.
    - **91**: Load index—how much weight each tire supports.
    - **V**: Speed rating—maximum speed the tire can safely handle (e.g., S = 112 mph, H = 130 mph; V = 149 mph; for a full list of speed ratings, check online charts). Driving above that speed rating can compromise tire integrity, potentially leading to dangerous blowouts.

Tread Wear Rating
- **What It Is**: A numeric code (e.g., 300, 500) indicating relative tread life. Higher number = potentially longer-lasting tread under standardized test conditions.
- **Not the Whole Story**: Different manufacturers use their own benchmarks. A 500 tread wear in one brand isn't always the same as another brand's 500, but it's still a handy comparison tool within the same brand line.

Deviating from OEM Tire Size
- **Speedometer Impact**: Altering the overall tire diameter can skew speed readings (the car thinks you're going 60 mph but you're actually doing 63! – still not a good excuse if you're pulled over).
- **Ride & Clearance**: Oversized tires might rub fenders; undersized tires can reduce ground clearance or handling stability.

Common Mistake: Upsizing Without Doing Your Homework
Big rims and low-profile tires might look cool, but they can stiffen your ride and skew your speedometer. Check with a pro or use an online tire size calculator if you're making major changes!

TYPES OF TIRES

All-Season Tires
- **Everyday Versatility**: Decent grip in moderate climates—mild winter, wet roads, moderate summers.
- **Trade-Off**: Jack-of-all-trades but master of none: not ideal for extreme heat or heavy snow.

Summer (Performance) Tires
- **Hot Weather Grip**: Excellent traction in warm or slightly wet conditions.
- **Downside**: Rubber stiffens in cold; traction plummets if temps approach freezing.

Winter (Snow) Tires
- **Specialized Compound & Sipes**: Softer rubber and deep grooves for ice and snow.
- **Why Swap?**: In harsh winter areas, they drastically improve braking and cornering.
- **Downside**: Driving them in warm weather speeds up tread loss.

All-Terrain & Off-Road Tires
- **Aggressive Tread**: Perfect for gravel, mud, rocky paths.
- **Downside**: Noisier, heavier, can reduce MPG and highway comfort.

Run-Flat Tires
- **Drive After Puncture**: Allows short-distance travel (low speed) if pressure is lost.
- **Cost & Comfort**: Pricier, often stiffer ride, but saves you from changing a flat roadside.

WHEEL CHOICES & UNSPRUNG WEIGHT

Steel vs. Alloy Wheels
- **Steel Wheels**: Heavier, cheaper, resilient. Common for winter sets or budget cars.
- **Alloy Wheels**: Lighter, better heat dissipation, more stylish—but pricier and can crack under severe impact.

Unsprung Weight & Ride Quality
- **What It Is**: Weight of wheels, tires, brakes not supported by the car's springs.
- **Impact**: Heavier wheels require more effort to accelerate or turn, possibly making your ride bumpier. Ultra-light wheels can also disrupt your suspension's intended balance.
- **Goal**: Match wheel/tire weight near OEM specs so your car handles and rides as designed.

Pro Tip: Moderation
Going from heavy steel to superlight alloy can alter handling. If you lighten unsprung weight too much, your springs/dampers might behave differently—sometimes uncomfortably.

TREAD WEAR & MAINTENANCE

Penny/ Coin Test
- **Simple Method**: Insert a coin into the tread. If you see too much of the coin's head or design, your tread is likely below safe depth.
- **Wear Bars**: Tires come with built-in bars at ~2/32" (1.6 mm). If they're flush with the tread, it's time to replace.

Rotation, Balancing & Alignment
- **Tire Rotation**: Moving tires from front to rear, left to right, for even wear.
- **Balancing**: Corrects small weight imbalances so your wheels don't vibrate at speed.
- **Alignment**: Keeps your wheels pointing straight, ensuring even tread wear.

Built-Up Snow or Ice
- **Wheel Balance Issues**: If snow or ice clumps inside your wheels, it can throw off balance, leading to steering wheel vibrations at higher speeds.

- **Fix**: Knock or rinse out snow/ice whenever you notice vibrations after driving in winter conditions.

SEASONAL & DRIVING CONTEXT

Swapping Tires
- **Summer vs. Winter Sets**: If you face hardcore snowy months, consider winter tires for those months, then switch back.
- **All-Season Shortcut**: Handy if your climate is mild, but performance suffers in heavy snow or heat extremes.

Towing & Extra Loads
- **Load Index**: Towing a trailer or hauling heavy gear? Ensure your tire's load rating can handle the weight.
- **Inflation Adjustments**: Sometimes recommended to slightly increase PSI within safe limits for towing.

Danger of Aquaplaning
- **What It Is**: Tires lose contact with the road, skimming on a thin layer of water.
- **Why It Happens**: Worn tread or high speed on wet surfaces.
- **Result**: Total steering and braking loss—scary! Keep tread depth healthy and slow down in the rain.

Common Mistake: Ignoring Minimal Tread
Low tread depth drastically increases aquaplaning risk, especially at highway speeds on puddled roads.

CHOOSING THE RIGHT TIRES

Driving Style & Climate
- **City Dwellers**: All-seasons or run-flats might suit year-round, assuming moderate winter.
- **Snowbelt Drivers**: Winter tires, no question—unparalleled traction on ice and snow.
- **Performance Enthusiasts**: Summer or performance tires for maximum grip in hot conditions, but mind temperature dips.

Budget vs. Quality
- **Cheaper Tires**: May wear out faster or have poorer grip in rain.
- **Premium Brands**: Typically, higher tread wear rating, better wet traction, and sometimes quieter.

- **Balance**: Factor in how long you'll keep the car, your daily conditions, and your tolerance for road noise or frequent replacements.

Pro Tip: Avoid Surprises

Make sure your tires' speed and load ratings match your vehicle's specs—pushing them beyond those limits can lead to blowouts!

Think of tires like your car's footwear: picking the right style for the season and surface can drastically improve safety, comfort, and performance. Whether you're all about that off-road life, braving snowy streets, or cruising sunny highways, a bit of knowledge on **tire sizing**, **tread wear**, **wheel choices**, and **seasonal swaps** ensures your car always has the right "shoes" for the job. Throw in regular maintenance—like rotations and alignment—and you'll roll confidently through every season and every road condition!

15. DECODE THE DASHBOARD: OR KEEP GUESSING AND HOPE FOR THE BEST

Have you ever looked at your dashboard and wondered if your car was trying to send you a secret message—like a flashy code you need to crack? Fear not! Think of it as your car's way of communicating. Some lights mean "Chill, everything's fine," while others scream, "Pull over now!" This chapter helps you decipher **common dashboard lights**, explaining which ones are urgent, which ones can wait, and the simple fixes that often make them disappear.

COLOR-CODED URGENCY

Red Lights: Immediate Attention
- **Meaning**: A serious issue that could threaten safety or cause significant damage if ignored.
- **Typical Lights**:
    - o **Brake System Alert**: (Brake fluid low, or parking brake engaged—if fluid is fine, consult a mechanic).
    - o **Powertrain Malfunction**: (Sometimes a wrench icon)—can indicate serious engine/transmission trouble. Pull over if it's accompanied by jerky shifts or reduced power.

Yellow/Amber Lights: Caution
- **Meaning**: Check soon, but you can usually keep driving short-term.
- **Typical Lights**:
    - o **Check Engine Light (CEL)**: Could be minor (loose gas cap) or major (sensor or misfire). Solid = see a mechanic soon, flashing = pull over or slow down.
    - o **Bulb Failure**: Indicates a burnt-out exterior light (headlight, brake light, turn signal). Fix soon for safety and legal reasons.
    - o **Collision Detection**: If it's amber, the system might be partially disabled or seeing an error—drive carefully.

Green/Blue Lights: Informational
- **Meaning**: Generally harmless status indicators or reminders you've engaged something.

- **Typical Lights**:
  - o **Rear Window Defroster**: Letting you know it's active. Turn it off once your view is clear.
  - o **4WD/AWD Engaged**: Tells you the system is on. Suitable for slippery roads; turn off if not needed to save fuel.
  - o **Child Lock**: Usually a small door/kid icon—reminds you the rear doors can't be opened from inside.

Pro Tip: Headlights at Night

A surprisingly common error is forgetting to switch from DRLs to full headlights after dark. If you're only seeing a green DRL icon, your rear lights might be off—remember to toggle them fully on!

COMMON DASHBOARD LIGHTS & WHAT TO DO

Brake System Alert (Red "BRAKE" or Exclamation in Circle)

- **Urgent?** Yes, if it stays on after releasing the parking brake.
- **Can I Drive?** Check brake fluid; if the level is fine but the light stays on, drive cautiously and see a mechanic.
- **Likely Fix**: Could be low fluid or worn brake pads. Parking brake not fully released is another quick check.

Oil Pressure (Red Oil Can)

- **Urgent?** Yes!
- **Can I Drive?** Usually no—pull over soon.
- **Likely Fix**: Check oil level and pressure sensor. Driving with zero oil pressure can toast your engine.

Battery/Charging System (Red Battery Icon)

- **Urgent?** Quite.
- **Can I Drive?** Briefly, but risk losing power steering, lights, etc.
- **Likely Fix**: Could be an alternator problem or loose battery connections. Inspect cables or have the charging system tested.

Engine Overheat (Red Thermometer/Wave)

- **Urgent?** Yes!
- **Can I Drive?** Stop before you warp the engine head.
- **Likely Fix**: Check coolant, radiator fans, possible thermostat or water pump failure.

Powertrain Malfunction (Wrench Icon or Gear Shape)
- **Urgent?** Quite—implies a serious engine or transmission issue.
- **Can I Drive?** If accompanied by reduced power or weird shifts, pull over soon.
- **Likely Fix**: Diagnostic scan to pinpoint fault; might be sensor or mechanical. Don't ignore it.

Bulb Failure (Outline of a Lamp with an "X" or Slash Through It)
- **Urgent?** Medium—driving without brake lights or signals can be dangerous (and illegal).
- **Can I Drive?** Yes, but fix promptly to ensure you're visible and signaling properly.
- **Likely Fix**: Replace the burnt-out bulb or check for loose connections.

Rear Window Defroster (Rectangle with Vertical Wavy Lines)
- **Urgent?** Not usually, just tells you the defroster is on.
- **Can I Drive?** Absolutely—this helps clear fog or ice. Turn off once done to save electrical load.

Low Fuel (Gas Pump Icon or "Low Fuel" Text)
- **Urgent?** Medium—means you're running low. Keep driving carefully, but fill up soon to avoid stalling.
- **Likely Fix**: Stop at a gas station. If it's blinking or you feel sputtering, you're cutting it too close!

Open Doors/Hood/Trunk Ajar
- **Urgent?** Generally low risk, but can be dangerous if a door suddenly opens.
- **Can I Drive?** Check that doors, trunk, or hood are fully latched to avoid them swinging open on the road.

Seatbelt (Red Person/Belt Icon)
- **Urgent?** Safety-critical—always buckle up.
- **Can I Drive?** The car may drive, but it's unsafe and often beeps annoyingly until you comply.

Airbag Warning (Person with a circle in front)
- **Urgent?** Medium—airbag might not deploy in a crash if light stays on.
- **Can I Drive?** Yes, but you lose critical safety protection. Get it checked soon.

Child Lock Icon (Car Door and a Stylized Child or a Padlock)
- **Urgent?** Low urgency, just a reminder.
- **Impact:** Rear passengers can't open doors from inside—a safety measure for kids.

ESP (Electr. Stability Program) or ESC (Electr. Stability Control)
- **Urgent?** Medium if it's off; your stability assist won't help in skids.
- **Can I Drive?** Yes, but be cautious on slippery roads.
- **Likely Fix:** Press the ESP/ESC button if you accidentally turned it off. If it's a fault, see a mechanic.

4WD/AWD Engaged (Green or Amber Car Drivetrain)
- **Urgent?** Typically, just informational—this system is active.
- **Should I Care?** Switch off if not needed to save fuel or reduce wear.

Tire Pressure (Exclamation Icon Inside of Deflated Tire Outline)
- **Urgent?** Medium. Underinflated tires affect handling and mileage.
- **Likely Fix:** Check and adjust PSI, reset the sensor if needed.

Steering Column (Steering Wheel Icon or Slashed Wheel)
- **Urgent?** High if it's red or locked. Could indicate power steering failure or a locked column.
- **Can I Drive?** Manual steering is possible if it's a power steering fault, but turning will be tough. Seek service soon.

Auto Start/Stop (Letter "A" With a Circular Arrow Around It)
- **Meaning:** Engine's auto stop/start system is engaged or disabled.
- **Drive?** You can proceed normally; just note the car might not shut off at lights if the icon indicates a fault or system is off.

Collision Detection (Car Silhouette with Radar Waves in Front)
- **Urgent?** Medium if it's off or faulted—your car won't brake automatically for you.
- **Driving Impact:** Drive with extra caution. Clean sensors or check for system errors if it's acting up.

ABS (Yellow "ABS")
- **Urgent?** Medium—basic brakes still work, but anti-lock features are down.
- **Can I Drive?** Yes, but expect skidding when braking on slippery roads if the system is off or faulty.

EXTRA SAFETY & TIPS

Flashing vs. Solid
- **Flashing**: Usually more severe (e.g., a misfire for check engine). Reduce speed or stop.
- **Solid**: Less urgent but fix soon to avoid bigger problems.

Keep Sensors & Cameras Clean
- **Autonomous Systems**: Lane assist or collision detection rely on clear sensors.
- **Dirty Bumpers**: A little mud can disrupt your fancy radar or camera—leading to error lights.

Pro Tip: Tidy Up
Clean your windshield, mirrors, and sensors regularly, especially in winter or off-road conditions. Many dash warnings vanish once sensors see clearly again! (for example, a parking sensor might act erratically if snow or mud is blocking it)

WHEN DASHBOARD LIGHTS FLICKER OR STAY ON

Quick Fix: Gas Cap & Fluids
- **Loose Gas Cap**: A top culprit for check engine lights. Tighten until it clicks.
- **Low Fluid (Coolant, Brake, Wipers)**: Topping up might make the light go away.

Pull Over vs. Keep Driving
- **Red**: Pull over promptly—oil pressure, overheating, brake system are no joke.
- **Yellow**: Drive cautiously to a shop or home if performance is normal. Check soon.
- **Green/Blue**: It's just status information—no panic required.

Temporary Indicators
- **Parking Brake**: If that light is on, ensure the brake is fully released.
- **Rear Fog Light**: Turn off if conditions no longer warrant it—nobody wants an overly bright rear lamp in clear visibility.

Common Mistake: Ignoring Low Coolant
Overheating can turn into a blown head gasket. Always investigate a coolant warning promptly to avoid engine misery!

DON'T PANIC... JUST READ THE MANUAL AND DIAGNOSE

Manuals & OBD-II Scanners

- **Owner's Manual**: Quick reference for specific icons. Don't guess if an odd symbol appears.
- **Diagnostic Tools**: Many auto parts shops offer free code scans for check engine lights—helpful if you're unsure what's behind them.

Keep Calm & Assess

- **Driving Feels Fine?** If it's a minor light (like washer fluid or seatbelt reminder), handle it soon but no need to freak.
- **Strange Noises / Power Loss?** That's more urgent. Pull over and investigate.

Your dashboard's "Christmas lights" might look festive, but they serve a serious purpose: telling you what's up with your car. Red typically screams "Stop now or pay later," yellow suggests "Check me soon," and green/blue is more "Just a heads-up!". Understanding these icons means you'll never be left guessing whether your car's just craving a bit more windshield washer fluid or on the brink of engine meltdown. Pay attention, address them promptly, and you'll cruise with confidence (and fewer "uh-oh" moments).

16. READY, SET... NOT YET!
DO THIS BEFORE YOU DRIVE AWAY

Ever jumped into a friend's car only to find the seat's so far back you need a footstool to reach the pedals—or so close you feel like hugging the steering wheel? Getting your **car's cabin** set up correctly before you hit the road is a big deal. It's about comfort, safety, and a better driving experience. In this chapter, we'll walk through the essential steps—**seat adjustment**, **mirror alignment**, and a few other finishing touches—so you can treat your car like it's your second home (one on wheels!).

SEAT POSITION, STEERING WHELL & COMFORT

Distance & Tilt: The "Wrist on Wheel" Trick
- **Why It Matters**: You need to reach pedals and wheel without straining—especially on longer drives.
- **Wrist Test**: Sit up straight, shoulders against the backrest. Extend your arm so your wrist rests on the top of the steering wheel. Your distance is likely correct if your arm can do that comfortably while shoulders stay back.
- **Pedal Reach**: Knees should have a slight bend when pressing pedals—avoid locking your legs. This helps maintain control and reduces fatigue.

Seat Height & Angle
- **Height**: Aim to see clearly over the dashboard without your head hitting the ceiling. Some prefer a higher vantage point for better visibility.
- **Angle**: Keep your thighs supported but not pinched. Too much recline can strain your arms; too upright can feel rigid.

Steering Wheel & Instrument Access
- **Tilt & Telescoping**: Position the wheel so you can grip it comfortably at around "9 & 3" or "8 & 4" without leaning forward.
- **Dash Visibility**: Make sure your seat/wheel placement doesn't block critical gauges or warnings.

Pro Tip: Lumbar Love
If your seat has lumbar support, tweak it until your lower back feels gently supported. Perfect for preventing aches on those long drives.

MIRROR MAGIC

Rearview Mirror
- **Positioning**: Tilt it so you see directly out the rear window—centered, with minimal head movement needed.
- **Day/Night Tilt Knob**: Some manual mirrors have a little lever underneath. Flip it at night to tilt the mirror and reduce glare from headlights behind you. You can skip this step if your mirror is equipped with auto-dimming technology.

Side Mirrors (a.k.a. Minimizing Blind Spots)
- **Traditional vs. Expanded**:
  - **Traditional**: You see the side of your car; easy to reference, but bigger blind spots.
  - **Modern "BGE" Approach**: (Blindspot & Glare Elimination). Tilt mirrors outward so you barely see the edge of your car, giving a wider view of adjacent lanes.
- **Practical Setup**: Sit normally, then tilt each mirror outward until your car's flank just disappears from view. This cuts down those sneaky blind zones. <u>A quick shoulder check remains essential</u>, but you'll spot vehicles sooner.

Common Mistake: Mirror Neglect
Setting your mirrors once and forgetting them, even after a seat adjustment. If you move your seat forward or backward, re-check those angles!

BUCKLING IN & STOWING STUFF

Seatbelts & Headrest
- **Buckle Up**: Secure the belt across your shoulder and pelvis—no "under the arm" tricks.
- **Headrest**: Align the top with the top of your head. This helps prevent whiplash if you're rear-ended.

Loose Items
- **Trunk or Storage**: Keep that laptop bag, sports gear, or water bottle from rolling under pedals or becoming airborne.
- **Cupholders**: Great for drinks, but avoid overfilling—nobody wants coffee on the dashboard.

Pro Tip: Seatbelt Height
If your car has an adjustable shoulder strap anchor, slide it so the belt crosses comfortably over your shoulder (not neck) and snug across your torso. This ensures optimal safety and ergonomics.

VISIBILITY & CLIMATE CONTROL

AC to Defog
- **Cold or Wet Weather**: Foggy windows? Turn on the AC. It dehumidifies the cabin air, clearing the windshield faster than hot air alone. Aim vents at the glass and let dryness work its magic.
- **Don't Block Vents**: That pile of mail or stuffed toys on the dash can obstruct airflow.

Lights Check
- **Auto vs. Manual**: If your car has auto headlights, verify they're truly on at dusk. If manual, flip them on as soon as it's dark or if conditions require them.
- **Beware DRL**: Daytime running lights don't always power taillights, so switch the main beams on if it's raining or twilight.
- **High Beam Reminder**: Always glance at your dash for the **blue headlight icon**—if it's lit in normal traffic, switch off those brights to avoid blinding oncoming drivers!

Pro Tip: Foggy Situation
Many folks forget that AC isn't just for cooling—it's a great demister in wet or cold conditions. If windows get hazy, hit that AC button, even if you also need the heat on.

GAUGES, WARNINGS & TECHNOLOGY

Dashboard Lights
- **Startup Self-Test**: Ignition on—most lights briefly illuminate. If any crucial one stays lit, investigate before driving.
- **Fuel/Battery Level**: Enough gas or charge for your trip? Plan accordingly. Running on fumes or 2% battery is stressful.

Infotainment & Navigation
- **Enter Routes Before Rolling**: Avoid fumbling with the touchscreen mid-drive.
- **Hands-Free Setup**: Pair your phone, test the microphone—keeps your eyes up and phone usage minimal.

Additional Safety Tech
- **Lane Assist or Forward Collision**: If you rely on them, confirm they're active. If they're off or malfunctioning, you'll see a dash icon. Keep sensors clean (snow or mud can confuse them).

FINISHING TOUCHES: READY TO DRIVE

360° Surroundings Check
- **Check Mirrors**: Are they angled right?
- **Shoulder Glance**: Before backing out, ensure no people, pets, or objects are behind you.

Release Parking Brake & Select Gear
- **Parking Brake**: If manual or foot pedal style, ensure it's fully disengaged. Watch for the brake light.
- **Gear or Drive Mode**: Shift to "D" or first gear calmly, hand on the wheel, foot on brake.

Pro Tip: Walk-Around Check
Before you hop in, do a quick lap around your car to spot any wheel obstructions (nails, broken glass, etc.) or ensure no children, pets, or objects linger where you might not see them. This is super important, which is why we're pointing it out twice!

Pro Tip: Double-Check Seat & Mirrors After Letting Others Drive
If you share a car, someone might tilt the seat way back or re-aim the mirrors. A quick readjustment ensures you're set.

Common Mistake: Sitting Too Close
Some new drivers think a super-close seat gives more control, but it can tire arms and hamper pedal feel. Keep a slight bend in arms and legs for the best blend of comfort and agility.

Before you zoom off, treat these steps like your personal pre-flight checklist. Making yourself "at home" behind the wheel is about more than plopping into the driver's seat. It's adjusting for **comfort** (so you don't cramp up after 20 minutes), **safety** (so your seatbelt, mirrors, and lights all do their jobs), and **focus** (so you're not scrambling to defog windows or readjust a seat mid-drive). By taking a minute to set up your seat, angle mirrors, and turn on crucial features—like headlights or AC for defogging—you'll transform your trip from fussy to fabulous!

PART II:

THE REAL-LIFE DRIVING SKILLS NOBODY TAUGHT YOU

17. TAKE YOUR FIRST STEP: STARTING YOUR CAR

Starting your car is a moment of transformation—from quiet metal box to roaring (or gently humming) vehicle. Whether you're dealing with a classic key ignition or a fancy push-button, taking just a few seconds to prepare ensures a smoother, safer drive. This chapter guides you through the **step-by-step process**—no fuss, no confusion. Ready? Let's ignite some excitement!

PREPARE YOUR LAUNCH PAD

Seat, Mirrors, & Seatbelt
- **Seat Setup**: You've already learned how to position it (Chapter 16), so just confirm it's still good—feet reaching pedals, wrist can rest on top of the wheel.
- **Mirrors**: Double-check if you can see behind and beside you. If you adjusted your seat again, readjust your mirrors, too.
- **Seatbelt**: Click it! The best safety device is the one you actually use.

Check the Gear & Parking Brake
- **Automatic**: Confirm the shifter is in **Park (P)**.
- **Manual**: Set it to **Neutral (N)**, foot on the clutch if needed.
- **Parking Brake**: Still engaged? That's okay for now—don't release it until the engine's up and running.

Pro Tip: Quick Surroundings Scan
Look around—make sure no kids, pets, or random objects lurk behind your wheels. A 10-second walk-around can prevent a nasty surprise.

THE IGNITION PROCESS

Key Start
- **Insert Key**: Slide it into the ignition—some cars have separate "ACC" (accessory) or "On" positions.
- **Dash Light Check**: Turn to "On" (but not "Start") for a second—watch dash lights do their self-test. If a red or urgent one stays lit, investigate before proceeding.
- **Turn to Start**: Turn the key further; you'll hear the engine crank.

Release once it fires up—don't keep cranking for ages or you risk flooding the engine or draining the battery.

Push-Button Start
- **Foot on Brake**: And if it's a manual, **clutch in** too.
- **Press the Button**: You might need to hold it briefly. The dash lights and engine (or electric motor) come alive.
- **No Crunchy Starter Sounds**: If the engine struggles, let go and try again calmly—some cars prevent repeated pressing for a few seconds.

Manual Transmission
- **Always Clutch**: Keep that pedal down while starting.
- **Neutral Wiggle**: Test the shifter to ensure it is indeed in neutral, then proceed.
- **Don't Rev Hard**: Let it idle a moment, gently letting oil circulate.

Common Mistake: Revving Immediately
Gunning the gas right after ignition can stress a not-yet-lubed engine. Give it a few seconds to stabilize; your engine (and wallet) will thank you.

COLD WEATHER & EV/HYBRID TWISTS

Cold-Start Tips
- **Brief Warm-Up**: Older advice suggested long idling—modern engines need only a short moment. Then drive gently to let everything warm evenly.
- **Battery Strain**: If your starter sounds weak in freezing temps, your battery might need a charge or replacement.

Hybrid & EV Startup
- **"Ready" Mode**: You may not hear an engine roar—just watch for a "READY" light. That means you're good to go.
- **No Gas Pedal Surprises**: EVs/hybrids can be silent at low speeds, so confirm the dash says you're in Drive before hitting the accelerator.

Pro Tip: Defog With AC (Refresher)
In cold or wet weather, flipping on the AC helps clear windshield fog quickly, even if you're also running heat. Dry air is your friend!

DASH LIGHTS & INITIAL CHECKS

Look for Urgent Warnings
- **Red icons**: (oil pressure, engine overheat, brake system) demand immediate attention.
- **Amber icons**: (check engine, tire pressure) suggest caution but might not stall your trip.

Fuel/Battery Status
- Enough gas? Or does your EV have enough charge? If it's borderline, plan a refill or charge soon.
- If a low fuel light or EV range warning is on, don't shrug it off—nobody enjoys a roadside run for gas or a tow.

Gauge Movement
- **Speedometer & Tach**: They shouldn't bounce erratically at idle.
- **Temperature**: If it's cold, expect a cool reading until you start driving.

RELEASING THE PARKING BRAKE & MOVING

Disengage Parking Brake
- **Handbrake/Lever**: Push or pull down fully until the "Brake" light on the dash disappears.
- **Foot Pedal**: Press it in and release—make sure the dash indicator goes off.
- **Check for Lights**: If the brake light remains, see if the handle is partially up or brake fluid is low.

Shift into Gear
- **Auto**: Move from Park (P) to Drive (D). Foot still on brake so you don't jerk forward.
- **Manual**: Clutch in, select first gear, and slowly release the clutch while giving light gas.

Shoulder Check & Mirrors
- Ensure no obstacles or people are behind/in your blind spots.
- Gently press the accelerator and begin rolling.

Common Mistake: Driving Off with the Parking Brake On
If you feel resistance or smell something burning, you may have left the brake partially engaged. Double-check that handle or foot pedal!

FINAL TOUCHES FOR A SMOOTH RIDE

Climate & Radio
- **Comfort Settings**: Adjust blower speed and temperature. If windows start fogging, remember AC can quickly clear them.
- **Music or Navigation**: Cue up your playlist or set your route **before** moving to avoid distraction.

Quick "Ready" Mindset
- **Posture**: Sit up, arms relaxed. Check wrist distance to the wheel.
- **Focus**: Resist phone temptations or rummaging in the glovebox— eyes on the road from the get-go.

Pro Tip: Listen to Your Engine
If your engine sounds off or starts stuttering at ignition, pop the hood or note the dash light. Early detection saves big repair bills later.

Common Mistake: Idling Forever in Winter
A short idle helps, but don't let your car sit for 10 minutes warming up. Modern engines prefer gently driving to warm all components evenly—plus it saves fuel.

Starting your car might seem routine, but it's the foundation for every drive. Give your ride a second to wake up, ensure you're all set, and hit the road with a smile—no stutters, no surprise squeals, just an easy roll out of the driveway!

18. GET A GRIP: HOW TO HOLD THE STEERING WHEEL PROPERLY

Imagine you're conducting an orchestra—every flick of your baton guides the musicians to play in harmony. Now swap that baton for a **steering wheel**, and your hands become the maestros of your car's every move. A slight turn, a gentle hold, and you orchestrate smooth lane changes and easy curves. In this chapter we'll dive into **hand positions**, **steering methods**, and **common pitfalls**, so you can handle curves and corners like a pro, with a perfect blend of confidence and finesse.

WHY GRIP MATTERS

Control & Comfort
- **Steady Hands, Steady Car**: Good grip means smooth steering inputs, making lane changes and turns feel effortless.
- **Less Fatigue**: A relaxed hold at the correct position reduces arm and shoulder tension, ensuring you're comfortable on long drives.

Airbag Safety
- **Proper Hand Placement**: If your arms are in the wrong spot when the airbag deploys, you risk injury from the force.
- **Thumbs Out**: Don't wrap your thumbs around the inside of the wheel spokes—a sudden jolt could sprain them.

Common Mistake: Death Grip
White-knuckling the wheel might feel secure, but it actually tires you out and slows your reaction if you need a quick correction. Loosen up—your shoulders and wrists will thank you.

HAND POSITIONS: 9 & 3 (OR 8 & 4)

The Modern Recommendation
- **9 & 3 o'clock**: Picture the wheel as a clock face. Placing your hands at left "9" and right "3" helps distribute control evenly.
- **Thumbs on the Outside**: Rest them along the rim rather than looping them inside—safer in case of an airbag or sudden wheel jerk.

8 & 4 Variation
- **Lower Grip**: Some people prefer 8 & 4 if their steering wheel and seat position allow. It's still balanced, though a tad more relaxed in posture.
- **Be Mindful of Elbows**: If your elbows hit the seat bolster or center console, revert to 9 & 3.

Pro Tip: Tire & Steering Feedback
A balanced hold lets you "feel" the road's texture and subtle changes in steering more clearly. You'll sense slippery patches or bumpy terrain sooner, helping you react smoothly.

STEERING METHODS

Hand-Over-Hand
- **Tight Turns**: Useful for parking maneuvers or U-turns, where you rotate the wheel significantly.
- **Smooth Execution**: Avoid flailing arms; pass one hand over the other gracefully to maintain control.

Push-Pull (Shuffle Steering)
- **Modern Instructor Favorite**: Also called "push-pull" or "pull-push." One hand pushes the wheel up, the other pulls it down—reducing crossed arms over the airbag zone.
- **Pros**: Good for gentle curves or moderate turns; keeps hands low and controlled.

Avoiding the "One-Hand Lean"
- **Palming the Wheel**: Stylish in movies, risky in real life—limited precision if you need a quick dodge.
- **Arm Out the Window**: Leaves you with one-hand control and slower reaction time.

SEAT & WHEEL ALIGNMENT

Keeping Shoulders Back
- **Shoulder Against Seatback**: You should steer without leaning forward—this gives consistent reach to the wheel.
- **Wrist-at-Top Check**: Rest your wrist on the wheel's summit; if you can do so while shoulders stay back, your seat is probably at a good distance.

Adjusting on the Go
- **Tilt & Telescoping**: Many wheels let you adjust angle and distance—tweak if you feel scrunched or overextended.
- **No Over-Lock**: Don't tilt so high that half the wheel is above your eye line.

Common Mistake: Cramped Arms
Sitting too close feels secure but can strain your arms and hamper smooth steering. Keep a slight bend in your elbows for fluid movements.

ADVANCED TIPS & SCENARIOS

Slippery Roads
- **Gentle Inputs**: Sudden steering jerks on ice or wet pavement can lead to skids. 9 & 3 helps you modulate small steering moves.
- **Two Hands Ready**: Refrain from letting one hand roam while you chat or handle your phone. You'll need both hands if you hit a slick patch.

Off-Road or Bumpy Terrain
- **Relax Grip Slightly**: White-knuckling over bumps transfers every jolt to your arms. Allow the wheel to move a bit, but keep a guiding hold.
- **Avoid Thumbs Inside**: A sudden wheel kick can sprain or break a thumb if it's hooked around the rim.

Unexpected Obstacles
- **Smooth Swerves**: If a pothole or debris shows up, you'll correct easily if you're at 9 & 3. Rapid, controlled steering can dodge hazards safely.

Check-ins & Comfort
- **Mid-Drive Adjustments**: If your shoulders ache or your wrists feel strained, pause somewhere safe and tweak your seat or steering wheel tilt.
- **Mirror Vigilance**: Good steering habits pair with frequent mirror checks—be aware of your surroundings as you turn or merge.

Building Muscle Memory
- **Practice**: In a safe parking lot, test hand-over-hand vs. push-pull. Learn your comfort zone but stay aligned with safe recommended positions.
- **Relax**: Shoulders down, arms slightly bent, hands at 9 & 3.

Pro Tip: Arms Down, Thumbs Out

Keep those thumbs resting lightly on the wheel's outer rim, not hooked inside. That's your best combo of comfort and airbag safety.

Common Mistake: One-Handed Swagger

Looks chill, but leaves you vulnerable if something unexpected happens. Keep both hands on the wheel for best control—and to impress your driving instructor, not your friends in the back seat!

Holding the steering wheel might sound trivial, but it's literally **how** you guide your car through every bend, lane change, or tricky merge. With the right posture (9 & 3 or 8 & 4), a relaxed yet firm grip, and an understanding of how to turn methodically, you'll drive with more finesse—and less fatigue. Think of it as the "magic touch" that turns mundane commuting into confident cruising.

19. WHEN EVERYTHING FEELS BACKWARDS: DRIVING IN REVERSE

Driving forward might feel second nature, but **going in reverse** can turn your perspective upside down. Suddenly, turning the wheel left sends your tail right, and everything looks… well, backward. But fear not! With a few simple strategies—and a lot of slow, steady movement—you'll learn to reverse properly. In this chapter, we'll explore **mirror use, positioning, and safety checks** so you can back up like a pro (even in tight spots).

WHY REVERSING FEELS WEIRD

Backwards Logic
- **Steering Flips**: When reversing, turning the wheel left moves the rear of your car left (which feels "mirrored"). Meanwhile, remember the front of your car will swing out in the opposite direction, so keep an eye on any obstacles in front if space is tight.
- **Mirrors & Orientation**: A quick glance might show a reversed world—especially in the side mirrors if you're not used to it.

Patience Is Key
- **Slow & Steady**: Good reversing is rarely about speed. Think of it like tiptoeing rather than sprinting.
- **Lower Gear**: In manual cars, staying in first or reverse gear with light clutch control helps avoid jerky lurches.

Pro Tip: Take It Easy
Reversing faster than a snail's pace can throw off your reactions. Creep along so you can correct if you spot a surprise obstacle.

POSITIONING & POSTURE

Seat & Mirrors
- **Already Set?**: We covered seat adjustments in an earlier chapter—just ensure you can comfortably twist your upper body to look behind (and slightly raise your seat for a better rear window view).
- **Side Mirrors**: Some drivers tilt them slightly downward when reversing to see curbs or parking lines. Just remember to reset them for normal driving later (or invest in power mirrors that tilt automatically when in Reverse).

Head Turn vs. Mirror Reliance
- **Look Over Shoulder**: For short distances, physically turning and looking out the rear window is most direct.
- **Long Reverses**: Mirrors are helpful, but keep checking each side to avoid drifting. If you sense something off, do a quick glance over your shoulder.

Common Mistake: Mirror-Only Backing
Relying on mirrors alone might miss hidden pedestrians or objects in your blind spot. A quick neck twist adds confidence and saves you from nasty surprises.

MIRRORS VS. BACKUP CAMERAS

Rearview Cameras
- **Obstacle Spotting**: Handy for seeing short objects or children behind the car.
- **Distance Distortion**: The camera might misrepresent how far away something really is. Rely on side mirrors for a second opinion.

360° Surround / Parking Sensors
- **Sensors**: Beeping faster as you approach an obstacle.
- **Dirty or Snowy?**: If sensors are covered, they could beep falsely or not beep at all, so keep them clean.
- **360° Systems:** Some newer cars offer overhead or multiple angle cameras. Still, do a quick head-turn for any last-second pedestrian or cat darting behind you.

SLOW & STEADY STEERING

Small Inputs
- **Gentle Movements**: Tiny steering changes translate big-time to your car's rear end. If you oversteer, you might swerve.
- **Front Swing-Out**: Remember, as you turn the wheel, your car's front corner can swing wide. Watch for curbs, parked cars, or walls.

Straight-Line Reverse
- **Keep the Wheel Centered**: If you only need to back up in a straight line, position the wheel dead center, then do small corrections if you drift.
- **Check Both Sides**: Don't just watch one mirror; flipping between left and right helps maintain a true line.

Pro Tip: Palm vs. Both Hands

It might feel tempting to palm the wheel while craning your neck, but using both hands (at least one on top, one at the side) gives more precise control if you need to brake or steer suddenly.

AWARENESS OF BLIND SPOTS & OBSTACLES

Pedestrians & Cyclists
- **Expect the Unexpected**: People seldom anticipate a reversing car. Be extra vigilant if your windows are tinted or your trunk is tall.
- **Kids & Pets**: They can dash behind you at the worst moment—take an extra second to glance around.

Low Objects
- **Tall Bumpers, Short Hazards**: Fire hydrants, posts, or curbs can lurk below your rear window's line of sight. The camera might catch them, but what if it's blocked by dirt?

Other Considerations
- **Tall SUVs**: More height = more blind zones. If your camera or sensors beep, stop. Then confirm visually if possible.
- **Rear Pillars**: Thick pillars, especially in SUVs, can hide entire people if you rely only on mirrors.
- **One More Shoulder Peek**: That final over-the-shoulder glance before rolling back can prevent collisions.

SPECIFIC REVERSE MANEUVERS

Driveway Back-Out
- **Inching Approach:** If a fence or hedge blocks your view, roll out incrementally, scanning side to side each time you move a foot or two.
- **Right-of-Way:** Street traffic doesn't have to stop for you, so yield until you're sure it's clear.
- **Angled Streets**: If your driveway is angled, align the wheel to exit straight, then steer once your front clears any gate or fence.

Tight Parking Spots
- **Slight Steering**: Start with the wheel centered, then add small turns once rolling. Too much turn at a standstill can cause your front to swing out unexpectedly.
- **Signal or Flashers**: In busy lots, consider using your hazard lights so passersby know you're maneuvering.

- **Shopping Carts**: Parking lots often have stray carts. Double-check behind you so you don't nudge a cart into someone else's bumper.

Parallel Parking & 3-Point Turns
- **Short Mention**: Detailed steps appear in the next chapter (Parking). For reversing, the gist is slow wheel rotation and frequent mirror checks so you don't tap the curb or other vehicles.

Common Mistake: Rushing A 3-Point Turn
If you hurry, you may not realize how close you are to a fence or curb behind you. Pausing mid-turn to do a thorough check can save your bumper.

COLD/WET WEATHER CONSIDERATIONS

Frosted Rear Window
- **Defroster On**: Clears your view. If side mirrors are heated, turn them on too for better side vision.
- **Rear Wiper**: Some hatchbacks/SUVs have one—use it if the window is soaked or snowy.

Fog & Rain
- **AC for Defog**: Even when reversing, turning on AC helps remove moisture from cabin air.
- **Reduced Traction**: Gentle on the accelerator—tires can slip if you abruptly accelerate backward.

Pro Tip: Practice in an Empty Lot
If reversing freaks you out, find a quiet spot and run short backing drills. Learn how the wheel reacts so you'll be more confident in real traffic.

Common Mistake: Mirror-Only Reverse (Again, because it's important!)
Cameras and mirrors are great, but they don't catch everything. The best combo is slow movement + frequent checks over your shoulder + listening for that beep if you have sensors.

Reversing might feel backward—because it literally is. Steering in reverse flips your usual sense of direction, but with a calm approach, thorough mirror checks, and a deliberate, snail-paced roll, you'll ace backing into driveways, parking spots, and quiet side streets. Keep an eye out for hidden obstacles, large vehicle blind spots, and random kiddos on scooters. Master these steps, and reversing becomes a simple act, not a nerve-wracking puzzle!

20. PARKING: WITHOUT THE PANIC ATTACKS

Parking is a rite of passage—nothing says "driver confidence" like nailing a parallel park in busy traffic or neatly sliding into that tight mall spot. But it's not always as simple as driving forward and stopping. In this chapter, we'll detail **parking basics** (angle, perpendicular, parallel), how to park on hills, when to use your parking brake (almost always!), and even how to tackle a **3-point turn** when you need to flip direction in a narrow street. Let's dive in—no more heart palpitations when you see a small parking space!

WHY PARKING SKILLS MATTER

The Perks
- **Fewer Scrapes**: Good parking avoids dings, scratches, and curb kisses that ruin tires or rims.
- **Reduced Anxiety**: Once you trust your parking, running errands becomes far less stressful.
- **Respectful Driving**: Centering your car within the lines and not hogging space is considerate to fellow drivers.

Confidence Booster
- **Tackling Tight Spots**: If you can park well in narrow spaces, you'll feel unstoppable.
- **Handling Surprises**: Sudden parallel spots or angled slots pop up everywhere—you'll be ready.

Common Mistake: Speeding Into A Spot
Attempting to park quickly is a recipe for near-misses. Slow is smooth, smooth is fast in the long run.

TYPES OF PARKING

Angle Parking
- **Where You See It**: Many lot aisles or side-street spaces angled at 30–45 degrees.
- **Approach**: Signal early, align your front wheel with the stall's beginning, and steer gently in.
- **Exiting**: Reverse slowly, watching traffic behind you. Angled spaces often mean one-way flow, but still double-check.

Perpendicular (90-Degree) Parking
- **Typical in Malls**: Wider turning radius than angle parking.
- **Steps**: Go wide enough before turning in so your car doesn't clip corners or other vehicles. Midway through, straighten the wheel to center.
- **Leaving**: Reverse carefully—cars on either side can block your visibility, so inch out until you can see clearly.

Pro Tip: Mental Markers

For angle or perpendicular parking, pick a reference point—like where the line meets your hood—so you know when to turn or straighten. Consistent reference = consistent results.

Parallel Parking
- **Intimidating for Newbies**: Squeezing between two parked cars along a curb.
- **Basic Steps**:
    1. **Signal:** Use your turn signal to alert drivers behind you that you're about to park.
    2. **Align**: Pull up beside the front car, roughly bumper to bumper (or your rear bumper to their rear). Switch to your hazard lights to signal that you'll be reversing, giving others a clear cue to leave you space for a safe maneuver.
    3. **Reverse & Turn**: Start rolling back while turning the wheel sharply toward the curb.
    4. **Angle & Straighten**: When your front aligns with the car's rear bumper, turn the wheel the opposite way to tuck in.
    5. **Adjust**: Move forward/back to center yourself.

Pro Tip: Reset For Success

If your first attempt leaves you crooked or too far from the curb, don't force it—just pull out and try again. A smooth second attempt is always better than awkwardly adjusting back and forth while blocking traffic.

Common Mistake: Trying To Parallel Park Front First

Attempting to nose into a parallel spot rather than backing in makes it nearly impossible to align your rear wheels properly. You risk scraping your front wheels against the curb, scraping other cars, struggling to straighten out, and often have to redo the maneuver anyway. The standard approach—pulling alongside the front car, then reversing into the spot—grants far better control and prevents fender benders.

PERPENDICULAR PARKING MANEUVERS & SAFETY

Front-In vs. Back-In
- **Front-In**: Simpler initial approach, but reversing out can be tricky if visibility is blocked by tall SUVs.
- **Back-In**: A bit more effort at first, but pulling out forward later is easier—especially in busy lots.

Checking Surroundings
- **Watch for Pedestrians**: They appear from behind cars or dash out in parking lots.
- **Use Mirrors & Cameras**: Side mirrors for the lines, backup cam for close obstacles, but keep an eye on your front corners if your wheel is turned.

Don't Hog Lines
- **Centering**: Keep your car aligned between the painted lines—crooked parking irritates everyone and might invite door dings.
- **Second Look**: If you realize you're angled, it's better to pull out and realign than settle for a sloppy position.

HILL PARKING CONSIDERATIONS

Uphill vs. Downhill with Curb
- **Uphill**: Turn your wheels **away** from the curb. If brakes fail, the back of your front tires will catch the curb, preventing the car from rolling.
- **Downhill**: Turn wheels **toward** the curb. The front tire touches it and prevents rolling.
- **No Curb**: For both uphill/downhill, angle wheels toward the shoulder to avoid rolling into traffic.

Using the Parking Brake
- **Second Line of Defense**: Engage your brake, even if you're in Park (automatic) or in gear (manual).
- **Prevent Rollback**: Saves your transmission from strain, especially on steep slopes.

Common Mistake: Forgetting to Turn Wheels
If you park on a slope without angling wheels, a brake failure could mean a runaway car. Don't skip this step—it's crucial safety insurance.

HARNESSING TECH: REVERSE CAMERAS & SENSORS

Cameras
- **Easy Spot**: Great for seeing low objects behind the bumper—like curbs or kids' bikes.
- **Caution**: Camera angles can distort distance. If it "looks close," it might be even closer.

Parking Sensors
- **Beep Patterns**: Faster beeps = you're near an obstacle. A solid tone often means "Stop now!"
- **Dirty or Snowy**: Sensors might beep nonstop if covered in grime. Clean them occasionally for accurate readings.

360° Bird's-Eye Systems
- **Confidence Booster**: See all around your car. Great for tight spaces.
- **Manual Check**: Don't fully rely on overhead cameras—small misjudgments can still lead to scrapes.

3-POINT TURNS: A PARKING-ADJACENT SKILL

Why 3-Point Turns?
- **Narrow Streets**: When you need to reverse direction but can't do a U-turn.
- **Similar to Parking**: Combining reversing and forward maneuvers in a tight space.

Steps to a 3-Point Turn
1. **Signal & Pull Over**: Slow down near the curb, keep an eye on traffic behind.
2. **Turn the Wheel Sharply to the Left** (assuming left turn-around): Signal your intent and give the right of way to surrounding traffic. Move forward slowly across the lane, aiming to reach the opposite curb or edge of the road.
3. **Stop Before Over the Edge**: Hard brake so you don't overshoot.
4. **Reverse Gear**: Turn the wheel fully the other way (to the right), back up carefully, checking behind.
5. **Forward Again**: Shift to Drive (auto) or first gear (manual), steer left once more to finish facing the opposite direction.

Key Watch-Outs

- **Traffic**: You do not have the right-of-way mid-turn. Make sure no cars are zooming up as you cross the lanes.
- **Obstacles**: Poles, fire hydrants, or mailboxes can surprise you near curbs. Go slow and watch mirrors.
- **Patience**: If you need a 4th or 5th move, that's okay. Better multiple small maneuvers than a single big "oops."

Pro Tip: Signal At Each Move

If you're turning the wheel back the other way or reversing, use your signals or hazard lights to alert any passing drivers. Clarity helps avoid confusion.

COMMON PITFALLS & QUICK FIXES

Crooked Final Position

- **Realign**: Better to spend 10 extra seconds readjusting your angle than risk annoying neighbors or damaging your car.
- **Practice**: A few "back-in, pull-forward, correct" cycles can become second nature.

Rushed Exits

- **Double Check**: Are you fully in the space with enough room to open your door? Did you lock your car properly if you're leaving it?
- **Parking Brake**: Even on flat ground, it's a good habit to set it—especially if you drive a manual.

Lane/Traffic Block

- **Don't Dilly-Dally**: If you're parallel parking on a busy street, don't chat on your phone mid-way. Finish the park swiftly but safely to minimize blocking.

From that initial "Oh no!" moment seeing a tight spot, to calmly slotting your car in with inches to spare, **parking skill** is all about practice and patience. Treat each step methodically: approach slowly, line up carefully, and make small steering adjustments. Whether it's a 3-point turn in a narrow lane or parallel parking on a busy street, these pointers will ensure every "break" you take is a well-parked one!

21. BLINKERS: BECAUSE OTHER DRIVERS CAN'T READ YOUR MIND

Imagine you're at a party, wanting to leave for the snack table, but you never say a word or give a hint. People might bump into you or block your way because they have no clue you plan on moving. **Blinkers** are your car's version of polite chatter: they announce your intentions so traffic flows smoothly. In this chapter, we'll explain why signals are essential, when to use them (spoiler: more often than you think!), and how to avoid confusing or annoying fellow drivers.

WHY SIGNALS MATTER

The Language of the Road
- **Blinkers = Communication**: They're a universal way to say, "Hey, I'm turning or changing lanes." Without them, others must guess your plan—leading to near misses or honking frustration.
- **Safety & Courtesy**: A well-timed turn signal can prevent collisions, ease traffic flow, and show you're respectful of others on the road.

Legal Requirement
- **Local Laws**: Most states require signaling before a turn or lane change—often specifying how many feet or seconds in advance.
- **Ticket Potential**: Failing to signal can get you pulled over or slapped with a fine, depending on where you live.

Common Mistake: "I'm Already Turning!"
Flicking your blinker on mid-turn is pointless—no one has time to react. Activate it early so drivers behind (and ahead) know your next move.

THE WHEN & HOW OF BLINKERS

Turning & Exiting
- **Approach**: If you're about 100 feet from your intended turn, that's typically enough space to warn others. If it's a high-speed road, signal even earlier.
- **Slowing Down**: Tap your brakes and turn signal around the same time, so drivers see brake lights and a blinker—they'll know you're about to slow and turn.

Lane Changes & Merging

- **Lane Switch**: Flick your blinker a few seconds before moving over—like giving a heads-up: "I'm going left/right now."
- **Merging onto Highways**: Turn on your signal as you accelerate on the ramp, letting highway traffic know you want in. They may (hopefully) adjust speed to accommodate you.

Ending Your Signal

- **Cancel the Indicator**: Some blinkers automatically turn off after a turn. But if you haven't turned the wheel enough or your system isn't that fancy, you might keep blinking unknowingly. Flick it off manually once you're done.

HAZARD LIGHTS VS. BLINKERS

Blinkers for Turning

- **Left or Right**: Single-side indicator showing the direction you're steering. Straightforward communication.

Hazard Lights

- **Both Sides**: All four turn signals flash—used for emergencies or if you're forced to stop in an awkward spot.
- **Not for Lane Changes**: Don't confuse people by hitting hazards to merge. It's misleading and can cause panic or extra caution from drivers who think you're in trouble.

Pro Tip: Double-Check Your Signal

Sometimes you might nudge the turn stalk by accident—leading to the opposite signal flashing. A quick glance at the dash arrow ensures you're not unintentionally telling people you're turning left when you plan to go right!

TIMING & DISTANCE

Early Enough—But Not Ridiculous

- **Rule of Thumb**: About 3-5 seconds before turning is usually good in city driving. On faster roads, signal a bit earlier so cars behind have more reaction time.
- **Too Soon?**: If you're half a mile away from your actual turn with multiple intersections in between, you might confuse drivers who see your blinker but don't know which turn you want.

Lane Changes on Highways
- **The "Two-Blink" Minimum**: Let it blink at least twice before you start drifting over. If traffic is heavy, wait for a small gap; your signal doesn't give you absolute right-of-way, but it helps others anticipate.

COMMON MISTAKES

Leaving It On
- **The Endless Blinker**: Sometimes after a gentle turn or lane change, it doesn't auto-cancel. Driving for miles with your blinker on confuses everyone around you. Keep an ear or eye out to switch it off.

Late Signaling
- **Last-Second Flick**: You're braking to turn, then—blip—the blinker. That's too late for cars behind you to adjust. Or for oncoming traffic to let you pass.

Wrong Direction
- **Oops**: If you have an older car or you're flicking the lever absentmindedly, you might flash left when you mean right. Check your dash indicator arrow to ensure you're not telling the wrong story.

Common Mistake: Forgetting You Still Must Yield
Signaling doesn't guarantee other drivers will (or must) let you in. It's a request, not a command. Always look to confirm your move is safe.

EXTRA POINTERS & COURTESY

Beware Over-Confidence
- **Blinker + Quick Swerve**: If you flick the signal but instantly move over, that's no real warning. Give it at least a couple seconds for drivers to notice.

Check Surroundings
- **Mirrors & Shoulder**: Even with signals on, do a final glance—some folks won't yield or may zoom up unexpectedly.
- **Nighttime & Adverse Weather**: Signaling is especially crucial in low visibility. Extra brake and turn signals help others spot you in fog or heavy rain.

City vs. Highway

- **City Streets**: Approaches are shorter, so maybe 3 seconds is enough.
- **Highways**: Speed is higher—signal sooner. Merging or lane-changing in quick traffic? The earlier they see your intent, the safer.

Pro Tip: Signal Even in Light Traffic
You may think, "No one's behind me, why bother?" But hidden or fast-approaching cars (or motorcycles) can appear. Better to over-communicate than to surprise someone at the worst moment.

DEVELOPING GOOD BLINKER HABITS

Practice Makes Predictable

- **Conscious Use**: For a week, mentally count "Signal—two—three—turn" each time. This helps internalize timing.
- **Driving With Friends**: Ask them to call you out if you skip a signal or turn it on too late. A bit of friendly teasing can build better habits.

Rewards of Good Signaling

- **Smoother Traffic**: Fewer abrupt brakes or swerves from others.
- **Fewer Honks**: When people see your blinker, they expect your movement—less confusion means less road rage.
- **Accident Reduction**: Many crashes happen simply because no one knew someone else was about to turn or merge.

Pro Tip: Get in the Habit
The moment you decide to turn or change lanes, use your signal—before you brake or move. It's a tiny act with big safety returns.

No one can read your mind on the road. Skipping your blinkers forces others to guess your next move—leading to honks, close calls, or even fines. But with a well-timed signal, you go from an unpredictable driver to a courteous road communicator. A simple flick of the lever makes all the difference!

22. SEE AND BE SEEN:
LEARN YOUR HEADLIGHT ETIQUETTE

Picture this: dusk settles in, streetlights flicker on, and you're cruising down the road. Your dashboard lights are glowing, so your headlights must be on, right? Not necessarily! Many cars have **daytime running lights (DRLs)** that **don't illuminate the taillights**, leaving you nearly invisible from behind. And if you're driving without proper headlights, you're a ghost on the road, startling other drivers and putting yourself at risk.

In this chapter, we'll talk about when to **turn your lights on** and when to **switch between high and low beams**. Ready to light up the road the right way?

DASHBOARD HEADLIGHT INDICATORS (Quick Refresher)
- **Headlights On**: A **green** headlamp icon with beams pointing forward—indicates your **low beams** are active.
- **High Beams On**: A **bright blue** headlamp icon—tells you that you're on **high beams** (and that you should switch to low beams if there's oncoming traffic).

WHY HEADLIGHTS MATTER

Visibility & Communication
- **Lighting Your Path**: Your headlights help you see obstacles and lane markings when it's dark or gloomy.
- **Being Seen**: Other drivers, cyclists, and pedestrians rely on your headlights to spot you, especially in low-light conditions.

Legal & Safety Basics
- **Rules & Regulations**: Most places require headlights from sunset to sunrise, or any time visibility is poor (e.g., rain, fog, snow).
- **Moving Objects**: A car with no headlights can blend into the night like a stealth ninja, scaring the daylights out of unsuspecting drivers.

Common Mistake: Daytime Running Lights (DRLs) Confusion
DRLs only illuminate the front in many cars—your taillights might remain off, leaving you nearly invisible from behind after dark. Always check if your "real" headlights are switched on.

HEADLIGHT BASICS

Low Beams
- **Primary Night Driving Light**: Dimmer, angled downward to avoid glare for oncoming cars.
- **Great for**: City streets, lighted highways, and standard nighttime or rainy conditions.

High Beams
- **Bright Illumination**: For poorly lit rural roads, where you need maximum visibility.
- **Etiquette**: Switch back to low beams when another vehicle approaches—no one likes to be blinded.

Common Mistake: Using High Beams in Fog or Snow

It might seem logical to crank up your high beams when visibility drops, but in fog, snow, or heavy rain, high beams actually make things worse. Instead of helping, the intense light reflects off moisture droplets or snowflakes, creating a blinding white glare that reduces your ability to see the road. This effect, sometimes called light scatter, can leave you more disoriented than if you had just stuck with low beams or fog lights. Solution? When conditions are hazy, switch to low beams and, if needed, activate your fog lights to cut through the mist.

WHEN TO USE YOUR HEADLIGHTS

Nighttime
- **From Dusk till Dawn**: The golden rule—if it's dark enough to struggle reading street signs, it's time for headlights.
- **Streetlights or Not**: Even a well-lit city can have patches of darkness; keep them on consistently.

Adverse Weather
- **Rain, Snow & Fog**: Lights help others spot you in swirling precipitation.

Daytime Exceptions
- **Heavy Rain or Stormy Clouds**: If visibility is poor, turning on headlights is a courtesy and a rule in many places.
- **Tunnels & Shadowed Areas**: Some roads wind through shady forests or under long overpasses—lights help you stand out.

Common Mistake: Forgetting to Turn on Headlights at Night
Dash lights on does not automatically mean headlights on. Double-check your headlight icon or the physical headlight knob.

HIGH BEAM ETIQUETTE

When They're Handy
- **Rural, Dark Roads**: No streetlights? Flick on high beams to spot hazards like deer, fallen branches, or potholes.
- **No Oncoming Cars**: Use them freely if you're alone on the road.

Switching Them Off
- **Approaching Vehicles**: Turn off high beams as soon as you see oncoming headlights or taillights in front of you—avoid dazzling other drivers.
- **Reflections**: If you see reflective signs or the glare of your own lights in another driver's mirror, it's time to switch.

Automatic High Beams
- **When to Trust It**: On empty, dark roads where you'd normally flip to high beams anyway. Let the system do the work so you can focus on the drive.
- **When to Override**: If your lights don't dim quickly for oncoming traffic (or if they're flipping on and off like a confused disco ball), take manual control—your fellow drivers will thank you.

Pro Tip: Look to the Right
When an oncoming car has stubbornly left high beams on, shift your gaze to the right edge of your lane to reduce glare and avoid getting blinded.

COMMON HEADLIGHT MISTAKES & QUICK FIXES

One Headlight Out
- **Danger**: Makes your car look like a motorcycle from a distance, confusing others about your car's width.
- **Fix**: Bulb replacements are usually cheap. Don't postpone it.

Headlight Aim
- **Poor Alignment**: Could be from an accident or general wear; if your beams seem to point at the sky or into the ground, get them adjusted.
- **DIY or Mechanic**: Some cars let you adjust with a simple screw; others need professional alignment.

Dirty or Cloudy Lenses
- **Reduced Brightness**: Over time, plastic headlight covers can fog up or get grimy. A quick cleaning or polishing kit can restore them.
- **Beware Over-Sanding**: Polishing kits are great but follow instructions—too much sanding and you might damage the protective coating.

TIPS: STAYING BRIGHT BUT NOT OBNOXIOUS

Quick Checks
- **At Startup**: Turn on your lights and walk around your car occasionally to confirm they're working.
- **Parked Car**: If you have manual lights, ensure you didn't leave them on—avoid draining the battery.

Flashing & Signals
- **Alerting Oncoming Traffic**: Some folks flash headlights to warn of hazards or remind them to switch off high beams. Know your local laws and norms (in some places, it's misunderstood).

Pro Tip: Light the Tunnels
Even in daylight, switch on headlights in tunnels or underpasses so other drivers can gauge distance better. DRLs alone may not be enough.

Common Mistake: High Beaming Approach
Accidentally leaving high beams on for oncoming traffic is a top annoyance—and a safety hazard. As soon as you spot headlights or taillights ahead, flick to low beams.

Headlights do more than just help you see—they make sure others see you, whether you're on a dark highway or a rainy backroad. Using low beams for everyday driving and reserving high beams for the right moments keeps the roads safer for everyone. The next time you question, "Should I turn them on?" the answer is probably yes—light 'em up and let others know you're there!

23. FOG LIGHTS: USEFUL IN THICK WEATHER, BLINDING OTHERWISE

Fog lights are one of the most misunderstood car features. Some drivers don't know when to use them, while others insist on driving with them **on all the time** like they're part of a fancy light show. So, what's the deal? In this chapter, we'll break down **what fog lights actually do, when you should use them**, and **why they can be more blinding than helpful if misused**. Ready to clear up the confusion?

DASHBOARD FOG LIGHT INDICATORS (Quick Refresher)
- **Fog Lights On:** A **green** or **amber** lamp icon with a wavy beam or diagonal slash—indicates **front** or **rear** fog lights are in use.

FOG LIGHTS 101

Position & Purpose
- **Low & Wide**: Fog lights sit below your normal headlights, casting a **broad, low beam**.
- **Low & Angled Downward**: Their design prevents the light from bouncing back into your eyes—common with high beams in fog.

Front vs. Rear Fog Lights
- **Front**: Helps **you** see in fog, heavy rain, or snow by lighting the ground close to your front bumper.
- **Rear**: A bright red light to ensure **others** can spot you in a soupy-whiteout (commonly found in European cars). Turn it off when the weather clears—it's blinding otherwise!

Common Mistake: Thinking Fog Lights Are Brighter Headlights
They're not replacement headlights. They're specialized for low-visibility. If it's clear out, you're just dazzling oncoming traffic.

WHEN TO USE FOG LIGHTS

Fog, Snow & Heavy Rain
- **Thick Mist**: If your visibility is severely limited (less than 300 feet), flick on fog lights **in addition** to low beams.
- **Heavy Snow or Rain**: Similar logic—fog lights help see the immediate road without the glare you'd get from high beams.

Not a Sunny-Day Accessory
- **Clear Weather**: Fog lights are **pointless** in normal conditions, adding extra glare.
- **Busy Traffic**: If it's not actually foggy, just rely on your standard low or high beams. Don't blind your lane-mates.

WHY NOT USE HIGH BEAMS IN FOG?

The Reflection Problem
- **Light Scatter**: Fog droplets reflect bright high beams back at you, forming a glowing white curtain. Yikes!
- **Poor Visibility**: High beams in fog can make you see less, not more.

How Fog Lights Fix This
- **Low Angle**: Fog lights send light under the fog layer, letting you trace the road without that glare.
- **Better Edge Definition**: You'll see lane lines and curbs more clearly than if you were blasting full beams.

Pro Tip: Low & Steady Wins
For fog, keep your **low beams + fog lights** on. Skip the high beams. Trust us—your retinas (and oncoming drivers) will thank you.

REAR FOG LIGHTS: THE BRIGHT RED SAVIOR

Extra Bright—But Not Always Needed
- **What It Is**: A super-bright rear lamp that's basically as intense as brake lights, giving approaching cars a clear target to avoid rear-ending you in dense fog.
- **Turn It Off in Clear Weather**: If it's no longer foggy, that bright red glare irritates drivers behind you.

A Rare Feature (In Some Regions)
- **European Models**: Common. Often a single lamp on one side of the rear.
- **North America**: Many cars skip it. If your dash doesn't show a rear fog icon, you probably don't have one.

COMMON MISUSES OF FOG LIGHTS

Fog Lights as "Extra Driving Lights"
- **Annoying for Others**: Running them 24/7 in perfect weather blinds oncoming traffic, and it's sometimes illegal.

- **Zero Performance Benefit**: Fog lights don't magically brighten your distant view in clear conditions.

Forgetting Rear Fog
- **Constant Red Beam**: People behind you think you're braking or have an electrical glitch.
- **Outcome**: Confusion, possible road rage. Shut it off once visibility returns.

Check Local Rules
- **Some Places Prohibit**: Using front or rear fog lamps in normal conditions might earn you a warning or ticket.
- **Dim or Off**: Many cars require manual toggling on/off. Don't expect them to turn off automatically.

FINAL THOUGHTS & ADVICE

Fog Lights: A Specialty Tool
- **They Shine in One Scenario**: When thick fog, snow, or rain hamper your low beams. Otherwise, they're just an unhelpful glare.
- **Pair with Low Beams**: Keep your standard headlights on for general visibility, use fog lights to highlight the ground directly ahead.

Respect Other Drivers
- **Courtesy**: Turn them off if the weather clears or if oncoming drivers are flashing their lights because they're blinded.
- **Check Reflection**: If your lights reflect heavily off the road or other objects, that might be a sign you don't need fog lights.

Common Mistake: Leaving Them On
Forgetting you toggled fog lights on last night? Next morning's drive could see you inadvertently blinding folks on a clear day. Always glance at your dash icons when you start the car.

Fog lights are like **your car's reading glasses**—amazing in the right situation, but weird and unnecessary all the time. Knowing **when to use them and when to turn them off** will make your driving safer, smoother, and less annoying for everyone else on the road. So, next time you see fog rolling in, go ahead and flip them on—but if it's a clear night, **give them a break!**

HEADLIGHTS VS. FOG LIGHTS: WHEN TO USE WHAT

Condition	Low Beams	High Beams	Fog Lights
Clear Night	Yes	Yes (if no traffic)	No (they're blinding to others)
Foggy Weather	Yes	No (creates glare)	Yes
Heavy Rain	Yes	No (bounces off rain)	Maybe (only if visibility is bad)
Snowy Roads	Yes	No (reflects back)	Yes

24. AC SMARTS: KEEPING COOL WITHOUT BREAKING A SWEAT

Have you ever opened the car door on a hot summer day and felt like you just opened an oven? Or struggled with foggy windows on a rainy morning, desperately wiping them with your sleeve? Your car's air conditioning isn't just about staying cool—it's also a game-changer for keeping visibility clear and maintaining a comfortable ride year-round. In this chapter, we'll explain **how to maximize your AC's efficiency, why it's useful in all seasons**, and **common mistakes to avoid,** so you can drive comfortably without wasting fuel or freezing your passengers.

WHY YOUR CAR'S AC MATTERS

Comfort & Safety
- **Stay Cool & Alert**: Being too hot in the driver's seat can wear you down mentally, leading to fatigue or cranky decision-making.
- **Defogging Champion**: AC dehumidifies the air, clearing fogged-up windows in seconds—crucial when rain or humidity causes instant windshield haze.

More Than a Luxury
- **Visibility**: Clear windows aren't just nice—they're a safety essential.
- **Seasonal All-Rounder**: AC helps in hot summers and damp winters. If it's musty or muggy inside, flipping on AC can save you from sweaty or foggy misery.

Common Mistake: Ignoring AC in Winter
Thinking you only need AC in summer overlooks its dehumidifying powers for defogging. Even on a freezing day, pairing AC with heat can banish windshield fog fast.

AC BASICS & SETTINGS

Manual vs. Automatic Climate Control
- **Manual**: Manage fan speed, temperature knob, and vent direction.
- **Auto**: Set a preferred temperature (say, 72°F/22°C), and let your car's system handle the blower speed, air distribution, etc. Great for those who like "set it and forget it."

Recirculation vs. Fresh Air

- **Recirculation (the "U-turn" icon)**: Re-uses cabin air, cooling it faster in searing weather. But it can get stale or humid if used too long.
- **Fresh Air**: Brings in outside air—good for long drives to avoid stuffiness.

Pro Tip: Find Your Sweet Spot

On sweltering days, start with recirculation to cool things down fast. After a few minutes, switch to fresh air to keep the cabin feeling crisp.

DEFOGGING & DEHUMIDIFYING

AC for Fogged-Up Windows

- **Magic Combo**: AC + defrost vents = quick glass clarity. The AC pulls moisture from the air, preventing condensation on glass.
- **Rear Defroster**: Activate the heated lines on your rear window if they're foggy. Some cars have heated side mirrors too.

Winter & Rainy Conditions

- **Yes, Even in Cold**: If your windshield steams up, flip the AC on (with heat if you like). It's not about making cold air; it's about drying the cabin air.
- **Quick Clear**: You'll be amazed how swiftly the fog vanishes when the AC's dehumidifying action kicks in.

FUEL & EFFICIENCY CONCERNS

AC vs. MPG

- **Slight Fuel Use**: AC does add a bit of load on the engine, so your MPG (or range, for EVs) can drop a little.
- **Better Than Drag**: On highways, driving with windows wide open can cause aerodynamic drag, sometimes costing more fuel than AC.

Mild Days

- **Windows Down, AC Off**: If temps are comfy and you're not on the freeway, fresh air might be enough.
- **Tune to Comfort**: Everyone's threshold varies. Don't sweat it—if you need cooling, go for it. Safety (and sanity) often outweighs small fuel savings.

Common Mistake: Max AC All the Time

Blast AC at max setting initially to cool a hot car, sure—but once you're comfy, dial it back. Constant max usage can freeze out passengers and overwork your system.

HOT WEATHER TIPS

Vent the Heat First
- **Open Doors/Windows**: If your car's been roasting in the sun, let the hot air escape before cranking the AC. It helps cool faster and saves a bit of energy.

Sunshades & Parking
- **Shade Hunting**: Parking under a tree or using a windshield sunshade reduces the cabin heat buildup.
- **Rear Sunshades**: Some cars have built-in retractable shades— helps keep the backseat cooler, too.

COMMON AC PITFALLS

Aiming Vents Wrong
- **Face vs. Body**: Constant frigid air blasting your face can be uncomfortable or cause dryness. Adjust vents to diffuse cool air around you.
- **Passenger Comfort**: If you have dual-zone controls, let your co-pilot set their preferred temp.

Musty or Moldy Smells
- **Moisture in the System**: Bacteria or fungus can grow if the AC drain is clogged.
- **Solution**: Run the fan without AC occasionally to dry internal parts, or seek professional cleaning if odors persist.

Neglecting Filter Changes
- **Cabin Air Filter**: If it's clogged, airflow weakens and your AC strains. Replace it every 12k-15k miles or as recommended. A fresh filter = crisp, clean breezes.

DASH & BUTTON INDICATORS

AC or Snowflake Icon
- **Compressor Activation**: Lights up when the AC is actively cooling. If it's off, you're just blowing air at ambient temperature.

- **Some Cars Auto-Enable**: In defrost mode, the AC might come on automatically to clear glass.

Recirculation Arrow

- **U-turn Arrow**: Means you're cycling cabin air instead of pulling from outside. Great for quick cooldowns, but switch to fresh air eventually.

Pro Tip: Listen for the Click
On some older cars, you might hear or feel a slight "click" or engine rev change when the AC compressor kicks in—that's normal.

MAINTENANCE & SERVICE

Refrigerant Top-Ups

- **Warm Air?**: If your AC blows lukewarm instead of icy, your refrigerant might be low or you could have a leak.
- **Certified Help**: AC systems can be complex—refrigerant leaks aren't always simple to DIY fix.

Seasonal Checks

- **Pre-Summer Inspection**: A quick check ensures your AC's ready for hot days. Better to find a problem early than swelter when temps spike.

Pro Tip: Quick "Defog Mode"
In rainy or cold weather, set your HVAC to defrost with AC on and fan medium-high. Watch your windshield go from cloudy to crystal-clear in seconds.

Your car's air conditioning isn't just a summertime luxury—**it's your year-round ally** for comfort and clear windows. Whether you're stuck in traffic on a scorching day or fending off fogged-up glass in winter, **knowing how to use and maintain your AC** can make every drive less sweaty and more enjoyable. So don't sweat it—flip that switch!

25. STAY IN THE ZONE: POSITIONING YOUR CAR INSIDE THE DRIVING LANE

Think of driving as a waltz: you and your car glide along in your own space (lane), occasionally adjusting position to avoid a partner's misstep (oncoming traffic) or an obstacle in your path (parked cars, roadside construction). **Lane positioning** isn't just about staying perfectly centered. Sometimes, you **shift** or **offset** your car to give extra clearance, reduce blind spots, or safely pass hazards. In this chapter, we'll show you **why** lane discipline matters, **how** to keep your wheels centered, and **when** it's smart to move away from the exact middle—without crossing the line into other lanes. Ready to waltz?

WHY LANE POSITIONING MATTERS

Safety & Predictability
- **Clear Boundaries**: Other drivers expect you to remain in your lane, so drifting is unpredictable and dangerous.
- **Avoid Sideswipes**: Holding a steady center line drastically cuts the risk of brushing adjacent vehicles.

Traffic Flow
- **Smooth Merges**: If you stay centered (or at a predictable offset), merging cars can judge space better.
- **Less Panic**: Your lane discipline calms drivers behind or beside you—they see you controlling your space confidently.

Common Mistake: Distracted Drifting
Checking your phone or rummaging for snacks can cause unintended lane departures. Keep those eyes forward and maintain your lane.

BASIC LANE-CENTERING TECHNIQUES

Visual Reference Points
- **Look Ahead**: Your hands follow your eyes. Staring directly at lane lines can cause you to overcorrect. Aim your gaze **down the road**, letting peripheral vision track the lines.
- **Steering Smoothly**: Minimal inputs keep you from swerving. If you see the lane line creeping too close, a gentle nudge on the wheel is enough—no big arm motions.

Use Your Mirrors
- **Side Mirror Glances**: Quick checks confirm if you're hugging one side. If you see a lot of empty pavement on one side and no space on the other, shift slightly.
- **Don't Lock Your Arms**: Stay relaxed—tense grips lead to jerky corrections.

Pro Tip: Practice in a Calm Spot
Head to a quiet road or large parking lot, pick a center reference, and practice staying aligned. Over time, you'll develop a natural sense of "where your wheels are."

DEALING WITH WIDE OR NARROW LANES

Wide Lanes
- **Temping to Drift**: Extra space can lull you into meandering. Keep a mental anchor on the center—like a dotted line or a seam in the pavement.
- **Beware Overconfidence**: If you're drifting around, you might surprise a passing car that expects you to be near-lane-center.

Narrow Lanes or Construction Zones
- **Precise Control**: Construction cones, barricades, or narrower lanes demand slower speeds and steady focus.
- **Stay Alert**: Keep scanning—other drivers might drift or swerve unexpectedly to avoid debris.

OFFSET POSITIONING & WHY IT'S USEFUL

Shifting for Safety
- **Big Vehicles**: If you're next to a truck or bus, slide a bit away within your lane to increase space. Still remain in your lane, but give them a bit more breathing room.
- **Emergency Lane Obstacles**: If a car is stopped on the shoulder or you see pedestrians near the road (where no sidewalk exists), shift to the far side of your lane and **slow down**. This extra clearance helps avoid accidents.

Handling Road Construction
- **Can't Change Lanes?**: If barriers or traffic prevent moving over, offset your position away from workers, cones, or barriers. **Reduce speed** to react more quickly if something changes suddenly.

Avoiding Potholes or Debris

- **Minor Lateral Movements**: A slight lean within your lane can bypass a pothole without a dramatic swerve. Just confirm your side mirror check so you don't drift too close to another car.

Common Mistake: Over-Offsetting

Shifting too much can push you across the center line or into the next lane. Make small, deliberate movements—your lane's center is still your home base.

TWISTY ROADS & CURVES

Positioning on Curves

- **Entering a Curve**: Start near the center of your lane, turning smoothly to follow the curve. Avoid hugging the curb or crossing the center line.
- **Exiting**: Gently straighten out, staying centered again—no abrupt flicks of the wheel.

Center Line Danger

- **Crossing in a Curve**: If you misjudge speed or angle, you might veer into oncoming traffic, risking head-on collisions.
- **Slow Down**: On unfamiliar, winding roads, better to reduce speed and keep your line tight than to overdrive and drift out.

Pro Tip: Look Where You Want to Go

On a curvy road, turn your eyes toward the curve's exit. This helps guide your hands to steer precisely around the bend, staying safely in-lane.

Common Mistake: Ignoring Curves at Higher Speeds

Speed amplifies every small steering error. If you approach a twisty road too fast, you risk crossing center lines or running onto shoulders. Slow down to maintain your lane's dance rhythm.

EXTRA TIPS FOR LANE DISCIPLINE

Slowing Down for Safety

- **Better Reaction Time**: If you must offset near a stopped car or a pedestrian, ease off the gas. Speed can magnify any small steering error.
- **Personal Bubble**: In narrow lanes, going slower gives you more time to spot hazards like merging traffic or door openings from parked cars.

Communicate via Signals
- **Lane Changes**: If shifting within your lane isn't enough to avoid an obstacle, signal before changing lanes.

Watch for Markings
- **Reflectors at Night**: In dim conditions, rely on reflective markers or cat's eyes (reflective markers) that highlight lane boundaries.

COMMON PITFALLS & REALIGNMENTS

Over-Correcting Drifts
- **Small Corrections**: If you notice you're too close to the center line, lightly adjust. Massive swings of the wheel can send you fishtailing or into another lane.
- **Stay Focused**: Daydreaming or fiddling with gadgets leads to drifting—snap back quickly with a gentle steering nudge.

Driving with a Single-Hand Lean
- **Cool Pose, Poor Control**: Resting an arm out the window or on the console might slow your reactions. Both hands on the wheel fosters more stable lane positioning.

Pro Tip: Anticipate Obstacles
If you see a disabled vehicle on the shoulder, shift smoothly within your lane (and signal if needed) while **slowing down**. This courtesy space reduces the chance of side-swiping an opened door or someone stepping out.

Perfect lane positioning is a blend of **predictability, minor steering corrections**, and **knowing when to shift within your lane** for safety's sake. Whether you're breezing down a wide highway or carefully navigating a narrow, winding route, treat your lane like your personal dance floor—keep your steps measured and elegant, and you'll avoid stepping on any toes (or bumpers!). Remember to slow down in tight or unpredictable situations, keep an eye on those lane lines, and **never** cross that center line on curves.

26. BLIND SPOTS: WHAT YOU CAN'T SEE CAN HURT YOU

Have you ever changed lanes, only to hear a blaring horn and realize another car was right there? That heart-stopping moment usually means you missed checking your **blind spot**. Think of a blind spot as a mini Bermuda Triangle for vehicles—they just... vanish from your mirrors. In this chapter, we'll explain why these sneaky zones exist, how to set up your mirrors correctly, and why a quick shoulder glance can save you from fender-benders (and embarrassment).

WHAT ARE BLIND SPOTS?

The "Invisible Zones"
- **Definition**: Areas around your car that mirrors don't capture, leaving you in the dark if you don't look over your shoulder.
- **Why They Form**: Car design (pillars, seatbacks, trunk height) and mirror angles naturally create spots no reflective surface can see.

Real Consequences
- **Surprise Collisions**: Another car, motorcycle, or even a cyclist can hide in these zones. A lane change or merge without checking can cause a sideswipe.
- **Heightened Risk**: Larger vehicles like SUVs or trucks often have larger blind spots.

Pro Tip: Anticipate Others' Blind Spots
Don't linger next to a big truck or bus—if you can't see the driver's face in their mirror, they likely can't see you. Pass or drop back to maintain a safe space.

MIRROR MAGIC (REFRESHER FROM PREVIOUS CHAPTER)

The Rearview Mirror
- **Framing the Back**: Tilt it to center your view out the rear window. If you see mostly headliner or trunk lid, adjust until you have a clear, full look behind you.
- **Tilt Feature (Day/Night)**: Some have a small lever/knob for reducing headlight glare at night—flip it if you're blinded by trailing cars.

- **Auto-Dimming**: If your mirror dims automatically, you can skip flipping any knob and enjoy glare-free night driving.

Side Mirrors
- **Traditional vs. Wide Setup**:
  - **Traditional**: You see a chunk of your car in the mirror. Convenient reference, but bigger blind spots.
  - **Wide/ "BGE" Method**: (Blindspot & Glare Elimination) Angle mirrors so you barely see your car's edge. This expands your peripheral view of adjacent lanes.
- **Fine-Tuning**: Sit in your normal driving position, then tilt each mirror outward until your car's flank just disappears from view. It feels odd at first, but covers more of the road.
- **Shift for a Better View**: Sometimes side mirror angles alone aren't enough. Lean forward or tilt your head slightly to catch those hidden corners—this quick adjustment often reveals sneaky vehicles lurking in your blind spots.

Checking Your Blind Spots After Mirrors Adjustment
- **Lane Switch Practice**: Look in side mirrors—car behind you transitions smoothly from the rearview mirror to the side mirror with minimal "dead zone."
- **Shoulder Check**: Mirrors help, but they aren't perfect. A quick glance over your shoulder remains essential.

Pro Tip: Aspherical Mirrors
Some cars use a split design on the outer edge of the side mirror (a slightly convex section) to further expand your field of view, reducing blind spots without a dramatic outward tilt.

Common Mistake: Mirror Stagnation
If you move your seat (or share a car), re-check those side mirrors. One inch of seat shift can create huge blind spots if your mirrors stay in the old position!

SHOULDER CHECKS: STILL A MUST

Why Mirrors Alone Aren't Enough
- **A Pillars & B Pillars**: Thick support pillars in modern cars can hide entire vehicles or pedestrians.
- **Tiny Targets**: Motorcycles and cyclists can vanish behind a rear pillar, only to reappear at your door.

The Simple "SMS" Technique

- **Signal**: Turn on your signal to give others a hint of your intentions.
- **Mirror**: Quick glance to your side mirror to see if it's clear.
- **Shoulder Check**: Lean slightly, glance behind you through the rear side window. If it's all clear, proceed.

Defensive Mindset

- **Expect Other Drivers' Blind Spots**: Don't hover in a truck's "no zone." If you must pass, do so promptly. (A truck's **"no zone"** refers to the **large blind spots** around a commercial truck or bus—particularly on the sides, front, and rear—where the driver can't see other vehicles.)
- **Use All Tools**: Some vehicles offer blind-spot detection lights or cameras—still do a shoulder check in case they fail or get blocked by grime.

LARGER VEHICLES & NO ZONES

Trucks & Buses

- **Sides & Rear**: Big rigs have huge swaths of invisibility—common accident triggers when people linger alongside.
- **Passing Strategy**: Quickly pass on the left when safe, maintaining a consistent speed. Minimize time in their blind zone.

SUVs & Vans

- **Rear Pillar Bulk**: The "C-pillar" can be extra wide, making it tougher to see smaller vehicles approaching diagonally.
- **Seat Height**: If you're driving a tall SUV, you have better forward visibility but can overshadow smaller cars next to you. Be mindful they can hide below your window line.

COMMON BLIND SPOT CHALLENGES

Motorcycles & Bikes

- **Slim Profile**: They hide easily behind a B-pillar or mirror edge.
- **Check Twice**: One swift shoulder glance might not register a small silhouette—be extra careful.

Fast-Approaching Vehicles

- **Lane-Change Surprise**: A car quickly overtaking you can appear out of nowhere. Constant scanning helps catch them before they zip into your blind spot.

Parking Lot Scrapes
- **Backing Out**: Blind spots aren't just for highways. Check side mirrors for angled parking-lot lanes or pedestrians crossing behind.

TECH ASSISTS: BLIND SPOT MONITORS, CAMERA SYSTEMS

Blind Spot Monitors (BSM)
- **Icons & Alerts**: Many cars flash a light on side mirrors or beep if someone enters your blind spot.
- **Limitations**: Sensors can fail or get blocked by snow or mud. Double-check with a shoulder glance.

360° Cameras
- **Top-Down Views**: Parking cameras that show obstacles all around—handy in tight spots.
- **Real-World Use**: Great for low-speed maneuvers, but won't help at highway speeds.

Radar & Lane-Change Aids
- **Warnings**: Some systems beep if you signal while a vehicle's in your blind spot. Handy backup, but never an excuse to skip physically checking.

TIPS TO AVOID BEING IN OTHERS' BLIND SPOTS

Don't Linger Beside
- **Pass with Purpose**: <u>If you're on a multi-lane highway, pass or fall back. Hanging at someone's rear quarter panel is risky.</u>
- **Truck "No Zones"**: If you can't see the driver's face in their side mirror, they don't see you either.

Adjusting Your Speed
- **Small Speed Changes**: A slight acceleration or deceleration can place you safely in their mirror coverage.
- **Defensive Positioning**: In heavy traffic, keep spacing so others don't suddenly merge into you.

Blind spots are like hidden pockets where other cars, bikers, or even pedestrians can vanish. Setting your mirrors widely, doing that crucial shoulder check, and anticipating big vehicles' no zones cut your risk of surprise collisions. Remember: even the fanciest camera or blind-spot tech isn't foolproof—**you** are the ultimate sensor!

27. MERGING: GET IN, FIT IN, DRIVE ON

Merging can feel daunting—like jumping onto a moving carousel. Yet, with a few clear steps and a dash of courtesy, you can blend right in without slamming brakes or causing near-misses. In this chapter, we'll explain how to **time your merges**, **coordinate speeds**, and avoid confusion.

WHY MERGING MATTERS

Smooth Traffic Flow
- **Purpose**: Merging is how different traffic streams become one. Doing it smoothly helps everyone maintain momentum, avoiding abrupt slowdowns or bottlenecks.
- **Courtesy & Confidence**: Nailing a merge showcases your awareness of surrounding speeds and gaps—reducing stress for you and the drivers around you.

Communication & Coordination
- **Signals**: Your blinker is how you "say hello" to drivers in the lane you're about to join. Flick it on early to give them time to react.
- **Position & Speed**: If you merge timidly at half their speed, you create a dangerous speed mismatch. If you rocket in too fast, you might spook them.

Common Mistake: Too Much Hesitation
Stopping at the end of a ramp or crawling at half-speed forces drivers behind (and in the main lane) to slam on brakes, risking rear-end collisions.

SIGNAGE YOU MAY ENCOUNTER

Yield Signs
- **Acceleration Lane + Yield**: Often found on busier highways, these ramps provide a short stretch to gain speed before merging. Still, a yield sign can appear—if traffic is dense or faster than you, be ready to slow or pause until you have a safe gap. Stay alert for ramps with very limited room to accelerate, especially in city areas.
- **Yield Without Acceleration Lane**: Often found on older or narrower roads where space is at a premium. You might have little room to build speed, so use your mirrors and timing to merge smoothly.

Stopping & Metering

- **Stop Sign:** Often placed where merging visibility is limited on high-speed roads or in areas with low traffic volume. Stop fully, check for an opening—because you're merging from a dead stop, accelerate decisively to match traffic flow.
- **One Car per Green Light:** Also called ramp metering, these signals regulate how many vehicles can enter a highway at once. You'll see them near busy urban interchanges during rush hour. Watch the lights closely—when it's your turn, go promptly and merge at a safe speed.

MERGING PREP: APPROACH & SIGNAL

Signaling Early

- **Let Them Know**: Turn on your signal a few seconds before you even begin to move over.
- **Don't Flick Last Second**: If your blinker only blinks once, drivers can't adjust or create space quickly enough.

Mirrors & Shoulder Checks

- **Thorough Scan**: Glance at side mirrors to spot any fast-approaching vehicles. Do a **shoulder check** for your blind spot just before moving over.
- **Confidence**: If you see a decent gap, smoothly align your car with that gap's speed.

Pro Tip: Use the Whole Ramp

If the ramp is long, keep accelerating until you match the highway speed. Don't merge halfway up if traffic is too close behind you—use every yard of that ramp to get in sync.

MATCHING SPEED & FINDING THE GAP

The Speed Dance

- **Goal**: Merge into traffic with minimal speed difference—reducing the "Oh no!" surprise factor.
- **No Over- or Under-Acceleration**: Roaring onto a 65-mph highway at 80 mph freaks out everyone, and creeping in at 45 mph can cause abrupt slowdowns. Aim for a happy middle ground.

Spotting an Opening

- **Look Ahead**: Watch how fast cars are traveling in the lane you want. Identify a gap well before your ramp ends.

- **Stay Alert**: If a semi is crawling, or a car is switching lanes, be ready to adjust your speed (slightly) to slip in behind or ahead of them.

Common Mistake: Stopping on the Ramp

Nothing unnerves trailing drivers more than a dead-stop car on a freeway entrance. It also shortens your distance for acceleration, making safe merging tougher.

CONSIDERING THE RIGHT OF WAY

Main-Lane Traffic vs. Merging
- **Typically, The Merger Yields**: Cars already on the highway/road have the right-of-way. Don't force them to brake abruptly just because you want in.
- **Polite Mergers**: If main-lane drivers slow too much or wave you in unnecessarily, it may confuse the flow. They have right-of-way; you manage your speed to slot in.

Don't Over-Yield
- **Avoid Confusion**: Sometimes, drivers in the main lane try to be nice by hitting the brakes to "let you in." This can disrupt traffic behind them, leading to honking or sudden stops.
- **Steady Flow**: If you see they're leaving a gap, merge carefully—but don't rely on main-lane traffic to slow down drastically for you.

SPECIAL CASE: MERGE RAMPS FOLLOWED BY EXIT RAMPS

Cross-Traffic Chaos
- **One Ramp In, One Ramp Out**: Some highways have merge ramps that immediately precede an exit ramp, creating crossing streams of traffic—merging cars might want **in**, exiting cars want **out**.
- **Focus & Extra Caution**: Speeds differ wildly; watch for vehicles zipping across your path from the left or right.

Communication & Space
- **Signal & Check**: Use the signals and keep your eyes on mirrors for cars quickly decelerating to exit.
- **Yield & Speed Management**: If your path crosses, a slight speed drop or acceleration can avoid a potential collision. Always watch for slowdowns—some might brake hard to catch the exit.

SPECIAL CASE: LEFT MERGE RAMPS INTO FAST-LANES

Fast-Lane Factor
- **Immediate Acceleration:** Merging into the left lane often means entering the quickest flow of traffic—be prepared to match higher speeds.
- **Limited Cushion:** Gaps between cars may be smaller. Make sure you can squeeze in safely.

Speed Adjustments
- **Smooth Transitions:** If traffic is flying by, a quick but controlled acceleration is essential. Avoid over-correcting or slamming the brakes.
- **Stay Alert:** Even with your signal flashing, some vehicles won't yield. Be ready to adjust speed or position at the last second.

Pro Tip: "Speed Harmony"
The name of the merging game is **reducing relative speed difference**. That is, keep your speed close to traffic flow so merges and exits happen smoother, with minimal abrupt stops or rocket launches. Even if it seems counterintuitive, accelerating to close the speed gap with other traffic can make merging significantly easier.

WHAT IF TRAFFIC IS CONGESTED?

Patience & Signals
- **Early Blinker:** Let others know you want in. In bumper-to-bumper traffic, a driver might (hopefully) grant you space.
- **Don't Force Gaps:** Pushing your nose in might cause sudden stops behind you. Ease in, maintain slow forward motion, and be ready to brake.

Eye Contact & Common Sense
- **A Quick Wave:** Sometimes a friendly wave or mutual nod helps. People respond better to courtesy than aggression.
- **Stopping at Ramp End:** If traffic is crawling at 5 mph, you may need to creep carefully until you find a spot. Stopping is not ideal, but in jammed traffic, speed differences are smaller, so it's less dire—still watch behind you!

DRIVING PAST MERGE LANES

Check Your Right Mirror
- **Merging Vehicles**: If you're in the right lane of a highway and see a merge ramp, glance at your **right mirror**. Are cars accelerating in? Adjust slightly—maybe move left if safe.
- **Reduce Surprise**: Being aware avoids last-second lane changes or brake slams if a merging driver misjudges speed.

"Slowing Down" Myths
- **Don't Over-Brake**: Slowing too much in the main lane can catch following cars off guard, leading to rear-end collisions. A mild speed adjustment might help, but big slowdowns can be dangerous.

COMMON MERGING MISTAKES & REMINDERS

Late/No Signal
- **Blinker Is Your Friend**: Flicking it at the moment you move is too late. People need time to react and create space.
- **If in Doubt, Keep Signaling**: Even after you start merging, let it blink a little—some drivers react late.

Over- or Under-Speeding
- **Misreading Flow**: Zooming onto a 60 mph highway at 80 mph confuses everyone; crawling in at 40 mph is equally hazardous.
- **Aim for the Middle**: Matching traffic speed is the best approach.

Stopping Abruptly or "Hesitation Hang"
- **Ramp End**: If you freeze and stop, you block everyone behind you and risk a rear-end collision.
- **Decision**: If you feel it's too tight, take a breath, find another gap, but maintain some forward momentum if possible.

Common Mistake: Forgetting to Cancel Signal
After you merge, turn off your blinker! Otherwise, drivers might think you intend to keep moving across lanes, creating confusion.

Pro Tip: Signal Your Intention to Exit
Don't forget to also use your turn signal when exiting the highway. Simply slowing down or braking without indicating can catch other drivers off guard and cause dangerous situations.

Merging is your car's way of saying, "Hi, nice to meet you!" to traffic already flowing on the road. By **signaling early**, **matching speed**, and **finding a good gap** before you arrive at the merge point, you waltz into the lane with minimal fuss. Remember not to rely on main-lane drivers hitting the brakes—**you** typically yield to them, but courtesy from both sides helps. Whether you're dealing with tricky ramp crossovers, congestion, or simple merges from a side street, keep an eye out, stay smooth, and let your blinker do the talking.

Bonus Pro Tip: Zipper Merge in Construction Zones

When two lanes narrow into one, **don't jump over the moment you see an "End Lane" sign.** Instead, use the entire length of your lane until you reach the merge point—this is often called a "zipper merge." By waiting until the lanes actually converge, you help keep traffic flowing steadily, rather than creating an early bottleneck. Once at the merge, alternate with cars in the other lane—one from your lane, one from theirs—ensuring a smoother, faster transition for everyone.

28. PASSING ETIQUETTE: WHEN IT'S COOL AND WHEN IT'S JUST DANGEROUS

Ever been stuck behind a slowpoke, staring at their bumper as if it's the only view you'll have for miles? You're itching to go faster, but how do you get around them without turning the road into a dangerous game of chicken? **Passing** is your ticket to escaping tailgating frustration, yet it demands the right timing, speed, and courtesy. In this chapter, we'll explore **when** to pass, **how** to pass efficiently, and **why** a good pass is like slipping out of a crowded movie theater row: quietly, safely, and without stepping on toes.

WHY PASSING MATTERS

Efficiency & Safety
- **Avoid Bottlenecks**: If you're stuck behind a vehicle going well under the speed limit, passing can help maintain a safer, steady flow of traffic.
- **Reducing Tension**: Nothing causes road rage like crawling behind a snail on wheels. A timely overtake can save everyone's nerves (including yours!).

Courtesy on the Road
- **Smooth Merges & Lane Swaps**: Overtaking quickly (but safely) frees up the lane for trailing cars.
- **Predictable Moves**: A well-executed pass is better than tailgating or abruptly swerving around the slower car.

Common Mistake: Tailgating Before Passing
Driving inches from someone's trunk to "pressure" them into going faster is risky and often illegal. Back off slightly so you have the space to accelerate and move over when it's actually safe.

CHECKING THE CONDITIONS

Road Markings & Legal Zones
- **Dashed vs. Solid Lines**: A solid line means **no passing**—could be a curve, hill crest, or other hazards. Dashes allow passing if it's safe.

- **Signs & Signals**: Watch for "No Passing" or "Passing Lane Ahead" signs. Most areas have designated passing lanes in hilly regions; slower vehicles are expected to stay in the right lane.

Visibility & Oncoming Traffic
- **Clear Distance**: If you're on a two-lane road, you need enough sightline to ensure no one's coming the other way.
- **Curves & Hills**: If the road is bending or cresting, skip the pass—cars can appear in seconds.

Nighttime Passing Hazards
- **Reduced Depth Perception**: Darkness makes it tougher to judge the distance or speed of oncoming traffic, especially if their headlights obscure how close they actually are.
- **Lane Marking Confusion**: Road lines and signs are harder to see, raising the chance of drifting into the opposite lane.
- **Glare Issues**: High beams or oncoming headlights can momentarily blind you, making a quick pass more dangerous.
- **Hilly Roads**: If the terrain is rolling up and down, oncoming cars' headlights may remain hidden until they crest a hill, leaving you little time to react.
- **Caution**: If you must pass, use your **low beams**, confirm a clearly visible gap, and be ready to back off if anything feels uncertain—better to wait behind a slow car than risk a dicey overtake in the dark.

Speed of Other Vehicles
- **Slower Ahead?**: Make sure the cars ahead aren't about to turn or speed up. Misjudging their moves could leave you side-by-side with them when an oncoming car shows up.
- **Busy Road**: If traffic is dense, sometimes waiting it out is wiser than weaving in and out.

Pro Tip: Aim for Minimal Speed Difference
You need a bit more speed to pass quickly, but don't rocket 30 mph faster than everyone else—overkill speeds can alarm the driver you're overtaking and others on the road.

Common Mistake: Lingering Beside the Other Car
Driving parallel to them for ages is stressful for both parties. Complete the pass swiftly (within legal limits) to minimize time spent in the oncoming or extra lane.

HOW TO EXECUTE A PASS

Signal, Signal, Signal
- **Blinker On**: Give a clear heads-up. Let it flash a couple times so folks behind or ahead know what you're doing.
- **Shoulder Check**: Right before moving, check your mirrors and glance over your shoulder to <u>confirm no one's about to pass you</u>—or if you're on a highway, that the next lane is clear.

Move Into the Passing Lane
- **Gentle Steering**: No need for a violent swerve. Keep a steady, controlled move into the adjoining lane.
- **Accelerate Smoothly**: Increase speed enough to go past the slower vehicle without lingering beside them.

Return to Your Lane
- **Check Mirrors**: Make sure you see the front of the passed car in your rearview mirror—it means you've cleared them.
- **Signal Again**: Flick your blinker to move back over.
- **Ease In, Don't Brake**: Don't cut back in and slam your brakes. Maintain or gradually adjust speed so you don't surprise the car behind you.

PASSING ON MULTI-LANE HIGHWAYS

The Left Lane Is Key
- **Standard Practice**: Overtake using the left lane, then return to the right lane once done.
- **Check for Speeders**: Look in your left mirror—some cars or motorcycles might be bombing down the left lane at warp speed. If they're close and moving faster, let them pass first.

Don't Hog the Passing Lane
- **Lane Courtesy**: Once you pass, move back right to allow faster traffic behind you to flow.
- **Avoid Middle Lane "Camping"**: If you're on a three-lane highway, keep right unless overtaking. Constantly sitting in the middle can block smoother traffic flow.

Exits, Ramps & Merges
- **Watch for Merging Cars**: If you're passing near an on-ramp, check your right mirror—cars may accelerate fast trying to merge.

- **Maintain Speed**: Drastically slowing in the right lane to "let them in" can confuse traffic. Remember, you have the right of way—maintain a steady pace or change lanes if possible.

SPECIAL SITUATIONS

Passing Large Vehicles (Trucks/Buses)
- **Longer Blind Spots**: Trucks can't see you if you hug close. <u>Hang back a bit, then pass decisively.</u>
- **Extra Room**: Their length means it takes more time to get fully around them—ensure you have enough distance to complete the pass safely.

Two-Lane Roads with Oncoming Traffic
- **Think "Zipper Timing"**: Judge the oncoming cars' speed—don't attempt a pass if an oncoming vehicle is closing the distance.
- **Slow Down If Unsure**: If your gap suddenly disappears, ease back behind the slower car. No shame in abandoning a pass to prevent a head-on.

Poor Weather & Low Visibility
- **Fog, Rain, or Snow**: Passing is riskier. If you can't see far enough ahead, it might be wiser to wait.
- **Road Slipperiness**: Hard acceleration on wet roads could spin your tires—exercise caution.

WHEN NOT TO PASS

Solid Lines & No-Passing Zones
- **Hills & Curves**: The road marking is telling you it's too dangerous to see oncoming traffic properly.
- **School Zones or Crosswalks**: You must not overtake another vehicle here (for example, a car stopped for pedestrians).

Heavy Congestion
- **Weaving Danger**: If everyone's crawling, constant lane changes and passes might cause fender-benders. Minimal gains, maximum risk.

Unexpected Obstacles
- **Animals or Debris**: If a slow car is dealing with an obstacle, be patient until you confirm it's safe to pass. They might swerve unpredictably.

Common Mistake: Assuming a Slower Car Will Stay Slow

Some drivers speed up randomly (maybe they were daydreaming). Mid-pass, you could find yourself stuck if they accelerate. Keep an escape plan.

GOAL: REDUCE RELATIVE SPEED DIFFERENCES

Merging & Exiting in the Passing Zone

- **Don't Over-Brake**: If you slow drastically while passing, you confuse traffic behind you.
- **Exiting Soon?**: If your exit is just ahead, maybe stay in your lane. Passing and then cutting right across multiple lanes is risky (and also rude!).

Eye on the Road Behind & Ahead

- **Mirrors**: Check both rearview and side mirrors to gauge approaching cars' speed.
- **Balance**: You want to pass quickly but not rocket by at a reckless speed difference.

Pro Tip: Don't Cut Them Off

If faster cars are already approaching in the fast lane, let them pass before making your move. Don't cut them off just because you feel like overtaking *right now*.

Common Mistake: Late or Non-Existent Signal

Swooping around a slow car without signaling can startle everyone. A blink or two beforehand lets cars around you anticipate the move. Be a courteous passer, not a surprise one!

Overtaking is your chance to say, "I really don't want to stare at your trunk anymore—time to move on!". But it's also one of the riskiest maneuvers if done without proper checks and signals. Follow **solid line rules**, ensure **clear visibility**, and match (or slightly exceed) traffic speed to complete the pass briskly. Whether on a multi-lane freeway or a narrow country road, courtesy and caution are your best friends: signal, accelerate smoothly, and return to your lane without cutting anyone off.

29. CHANGING LANES: EASY DOES IT, EVERY TIME

Think of changing lanes as a polite way of saying, "Excuse me, I'd like to be over there now," to the traffic around you. It's a straightforward move—signal, check, and go—but it often leads to confusion when done abruptly or without enough scanning for hidden cars. In this chapter, we'll focus on **smooth** and **safe** ways to move from one lane to another, **avoid blind spot surprises**, and **sync** with the traffic flow (because no one likes a rogue lane-swerving driver).

WHY LANE CHANGES MATTER

Traffic Flow & Efficiency
- **Don't Stall Progress**: If a lane is slow or blocked, shifting to a faster or clearer lane can ease congestion for everyone (including you).
- **Courtesy & Confidence**: Properly timed moves prevent abrupt slowdowns and startled fellow drivers.

Being Predictable
- **Signals**: Telling others you're about to move is like raising your hand in class—everyone's aware of your intention.
- **Steady Steering**: Small, consistent inputs help your car glide sideways rather than lurch.

CHECKING THE CONDITIONS BEFORE YOU MOVE

Mirrors & Blind Spots
- **Side Mirrors**: A quick glance identifies cars in your adjacent lane.
- **Shoulder Peek**: Even the best mirrors can miss vehicles in your rear quarters—especially motorcycles or smaller cars.

Lane & Speed Awareness
- **Don't Slam the Brakes**: Maintain speed while you merge. A sudden deceleration can cause rear-end confusion.
- **Observe Traffic Rhythm**: If the next lane is going faster, accelerate a bit to match them; if slower, ease off slightly.

Pro Tip: One Lane at a Time
If you need to cross multiple lanes, do it step by step. Signal, check, move one lane, stabilize, signal again. Skipping steps can lead to mid-lane collisions.

Common Mistake: Last-Second Flick
Flicking your blinker as you physically change lanes leaves zero reaction time for other drivers. Give them a heads-up at least a couple of seconds beforehand!

EXECUTING A SMOOTH LANE CHANGE

Signal Early
- **Blinker On**: Let it flash a few times before you drift.
- **Eye Contact?**: Sometimes, if traffic is dense, a quick glance at the driver next to you can help confirm they see you.

Move Over Gently
- **Align Speed**: Match or slightly adjust to the target lane's flow—don't surprise them by zipping 20 mph faster or slower.
- **Steer with Subtlety**: A calm, controlled drift is safer (and more pleasant for passengers) than a sharp yank on the wheel.

Cancel Your Signal
- **After the Move**: Don't leave your blinker flashing for miles. Turn it off once you're settled in your new lane.

Common Mistake: Hovering Over Lane Lines
Don't linger on the dividing line, half in, half out. Commit to the move once it's safe—occupying two lanes is a recipe for confusion.

HANDLING MULTI-LANE HIGHWAYS

The Left Lane for Passing
- **Standard Practice**: Keep right unless you're overtaking or the traffic layout forces you to stay left.
- **Faster Traffic**: Monitor your left mirror—cars (or motorcycles) might zoom up behind you. If they do, let them pass before you shift.

Checking the Right Mirror for Merge Ramps
- **Merging Cars**: When you see an on-ramp approaching, be extra mindful—some drivers accelerate rapidly onto the highway, possibly crossing your lane.

- **Steady Yourself**: If you can move left to let them in easily, do so. If not, maintain your speed or adjust slightly, but don't drastically slow down (others behind you might not expect it).

Exit Ramps & Lane Weaving
- **Busy Exits**: If you're in the right lane near an exit, watch for last-minute lane-changers who realize they need to exit ASAP.
- **Avoid the Frenzy**: If you see a cluster of cars aiming for the off-ramp, you might shift one lane left beforehand, if safe, to sidestep the chaos.

SPECIAL SCENARIOS & SAFETY CONSIDERATIONS

Heavy Traffic or Slowdowns
- **Patience Over Peril**: Resist frequent lane-hopping in gridlock. Gains are minimal, and risk is high.
- **Ensure Gaps**: Tail-to-bumper traffic means minimal space. Signal, wait for a slight gap, then move gently—no forced merges.

Construction or Narrow Lanes
- **Tight Spaces**: Shifting lanes in a construction zone can be tricky—often lanes are narrower and lined with cones or barriers.
- **Slow Down**: Give yourself more reaction time, especially if there's shifting traffic or you see a lane end sign up ahead.

Pedestrians & Cyclists
- **City Streets**: If there's a bike lane or sidewalk, ensure no one's popping into your lane from the right. Shoulder check for scooters, too.

Pro Tip: Always Think "Relative Speed"
The safest lane changes happen when your speed roughly matches the lane you're entering. Avoid giant speed differentials that unsettle surrounding drivers.

DANGERS OF MULTIPLE SIMULTANEOUS LANE CHANGES

Two Cars, One Lane
- **Center-Lane Collision**: If you and a driver two lanes over both aim for the middle lane at once, you're invisible to each other's blind spot.
- **Extra Checks**: Peek further across your mirrors or glance quickly to confirm no one else is making the same move.

Communication Gaps
- **Your Signal vs. Their Signal**: If you both flick the blinker at the same time, who yields? Typically, it's not a rule but a courtesy dance—one might slow, the other might speed up. Keep scanning for their position.

Minimizing Surprise
- **One Lane at a Time**: If you need to cross multiple lanes, do so in increments, repeating the signal and blind-spot check each time.
- **Situational Awareness**: Watch any car in the far lane that might want the same space. If you suspect it, delay your move or accelerate ahead.

FINISHING THE LANE CHANGE & SETTLING IN

Smooth Adaptation
- **Space Cushion**: Once in the new lane, maintain a safe following distance—don't jump over and ride someone's bumper.
- **Cancel Signal, Keep Pace**: If you drastically slow or accelerate after changing lanes, you might confuse trailing traffic.

Posture & Mirror Check
- **Stay in Your New Lane**: Resist the urge to keep weaving. If you're where you want to be, relax.
- **Look Ahead**: Re-center your focus on the road in front of you, ready for any fresh merges or obstacles.

Common Mistake: Losing Sight of What's Ahead
If you stay glued to your mirrors planning your next move, stopped traffic ahead can catch you off guard.

Switching lanes doesn't have to be nerve-wracking—**signal early, glance thoroughly**, and move with purpose. By keeping your speed in line with the traffic, you'll slide over smoothly instead of jolting the flow. Watch out for multi-lane hazards (especially if other cars might move into the same spot) and give merges or off-ramps space if you can. Ultimately, changing lanes is about courtesy, clarity, and confidence. Think of it as politely excusing yourself in a line—people appreciate a heads-up and a calm, decisive action.

30. TURNING: LEFT, RIGHT, AND EVERYTHING IN BETWEEN

Turning might sound straightforward—just rotate the wheel, right? But a well-executed turn involves **signal timing**, **speed control**, **lane choice**, and sometimes even **decoding local rules** (like whether you can turn right on red). Toss in the challenge of oncoming traffic on country roads, confusing one-way intersections, or pedestrians lurking in crosswalks, and you'll see why a good turn is part art, part science. In this chapter, we'll walk you through the essentials of making safe, smooth, and controlled turns.

WHY PROPER TURNING MATTERS

Safety & Predictability
- **Signaling Your Intent**: Blinking before you brake or turn helps other drivers and pedestrians know your plan.
- **Avoiding Collisions**: Being clear in your approach reduces the risk of side-swipes or fender benders from behind or the side.

Flow & Confidence
- **Smooth Traffic**: Last-second turns can catch other drivers off guard. Steady, predictable behavior keeps everyone calm.
- **Less Stress**: Mastering the technique means fewer honks, fewer near-misses, and more relaxed commutes.

Common Mistake: Over-trusting "They'll Stop for Me"
Just because you signal doesn't mean oncoming traffic (or crossing pedestrians) will automatically yield. A good turn acknowledges you share the road.

APPROACH & SIGNAL TIMING

Signal Early
- **Rule of Thumb**: In city settings, signal at least 100 feet (30 meters) before turning. On high-speed roads, consider starting even earlier.

Checking Mirrors, Especially on Country Roads
- **Rearview Mirror Check**: If you're slowing down for a left turn on a rural highway, be aware cars behind might attempt to pass. A quick glance can save you from a side collision.

- **Blind Spot**: Even if it's rural and less busy, a final shoulder check ensures no surprise speed demons behind you.

Pro Tip: Signal Then Brake

Flick on the blinker first, then ease into braking. Drivers behind you see your intention sooner and won't wonder why you're slowing down suddenly.

SPEED & STEERING TECHNIQUES

Slow Before the Turn
- **Brake on Approach**: Decelerate smoothly while still going straight. Steering while braking too hard can cause understeer or slides on slick roads.
- **Steady Wheel**: Once you enter the turn, avoid big speed changes—keep moderate throttle to maintain control.

Turning Methods
- **Hand-Over-Hand vs. Push-Pull**: Each method has fans. Either way, keep your arms out of the airbag zone, controlling the wheel smoothly through the arc.
- **Look Through the Turn**: If you're turning left, look down the lane you plan to occupy; your hands follow your eyes.

Common Mistake: Slamming Brakes Mid-Turn

If you panic mid-turn, you might stop abruptly and cause a rear-end collision. Anticipate your speed so you're set before the curve.

LEFT TURNS VS. RIGHT TURNS

Right Turns
- **Tighter Radius**: Usually requires less arc space but watch for pedestrians or a curb.
- **Bike Lanes**: In many cities, the right lane might share space with cyclists. Always shoulder-check for bikes—especially in your blind spot.

Left Turns
- **Crossing Oncoming Traffic**: The biggest hazard. Yield if you don't have a protected green arrow.
- **One-Way to One-Way**: If both roads are one-way, you can typically hug the left side and turn into the left lane of the new one-way (check local rules).

- **One-Way to Two-Way:** Choose your lane thoughtfully—typically, the leftmost lane is designated for left turns, meaning you'll end up in the left lane of the road you're entering. This keeps you clear of potential conflicts and lets you switch lanes later when it's safe. Watch out for oncoming cars turning right into the rightmost lane—this is why you don't immediately jump into that far-right lane during your turn.

Pro Tip: Read the Lane Markings

Intersections often have arrows and "ONLY" markings indicating which lanes turn left or go straight. Don't guess—follow the paint.

NAVIGATING THE CENTER TURN LANE

Proper Use & Purpose
- **Designed for Left Turns:** The center turn lane is exclusively for making left turns from the main road or safely entering it from a side street. You can pause here briefly while waiting for a safe gap in oncoming traffic.

Signal, Slow, Stop, Turn
- **Turning from the Main Road:** Signal first, then merge into the center lane before making your left turn into a driveway or smaller street. This prevents you from blocking through traffic as you wait.

Entering from a Side Road
- **Turning onto the Main Road:** You don't have to wait for both directions to clear completely. Turn into the center lane first, pause or roll slowly, then merge safely into traffic when there's an opening.

Pitfalls to Avoid
- **Keep It Brief:** The center lane is for turning only—not for merging, passing, or extended travel. Signal, check both directions, and avoid lingering too long to prevent confusion.
- **Watch for Other Cars:** Other drivers may also be using the center turn lane at the same time. Always check for oncoming vehicles before entering, and be ready to adjust if someone else is turning into the same space.
- **Wheels Straight While Waiting:** Avoid turning the wheels left in anticipation of your turn. If you're rear-ended, you could be pushed into oncoming traffic, so keep them aligned forward until it's actually time to move.

INTERSECTIONS & CROSSWALKS

Pedestrians
- **Always Watch**: Scan crosswalks before finalizing your turn. Stopped cars might hide a pedestrian stepping off the curb.
- **Legal Duty**: Pedestrians in a crosswalk (marked or unmarked) generally have the right-of-way.

Traffic Lights & Signs
- **Protected vs. Unprotected**: A green arrow for left turns means oncoming traffic is stopped. No arrow? You must yield to them.
- **Turn on Red**: Many places allow right turns on red (after a full stop), but check for "NO TURN ON RED" signs. Some states forbid turning left on red from a one-way to another one-way, while others allow it under certain conditions.

Hazard of Turning on Red from the Second Lane
- **Double Right Turn Lanes**: If you're not in the rightmost lane, turning right on red can be illegal or unsafe—drivers in the far-right lane might also turn.
- **Lane Confusion**: It can lead to two cars turning onto the same path. Unless signs say otherwise, stick to the rightmost lane to turn on red.

ROUNDABOUTS & COMPLEX TURNS

Roundabout Basics (more details in the next chapter)
- **Yield on Entry**: Vehicles inside the roundabout have priority.
- **Signal on Exit**: Indicate your exit to let other drivers know.
- **Lane Choice**: Some multi-lane roundabouts have specific lanes for different exits. Read signs or road markings carefully. We'll dive deeper into safely maneuvering roundabouts in the next chapter.

Multi-Lane Turns
- **Designated Lanes**: Large intersections might have two or more turn lanes. Pick one early and stay in it. Drifting across lane lines mid-turn can cause side-swipes.
- **Follow the Arrows**: Painted arrows often show which lane leads to which direction.

Common Mistake: Crossing Lanes During the Turn
If you start in the left turn lane, don't end up in the rightmost lane once you've turned—unless signage specifically allows it.

TURNS ON COUNTRY ROADS

Checking the Rearview Mirror
- **Left Turn on Country Roads**: Cars behind might try to pass you on the left if they see you slowing. Double-check your mirror and left blind spot for any impatient drivers. Signal early to give drivers behind you plenty of time to react and slow down.
- **Wide Shoulder**: When making a right turn, if it's safe and the shoulder is wide enough, signal first, then ease slightly right to keep cars behind you from braking hard—reducing the risk of being rear-ended.

No Surprises
- **Early Signal**: Give extra notice if you see an upcoming driveway or side street. Drivers behind you might be traveling at high speeds.
- **Hilly Terrain**: Turning just past a hillcrest can be risky since the driver behind might not see you stopping—be extra careful with left turns on hills.

COMMON TURNING PITFALLS

Oversteering/Understeering
- **Jerky Motions**: If you over-rotate, you risk swinging wide into oncoming lanes. If you under-rotate, you might curb your wheels or clip a parked car.
- **Smooth Arc**: Maintain a gentle, consistent rotation of the wheel.

Late or No Signal
- **Sudden Brakes**: If drivers only realize you're turning when your brake lights go bright, it's too late. Flick that blinker early.

Turning Too Wide or Tight
- **Clipping the Opposite Lane**: A wide left turn can cross into oncoming traffic.
- **Jumping the Curb**: A tight right turn could mount the sidewalk or corner. Eye your turn radius carefully.

Misjudging Oncoming Traffic Speed
- **Wait & Evaluate**: Cars heading your way could be moving faster than they appear. If you're unsure, take an extra moment before turning—caution always beats a close call.

Common Mistake: Forgetting Pedestrian / Cyclist Lanes
Many right-turn lanes cross bike lanes or crosswalks. If you ignore them, you might sideswipe a cyclist or force a pedestrian to jump back.

TIPS: LOOK WHERE YOU'RE GOING & SPEED CONTROL

Turn Your Head, Not Just Your Eyes
- **Direction of Travel**: If you're making a left turn, gaze into the lane you'll land in, scanning for obstructions or halted cars.
- **Maintain Balance**: Quick glances at mirrors, but your main focus is forward—where your car is heading.

Weather & Night Adjustments
- **Slippery Roads**: Slow earlier, turn gently, and don't mash the throttle mid-turn.
- **Night Turns**: Use headlights or streetlights to gauge turn angles. Keep your eyes peeled for poorly lit signs or pedestrians.

A well-executed turn requires **planning** and **precision**—signal early, adjust your speed, and watch for hidden hazards like pedestrians or surprise pass attempts on rural roads. In city driving, be mindful of bike lanes, "No Turn on Red" signs, and proper lane positioning, especially on one-way streets. By anticipating your route, looking through the turn, and staying aware of your surroundings, you can make every turn smooth, safe, and stress-free. Turning isn't just a quick flick of the wheel—it's a skill worth mastering!

31. CIRCLES OF CONFUSION, SOLVED: ROUNDABOUTS MADE EASY

Roundabouts can appear daunting—a circular exchange where everyone merges and exits in a steady flow, with no traffic lights to boss you around. But once you master **how** and **when** to yield, **where** to look, and **which lane** to choose (in multi-lane roundabouts), you'll realize they're designed for **fewer stop-and-go moments** and smoother commutes. In this chapter, we'll walk you through the basics of **approaching**, **circulating**, and **exiting** a roundabout, plus dispel myths about signaling. The end goal? Confident, swirl-free driving that helps you glide around these circles like a waltz, not a demolition derby.

WHY ROUNDABOUTS EXIST

Reduced Collisions & Congestion
- **Fewer High-Speed Crashes**: Roundabouts encourage lower speeds, which means fewer T-bones and head-on collisions—common in standard intersections.
- **Better Flow**: No long red lights or 4-way stop signs; cars enter and exit at a slow roll, often shortening queue times.

Courtesy & Awareness
- **Everyone Yields**: Vehicles inside have priority. New arrivals must find a gap—no one's left fuming at a forever-red light.
- **Lower Stress**: Once you trust the roundabout system, it can be calmer than large multi-turn intersections.

Common Mistake: Stopping in the Circle
Unnecessary stops in the roundabout confuse drivers behind you and can trigger minor rear-end collisions. Unless there's an actual hazard, keep rolling.

APPROACH & YIELD STRATEGY

Slow Down & Check Lanes
- **Approach Gently**: Let off the gas as you near the roundabout. Prepare to brake if needed.
- **Yield to Traffic in the Circle**: Glance left to see if a gap exists. If cars are flowing, wait. If it's open, roll in.

Signaling When Approaching
- **Common Misconception**: Many drivers think they must signal as if turning left or right to enter. Actually, you typically **don't** signal to enter a roundabout (since you're not making a "turn" into a separate road).
- **Exception—Lane Change**: If the approach has multiple lanes and you need to move from one lane to another **before** entering (say, the left lane if you plan to take the second or third exit), then you'd signal your lane change. But the act of entering the roundabout itself isn't signaled the same way as a normal intersection turn.
- **Exception—Bypass or Adjacent Lane**: If the approach includes a separate lane that either bypasses the roundabout or merges into it, you'll need to signal if you're changing over from the main approach lane. For example, some roads have a slip-lane allowing you to avoid the roundabout altogether or to merge into it from a different angle. In these cases, **use your signal** to show that lane change. Once you're already aligned with the roundabout entrance lane, however, you typically don't signal again just to "enter" the circle—your blinker is reserved for lane changes or exit signals.

Pro Tip: Focus on Lane Position

If it's a multi-lane approach, confirm which lane leads to which roundabout exit. You might shift lanes first (with a brief signal) before the actual entry.

LANE CHOICE (MULTI-LANE ROUNDABOUTS)

Picking the Correct Lane
- **Road Signs & Markings**: Usually indicate which lane is for going straight, turning right, or turning left around the roundabout.
- **Stay in Your Lane**: Once you commit, don't drift across lane lines inside the circle—that's a sure way to sideswipe or startle neighbors.

Yield Inside the Circle
- **You Already Have Priority**: If you're circulating within the roundabout, you outrank approaching traffic.
- **Watch for Lane Changers**: Some drivers might realize "Oops, I'm in the wrong lane!" and shift abruptly. Keep scanning your mirrors and blind spots.

Common Mistake: Lane-Hopping Mid-Roundabout
Resist the temptation to cross from an inner lane to outer lane (or vice versa) inside the circle. Complete your intended path, then exit or circle again if needed.

CIRCULATING & SIGNALING

Drive Steadily Around
- **Gentle Steering**: Roundabouts typically need only light, constant steering input. No jerky wheel yanks, please.
- **Maintain Low Speed**: This is not a racetrack—everyone's depending on moderate, uniform speeds.

Signaling on Exit
- **Why Signal at All?**: Indicating your exit helps vehicles behind you—and those waiting to enter—know you're leaving.
- **Timing**: Flick your right blinker a bit before your intended exit, letting the driver behind anticipate your move.

Common Mistake: Forgetting to Signal When Leaving
Exiting without signaling forces cars waiting to enter to guess your plans. They might hold up traffic or jump in front of you unexpectedly.

ROUNDABOUT EXITS & CROSSWALKS

Pedestrians & Cyclists
- **Yield to Crosswalks**: Pedestrians typically cross each entrance or exit leg. If someone's waiting or stepping in, you must pause.
- **Watch Out for Cyclists in the Circle**: Some ride around as if they're another vehicle; others use sidewalks or crosswalks. Stay alert for either approach.

Merging & Lane Management
- **If Two Lanes Exit**: Follow your lane's path—don't cut across the outer lane's exit if you're in the inner lane.
- **Returning to Main Road**: Once you exit, accelerate gently back to appropriate speed, scanning mirrors for merging traffic.

SPECIAL SCENARIOS & MISTAKES

Stopping When You Shouldn't
- **Unnecessary Halts**: If the roundabout is free, go! Stopping abruptly can cause rear-end collisions, especially if the driver

behind expects you to continue.

- **Confusing Oncoming Drivers**: Halting mid-circle can cause them to guess incorrectly and lead to near-misses.

Oversized Vehicles

- **Give Them Space**: Large trucks or buses may partially straddle lanes. Don't crowd them or try to squeeze by inside the roundabout.

Poor Visibility or Night Driving

- **Dim Streets**: Look for the roundabout signs early, especially if lights are minimal.
- **Slow & Easy**: If you can't see well, reduce speed further—other cars might appear from around the bend in the circle.

DANGER OF SIMULTANEOUS LANE CHANGES

Lane Crossing Collisions

- **Same Exit or Next Lane?**: In multi-lane roundabouts, two cars might both shift for the same exit from different lanes, blind to each other's move.
- **Extra Vigilance**: Double-check your blind spot and read other drivers' body language (their speed or half-lane drift) before exiting.

"Play It Safe" Mindset

- **Better to Circle Again**: If you miss your exit or your lane positioning gets confused, just continue around one more time rather than forcing a dangerous swerve.

PUTTING IT ALL TOGETHER: LOW SPEED, YIELD, FLOW

Reducing Stress & Maintaining Control

- **Low Speeds**: Roundabouts are the place for 15–20 mph, not highway speeds.
- **Flow Over Force**: Ease in when it's clear, circle politely, and exit without slamming brakes or signals last second.

Reassure Others with Courtesy

- **Signal on Exit**: A quick blink to say, "I'm leaving here, heads up!" to cars behind and those waiting to enter.
- **Maintain Spacing**: Keep a safe gap from cars in front—no tailgating in a circle.

Common Mistake: Guessing Lane Without Checking Signs

Roundabouts often have arrow markings or overhead boards telling you which lane goes left vs. straight vs. right. If you guess, you risk mid-roundabout confusion or last-second merges.

Pro Tip: Don't Signal on Entry—Unless Changing Lanes

Many drivers unfamiliar with the roundabout etiquette flick their blinker thinking they must "turn left" into a circle. You only signal if you need to shift lanes on approach (e.g., to the left lane for a further exit). Otherwise, keep your signals for exiting or lane changes.

Roundabouts can seem chaotic at first glance, but with **low speed**, **proper lane choice**, and **courteous yielding**, you'll find they're smoother than traditional stoplight intersections. Avoid the biggest pitfalls—**stopping** unnecessarily, **signaling** incorrectly, or **drifting** lanes mid-circle—and you'll sail around gracefully. Remember: it's about matching the rhythm of other cars, lightly tapping your signals when exiting, and letting that circle do its traffic magic. After a few successful loops, you'll appreciate how roundabouts truly help the world (of traffic) go round!

32. INTERSECTIONS: WHERE CONFUSION AND RIGHT-OF-WAY COLLIDE

Intersections are like the social hubs of driving—where you meet everyone else coming from different directions. And much like mingling at a busy party, you need to read signals, take turns, and avoid stepping on toes. Some intersections are calm, two-road affairs with a simple stop sign, while others can be multi-lane monsters sporting advanced turn arrows, confusing merges, and "no right turns on red" rules. In this chapter, we'll walk you through **recognizing intersection types**, **right-of-way basics**, and **common pitfalls** so you can cross paths with others safely and smoothly—like a pro who knows exactly when to yield and when to go.

WHY INTERSECTIONS MATTER

Collision Hotspots
- **Frequent Crashes**: Many accidents happen where roads meet, often due to drivers misjudging right-of-way or rushing a changing light.
- **Conflicting Directions**: Vehicles can come from multiple roads, crossing lines, or turning in every which way.

Varying Complexity
- **One-Lane vs. Multi-Lane**: A basic four-way stop is easier to manage than a five-lane metropolis intersection with turn arrows, slip lanes, and pedestrians weaving through.
- **Traffic Flow**: Mastering intersection rules helps keep traffic gliding along rather than slamming into each other.

Common Mistake: Trusting Others Implicitly
Never assume another driver will stop or yield just because they're supposed to. Always verify with your own eyes that they are indeed halting before you proceed.

TYPES OF INTERSECTIONS

Controlled
- **Lights or Signs**: Stop signs, yield signs, or traffic lights direct who goes first.
- **Roundabouts**: A circular intersection with yield-on-entry rules.

Uncontrolled
- **No Signs or Lights**: Common in rural or quiet residential spots. Drivers rely on courtesy and right-of-way rules—like yielding to the vehicle on the right if you both arrive simultaneously.

Multi-Lane & Complex
- **Turn Lanes & Arrows**: You might see separate lanes for right turns, left turns, or "straight only." Painted arrows or overhead signs guide you.
- **Slip Lanes & Merging**: Some intersections have small bypass lanes to let right-turners avoid waiting at the main light. Always watch for merging traffic or crosswalks.

Pro Tip: Read the Road
Pay attention to lane markings and overhead signs—before you reach the intersection—to choose the correct lane for your desired direction.

RIGHT-OF-WAY BASICS

Stop & Yield Signs
- **4-Way Stops**: The first car to arrive goes first. If two arrive together, the one on the right proceeds. If confusion reigns, eye contact can help decide who waves the other on.
- **Yield Sign**: Slow down, give priority to crossing traffic, and go only when clear.

Traffic Lights
- **Green, Yellow, Red**:
  - **Green**: Go if safe, but watch for stale greens turning yellow.
  - **Yellow**: Clear the intersection if you're already in it or prepare to stop if you haven't crossed the stop line yet.
  - **Red**: Full stop. Right on red is often allowed after a complete stop (unless there's a "No Turn on Red" sign).
- **Arrows**:
  - **Protected Left/Right**: Oncoming traffic is stopped; you have a dedicated turn arrow.
  - **Unprotected**: You must yield to oncoming cars before turning.

Pedestrians & Cyclists
- **Crosswalk Priority**: If someone is in the crosswalk or about to enter, let them pass—don't inch forward intimidatingly.

- **Bike Lanes**: Especially turning right—check your side mirror and blind spot for cyclists continuing straight.

Common Mistake: Assuming a Green Light = Guarantee
Green means "go if safe"—not "go blindly." Always glance for turning vehicles, red-light runners, or pedestrians still crossing.

APPROACH & OBSERVATION

Scanning Early
- **Look for Signs**: "No Left Turn," "One Way," or special time-based rules (e.g., "No Turn on Red 7AM–9AM").
- **Speed Adjustment**: Easing off the gas before you're right upon the intersection helps you respond if lights change or traffic stalls.

Lane Choice
- **Plan Ahead**: If you know you'll turn left in a few blocks, start moving to the left lane early (when safe).
- **Multiple Turns**: Some intersections have multiple left-turn lanes—pick one that leads to the lane you want afterward.

Pro Tip: Watch Brake Lights
If cars ahead slow down unexpectedly, they might be planning a turn. Anticipate possible confusion and be ready to react.

TRAFFIC LIGHTS & SIGNALS

Reading the Lights (Refresher)
- **Green**: Go, but remain watchful. If you see cross traffic not slowing, they might be about to run a red.
- **Yellow**: Decide quickly—speeding up last-second can cause T-bones if oncoming or cross traffic jumps the gun.
- **Red**: Stop fully behind the line (or crosswalk). Only turn right (or left from a one-way to another one-way) if local laws allow and safe.

Right on Red (and the "No Turn on Red" Clause)
- **Check for Signs**: A "No Turn on Red" sign overrides the usual rule—stop and wait for green.
- **Pedestrians**: Even if turning is allowed, you must yield to crossing pedestrians or bikes.
- **Second Lane Right Turn**: If you're in a middle lane and want to turn right on red, that's usually not permitted—it's typically for the far-right lane only.

Attempting a right turn on red from a lane not designated for it risks side-swiping cars in the actual right-turn lane or conflicting with through traffic.

4-WAY STOPS & UNCONTROLLED INTERSECTIONS

4-Way Stop Flow
- **Arrival Order**: First in, first out. If you and another arrive at the same time, yield to the driver on your right.
- **Polite Eye Contact**: If in doubt, a friendly wave can settle who goes next. Don't wave them on if they're clearly letting you go.

Uncontrolled Crossings
- **Slow & Scan**: No sign or light means you rely on caution. Approach with foot near the brake, looking all directions.
- **Right-of-Way**: Typically, yield to traffic from your right if you arrive simultaneously. But courtesy can vary; watch for others ignoring the rule.

MULTI-LANE INTERSECTIONS

Designated Turn Lanes
- **Arrows Painted**: If an arrow says "left only," do not attempt to go straight from that lane. Similarly, for right-turn-only lanes.
- **Stay in Your Lane**: If two lanes can turn left simultaneously, keep your lane throughout the turn—don't drift into the adjacent lane.

Hazards
- **Wide & Complex**: More lanes = more chance someone else might misinterpret signals or shift lanes unpredictably.
- **Watch Opposite Turners**: Oncoming left-turners might attempt a quick turn before you clear.

Common Mistake: Turning from the Wrong Lane
"Oops, I need that left turn"—some drivers forcibly cross lanes at the last second, risking collisions. Plan early to avoid last-minute lane changes.

SLIP LANES

What Is a Slip Lane?
- **Bypass for Right Turns**: A slip lane is a separate lane that allows vehicles to turn right without entering the main intersection.

- **Separated from Traffic Flow:** Often marked by an island or painted lines, guiding turning vehicles away from straight-moving traffic.
- **Improves Efficiency:** Helps keep intersections moving smoothly by reducing congestion for drivers continuing straight.

Using a Slip Lane Correctly

- **Yield, Don't Stop Unnecessarily:** Most slip lanes have a **yield sign**, meaning you should **slow down and merge when safe—** not come to a full stop if traffic is clear.
- **Check for Pedestrians:** Many slip lanes include **crosswalks**, so always yield to anyone crossing before merging.
- **Merge Smoothly:** Use your turn signal and check your blind spots before merging into the main road—don't cut off faster-moving traffic.

Common Mistakes & Hazards

- **Stopping When Clear:** If there's no traffic or pedestrians, keep moving—stopping unnecessarily disrupts flow.
- **Forgetting to Look Left:** Even though you're turning right, **check for oncoming traffic from the left** before merging.
- **Slow or Hesitant Merging:** Hesitating too long can confuse other drivers or force sudden stops—be decisive but cautious.

COMMON INTERSECTION PITFALLS & SOLUTIONS

Running Yellow or Red

- **Be Realistic:** If it's clearly yellow turning red, **don't** accelerate blindly. Missing the light by a second can lead to T-bone collisions.
- **Block the Box:** If there's not enough space to clear the intersection, remain behind the line. Nobody likes a cross-gridlock standoff.

Intersection U-Turns

- **Check Signs:** Some intersections prohibit U-turns. Even if allowed, watch for cars turning right on red who might not anticipate your move.
- **Wide Arc:** If you have multiple lanes, ensure you don't swing into a lane with oncoming traffic.

Pedestrian Surprise
- **Looking Left/Right**: Even if your main hazard is a green arrow or cross traffic, a quick sideways glance can catch a pedestrian stepping off the curb.

Common Mistake: Inching into Crosswalks
Some drivers creep forward, ignoring that pedestrians might have the walk signal. Hitting a foot is as bad as hitting another car—always yield in crosswalks.

ADVANCED TIPS

Look for Clues
- **Opposite Light**: If cross traffic's light turns red, yours will likely turn green soon—be ready, but wait for the actual green.
- **Night or Weather**: In dim conditions, watch for headlights or reflective surfaces that reveal hidden cars. Slow down if uncertain.

"Speed Harmony"
- **Keep Up or Slow Appropriately**: Zooming through a yellow or crawling unpredictably confuses everyone. Maintain a pace that matches the intersection flow.

Pro Tip: Stay Cool Under Pressure
If you're in the wrong lane or the light is about to change, better to go straight or proceed carefully rather than forcing a turn you're not lined up for. You can always loop around the block.

Pro Tip: Anticipate Light Changes
If the crosswalk countdown is near zero, your green light may switch soon. Keep an eye on crosswalk signals as an early hint so you're not caught mid-intersection when it flips to red.

Intersections are the crosswords of driving—multiple directions, signals, and potential conflicts. By **knowing right-of-way rules**, **signaling early**, **checking for pedestrians**, and **reading the road signs**, you'll navigate them with confidence. Whether it's a quiet four-way stop or a bustling multi-lane junction with slip lanes, approaching with caution, courtesy, and a clear plan ensures smoother traffic flow, fewer close calls, and a safer journey for everyone.

33. RAILROAD CROSSINGS:
SAFETY RULES YOU CAN'T IGNORE

You're rolling along, enjoying the drive, when those iconic **crossbuck signs** appear, or you spot the **flashing lights** and lowered gate. A **railroad crossing** is a literal crossroads: your path could intersect with a massive, hard-to-stop train. In this chapter, we'll learn how to **recognize**, **respect**, and **navigate** these crossing points safely—because in a battle of car vs. locomotive, the train always wins.

RECOGNIZING RAILROAD CROSSINGS

Signs & Signals
- **Crossbuck = Yield**: The white "X" sign means you must yield to trains. If it's just the sign (no lights/gates), look both ways—some areas lack active signals.
- **Flashing Lights & Gates**: Active gates, red lights, or bells signal an approaching train—time to stop.

Pavement Markings
- **"RR" Painted on Road**: A heads-up you're nearing tracks, often paired with a stop line.
- **Slow Down & Listen**: Turn down music or crack a window if needed—trains can creep up quietly, especially at slower speeds.

Common Mistake: Missing the Signs
Don't assume you'll hear a train—some run with minimal horn blasts. Always check for crossing indications.

APPROACH & STOP GUIDELINES

Slow & Scan
- **One Track or Several?**: If multiple tracks, be aware a second train might appear right after the first.
- **Look Left & Right**: Even with no flashing lights, still glance both ways. Not all crossings are high-tech.

Obey Active Warnings
- **Gates Down = Stop**: Never go around lowered gates—trying to "beat" the train is a huge risk.

167

- **Flashing Red Lights**: Same as a stop sign. Wait until they stop flashing and gates lift before proceeding.

Pro Tip: If in Doubt, Wait It Out

Taking a moment to stop is always smarter than risking it against a roaring freight train—trust me, it's a game you'll never win.

GATES & FLASHERS

Patience Matters
- **Trains Are Coming**: If gates lower and lights blink, the train is close—don't assume it's a malfunction.
- **Double Tracks, Double Hazard**: After one train passes, a second could roll by from the opposite direction. Only proceed when signals are fully off.

Resist Impulse
- **Never Zigzag Past Gates**: This isn't a daring stunt; it's an invitation for disaster.
- **Stay Calm**: If traffic is jammed near the crossing, keep the rails clear—don't box yourself in on the tracks.

Common Mistake: Assuming Gate Errors

Malfunctions are rare. If gates stay down unusually long, call the crossing's emergency number before risking a drive-around.

HANDLING A STUCK OR STALLED VEHICLE

Evacuate Immediately
- **Get Out**: If your car stops on the tracks and you can't move it, exit the car. Run away from the tracks at a 45° angle in the direction the train is coming from—debris typically flies forward.
- **Signal Authorities**: Look for an emergency contact sign near the crossing. Provide the crossing ID to help them stop or slow the train.

Push If Safe
- **Teamwork**: If you have time and help, pushing a stalled car off might be possible—but never risk your life if a train is near.
- **Call 911**: Even if you manage to move the car, let authorities know about any ongoing blockage.

Pro Tip: Stay Clear of Impact Zone
If a collision seems inevitable, distance yourself from potential flying wreckage—trains carry huge momentum.

LEGAL & SAFETY CONSIDERATIONS

Fines & Penalties
- **Serious Infractions**: Crossing against flashing lights or driving around gates can lead to heavy fines or license points. Some places even count it as a misdemeanor.
- **Unforgiving Physics**: Trains can't stop quickly, so it's on you to keep out of their path.

Trains Need Distance
- **Long Stopping Times**: A freight train might require over a mile to halt. By the time you see it, it's often too late for them to brake in time.
- **No Shortcuts**: Don't assume "it's slow, I can beat it." The train's velocity can be deceivingly fast.

Common Mistake: Overestimating Train Stopping Power
They aren't cars. That mass isn't going to halt swiftly for your quick dash across the tracks.

NIGHTTIME & POOR VISIBILITY

Extra Caution
- **Use Low Beams**: Overly bright lights can cause glare. You want to spot reflectors or crossing signals in time.
- **Weather Effects**: Fog or heavy rain dampens train noise. Slow down, open your window to listen, or carefully watch for crossing lights.

Reflective Strips
- **Gates & Signs**: Often have reflective tape visible by headlights— another reason not to speed through if you see something shining up ahead.
- **Take It Slow**: Rushing in low visibility is gambling with your car's front end.

Pro Tip: Turn Down the Tunes
If conditions are poor, lowering music or switching off distractions helps you hear an approaching train earlier.

SCHOOL BUSES & CERTAIN VEHICLES

Mandatory Stops
- **School Buses & Hazmat Loads**: By law, many must stop at all tracks—even if gates are not down and no train is visible. Don't get annoyed; they're just following required safety protocols.
- **Expect Delays**: Don't tailgate them; they'll definitely brake before the tracks.

Patience with Professional Drivers
- **Trucks**: Large or heavy loads sometimes need more time to accelerate across tracks. Give them space.

Common Mistake: Impatient Honking
Buses and hazmat trucks are abiding by strict rules. Honking only adds stress—relax.

COMMON MISTAKES & TIPS

Trying to "Beat the Train"
- **One of the Deadliest Choices**: The difference between "almost made it" and "crashed" is a fraction of a second. Not worth gambling your life.
- **Stop Means Stop**: Flashing reds aren't a suggestion.

Distractions & Overconfidence
- **Phones, Chatty Passengers**: Quick glimpses of a text might lead you to miss a lowered gate or flashing signal.
- **Watch Crossing Countdowns**: Some advanced systems might give you time estimates—still, remain alert throughout.

Don't Tailgate
- **Vehicle Spacing**: Keep enough distance from the car ahead so you don't end up stuck on the tracks if traffic stalls.

Your path might cross train tracks here and there, but remember—the rails belong to those massive engines first and foremost. By **recognizing signs**, **obeying gates**, and **never trying to beat a train**, you'll keep both your car and peace of mind intact. It's a small detour in time, but a giant leap in safety. Next time you see that crossbuck sign, slow down, look both ways, and tip your mental hat to the unstoppable force that is a locomotive—because sometimes, waiting really is the smartest move of all.

34. EMERGENCY VEHICLES: STEP ASIDE, SAVE A LIFE

Picture it: you're cruising along, enjoying the day, when suddenly you spot **flashing lights** in your rearview mirror—or hear the urgent wail of a siren. An ambulance? A fire truck? A police cruiser? In those few moments, it's up to you to **respond quickly, smoothly, and courteously**. Emergency vehicles need a clear path, so they can reach someone who might be in serious trouble. In this chapter, we'll walk through the essentials of **pulling over**, **yielding** properly, and **staying out of the way** so these heroes on wheels can do their jobs.

RECOGNIZE & RESPOND TO EMERGENCY SITUATIONS

Flashing Lights & Sirens
- **See or Hear**: Ambulances, fire trucks, and police cars typically announce themselves with bright lights and loud sirens.
- **Stay Cool**: Don't slam your brakes or swerve blindly—take a breath, check your mirrors, and plan your next move.

Legal Obligation
- **Yield the Right-of-Way**: In most regions, you must pull over to the right and stop (or at least slow to a crawl) when an emergency vehicle approaches with lights/sirens.
- **Main Goal: Give them a free lane**—they're racing to an urgent call, so your timely action really matters.

Common Mistake: Delayed Reaction
Waiting too long to slow down or signal confuses drivers behind you, who might not realize you're stopping.

PULLING OVER & SLOWING DOWN

Don't Panic
- **Check Mirrors**: First, see what's around you—cars behind, next to you, or in your blind spot.
- **Ease Off the Throttle**: Gently slow down, then drift toward the right curb or shoulder. Avoid abrupt braking that might surprise drivers behind.

Where & How to Stop
- **Right Side**: Typically, you move to the right shoulder. If you can't safely get right (due to parked cars or narrow roads), find the next best space.
- **Stay Still**: Once you're pulled over, remain there until the emergency vehicle passes completely—there might be more than one.

Pro Tip: Head Out of the Way Early
If you see flashing lights in your rearview from a distance, start moving aside sooner rather than waiting till the last second.

INTERSECTIONS & TRAFFIC LIGHTS

Don't Block the Box
- **Stop or Move Through?**: If you're at a green light but see an emergency vehicle heading your way, consider staying put (if safe) or fully clearing the intersection before pulling over.
- **No Middle-of-the-Road Stalls**: Never stop in the intersection itself—quickly pass through if the light permits, then pull over on the other side.

If They're Behind or Crossing
- **They Own the Intersection**: If an ambulance or fire truck is behind you at a red light, let them through by moving aside. If you see them crossing left to right, wait for them—even if your light is green.

HIGHWAYS & MULTI-LANE ROADS

Moving Over
- **Flashing Lights Approach**: On a multi-lane highway, shift lanes to the right if possible; if traffic is dense, slow down and use your hazard lights if needed.
- **Maintain Consistency**: Avoid big speed swings—other drivers might need a second to interpret your actions.

Don't "Chase" the Siren
- **Illegal & Dangerous**: Tailgating an ambulance to exploit its cleared path is both risky and often unlawful.
- **Keep Distance**: Stay well behind, as emergency vehicles might brake or change lanes suddenly.

Common Mistake: Slamming on Brakes in the Fast Lane

If the emergency vehicle is behind you, check mirrors and signal to the right-lane calmly. Don't force a chaotic slowdown that triggers rear-end collisions.

MULTIPLE EMERGENCY VEHICLES

One After Another
- **Anticipate More**: If you see one ambulance zoom by, another might be seconds behind, heading to the same call.
- **Stay Pulled Over**: Pause until you're sure no further sirens are approaching.

Return to Traffic Smoothly
- **Signal Back In**: Once the coast is clear, re-enter your lane with your blinker and a mirror check.
- **Gradual Acceleration**: Don't floor it—other drivers might still be recovering from the emergency pass.

SPECIAL SITUATIONS

Stopped Emergency Vehicles
- **"Move Over" Laws**: Many places require you to move one lane away or slow down significantly if a police or emergency car is pulled over with lights on.
- **Protect the Responders**: This ensures officers, paramedics, or tow-truck operators are safe from passing traffic.

Adverse Weather
- **Harder to Hear Sirens**: Heavy rain, snow, or wind might drown out sirens—keep your eyes peeled for any reflection of flashing lights.
- **Slippery Roads**: Stop carefully to avoid skidding. Early signals help other cars react.

COMMON PITFALLS & HOW TO AVOID THEM

Sudden Panic Moves
- **Abrupt Swerves**: Jerky movements can cause pileups behind you. Plan a quick but controlled pull-over.
- **Halting in the Middle**: If the emergency vehicle is behind you, please don't freeze in your lane—transition gently to the right.

Distraction or Loud Music
- **Ear on the Road**: Keep volume moderate enough to catch sirens—missing that wailing sound means you'll only notice lights at the last second.
- **Phone Down**: In an emergency scenario, your reaction time needs to be near-instant. Don't text or rummage for something.

Common Mistake: Expecting Everyone Else to Move
Don't assume other drivers will yield perfectly. Some might hesitate or be equally panicked. You do your part safely and watch for them too.

FINAL TIPS FOR SAFELY YIELDING

Check & Signal
- **Mirrors**: A glance first—never just yank the wheel.
- **Blinker**: Indicate your intention to pull over, so traffic behind sees what's happening.

Smooth Return
- **Mirror & Merge**: After the emergency vehicle passes, signal again to rejoin traffic. Ensure you're not cutting someone off who also wants to get moving.

Pro Tip: Better Safe Than Sorry
If you're unsure whether you need to pull over, do it anyway—err on the side of caution. The faster emergency responders can move, the better their odds of saving lives.

Pro Tip: Yield to Volunteer Responders
When you see flashing blue or green lights—often used by volunteer firefighters or EMT's on personal vehicles—remember that while they're not legally considered emergency vehicles (and so, they still need to obey all traffic laws), they're still rushing to help someone in need. Moving over or yielding, even if not required, is a simple act of respect that could save precious seconds.

Seeing flashing lights and hearing sirens can spark instant adrenaline, but your job is to **stay calm, move aside, and let them pass**. Whether it's in a tight city street or on a broad freeway, **yielding** properly keeps the roads safe and frees up vital moments for responders to tackle emergencies. Remember: no abrupt stops or frantic swerves—just a purposeful pull-over, a patient pause, and a smooth re-entry once they zoom on by. That simple courtesy might make a life-saving difference!

35. BIG RIGS, BIG RULES: DRIVING AROUND LARGE VEHICLES

When a snow plow or tractor trailer rumbles past, you're reminded of just how small your car can feel. But navigating around big vehicles doesn't have to be intimidating if you understand their quirks: **wide turning circles**, **gigantic blind spots**, **slower stops**, and sometimes **flying salt or gravel** from snow plows. In this chapter, we'll cover how to safely share the road with these giants. By respecting their limitations (and your own), you'll avoid sideswipes, misjudged gaps, and those white-knuckle moments no driver enjoys.

WHY LARGE VEHICLES REQUIRE SPECIAL CAUTION

Limited Visibility & Blind Spots
- **No Zones**: Trucks and buses often have significant "no zones" around their front, sides, and rear—if you can't see the driver's mirrors, they likely can't see you either.
- **Tall Vehicles**: If your ride is small and they're extra tall, there's a good chance they might not spot you if you hang out next to them.

Longer Stopping & Turning
- **Heavy Means Momentum**: A loaded truck or bus needs more distance to brake. Give them space so you're not in their crash zone if they need to stop fast.
- **Wide Arc**: Big rigs often swing wide, especially making right turns—so no scooting up on their right side if they're turning.

Common Mistake: Lingering Alongside
Hanging out in a truck's blind spot or near its massive trailer is dangerous—pass quickly (but safely) or stay well behind.

TRUCKS, TRACTOR TRAILERS & BUSES

Give Them Room
- **Stay Back**: If you follow too closely, you won't see traffic or hazards ahead of them, and you vanish from their rearview.
- **Proper Passing**: Speed up decisively to overtake—don't dawdle next to the cab where the driver can't see you.

Wide Turns & Blind Spots
- **Right Turns**: Watch out for signals indicating they're swinging wide to the left before turning right. Don't slip into that gap.
- **Left Turns**: Similarly, they may start from a middle lane to avoid curbs. Respect the space they need.

Danger of Being Sideswiped
- **Tall Vehicles**: If you're in a tiny sedan or compact, a tall truck might not notice you. Their sideways mirror angles may miss your car entirely—be extra cautious in multi-lane changes.

Pro Tip: Mirror Check
If you're behind a tractor trailer, try to offset your car slightly to one side so you see its side mirror—then they can see you, too.

SNOW PLOWS

Blades, Salt, & Debris
- **Wide Blades**: Plows have huge front blades extending beyond the truck's normal width—stay back so you're not clipped if they shift.
- **Salt or Sand Spray**: They sometimes fling salt, sand, or snow from the plow. Keep a safe distance to avoid windshield dings or reduced visibility.

Passing a Plow
- **Impaired Vision**: Snow swirling around makes it hard to see. If you must pass, ensure you have enough clear road and that oncoming traffic is absent.
- **Slower Speeds**: Plows move deliberately slow. Don't rush around them on slick roads—give them the courtesy to clear your path.

Common Mistake: Tailgating Plows for "Cleared Road"
Driving too close behind the plow might tempt you for a clear lane, but if they hit a patch of ice or swerve, you're in trouble—plus salt chunks can ping your car.

SAFETY AROUND WIDE LOADS & OVERSIZED HAULS

Escorted Loads
- **Pilot Cars**: Often, you'll see lead or follow cars with flashing lights guiding a massive, oddly shaped load.
- **Never Squeeze Between**: If there's a gap, it's for them to maneuver—don't slip in or you risk being pinned if they turn.

Hazard Markings
- **Reflective Flags & Signs**: Trucks carrying oversize cargo might have bright red flags at corners or special signage indicating wide or tall load.
- **Your Best Move**: Keep well behind or pass with ample clearance, ensuring you're not overshadowed by something that overhangs the lane.

FOLLOWING DISTANCE & VISIBILITY

Adjusting Your Space
- **Longer Reaction Times**: Big vehicles can brake unpredictably—like for weigh stations, steep grades, or a slow bus stop. Maintain extra following distance.
- **Avoiding Spray, Dust or Debris**: If it's a dump truck, expect dust or debris. Keeping your distance behind big rigs improves your visibility—especially in wet weather—and helps protect your windshield from flying debris or loose rocks kicked up by the tires.

Wind Gusts
- **Air Turbulence**: Large trucks push a wall of air. When passing or being passed, keep both hands on the wheel to stay stable.
- **Stay Steady**: Don't overcorrect if you feel a sudden push—your car will settle once you move beyond the truck's wake.

Common Mistake: Underestimating Speeds
Big rigs can accelerate faster than expected on a downhill or open highway; so be careful around them.

TIPS FOR MANEUVERING ALONGSIDE BIG VEHICLES

Passing Approach
- **Signal Early**: Let them know you intend to move around them.
- **Swift but Safe**: Linger in their blind spot as briefly as possible. Keep an eye on oncoming traffic (for 2-lane roads) or faster cars in the passing lane.

Communication
- **Headlight Flashes or Horn Taps**: Sometimes truckers use signals to let you pass, but rely on your own checks to confirm.
- **Respect Their Lane**: If they move left slightly, it could be to avoid obstacles—don't panic, just hold your lane unless they signal otherwise.

Safe Stopping Distance

- **Respect Their Gap**: On highways with fast-moving traffic, you might notice large gaps between a tractor-trailer and the vehicle ahead. That's intentional—experienced truck drivers maintain extra space for safe stopping. While it may be tempting to merge into that gap, be mindful of the risks if traffic suddenly slows or stops.

COMMON PITFALLS & HOW TO AVOID THEM

Riding the Blind Spot

- **Danger Zone**: Beside or behind big vehicles where the driver can't spot you. Solve it by either passing or dropping back.
- **Watch the Mirrors**: If you can't see the truck/bus mirrors, they can't see you.

Abrupt Cuts in Front

- **No Sudden Lane Swaps**: Completing a pass then braking is a recipe for a rear-end collision—trucks don't stop on a dime.
- **Ensure Clear Space**: If you can see their entire front in your rearview mirror, that's usually safe to merge back.

Failing to Slow in Narrow Lanes

- **Meeting a Tractor Trailer**: If you're on a narrow two-lane, reduce speed and edge right, giving them the center if needed.
- **Hills & Curves**: The driver might not see you until they crest the hill or round the bend—be prepared to yield or pull aside.

Pro Tip: Watch the Rear "Swing"
When a big truck or bus makes a turn, its rear wheels can track inward differently than the front. Give them space on corners so you're not sideswiped by a trailer.

Common Mistake: Ignoring School or Tour Buses
Overlooking that a bus might stop frequently or children might appear out of nowhere is a huge hazard. Treat them both with extra caution!

Whether it's a **snow plow** flinging salt, a **tour bus** loaded with tourists, or a **tractor trailer** hauling steel coils, big vehicles command extra respect. They have wider blind spots, heavier braking demands, and monstrous turning radiuses. Driving around them safely means **anticipating their movements**, keeping your distance, and never trying to outmaneuver them in tight spaces. Give each other room, stay visible, and you'll coexist with the big rigs just fine—no honking intimidation or sudden swerves needed!

36. RUSH HOUR RULES:
BUSY COMMUTE SURVIVAL GUIDE

Imagine you're at a mega-concert, shoulder-to-shoulder with strangers, trying to move through the crowd without stepping on anyone's toes. **Busy traffic** feels exactly like that, except you're in a car—everyone jockeying for position, frequently stopping, occasionally shouting. Stressful? It can be. But with **smart moves** and a **cool head**, you can navigate the busiest traffic jam. In this chapter, we'll show you how to keep your cool, maintain safe distances, and even handle aggressive drivers like a pro. After all, driving in heavy traffic shouldn't leave you exhausted; it should just be part of the ride.

WHY BUSY TRAFFIC IS STRESSFUL

Density & Chaos
- **Cars in Every Direction**: More vehicles mean more potential blind spots, random lane changes, and abrupt stops.
- **Low Speeds, High Stress**: The paradox: you're barely moving, but your tension skyrockets if you're worried about fender-benders.

Patience & Perspective
- **Realistic Expectations**: Rush hour is called that for a reason—accept slower progress.
- **No Racing**: Weaving in and out rarely shaves more than a few seconds off your arrival time but can quadruple your risk of collisions.

Common Mistake: Driving Aggressively to "Beat" Traffic
Tailgating or abrupt lane changes might feel like you're winning, but it only raises tension (and your accident odds). Breathe, relax, and let the flow carry you.

MAINTAINING PROPER FOLLOWING DISTANCE

Why Space Matters
- **Time to React**: In stop-and-go traffic, cars might slam brakes unexpectedly. Leave enough space to avoid frantic last-second stops.

- **Avoid Chain Reactions**: If you maintain a safe gap, you won't cause a rear-end pileup if you have to brake quickly.

Striking a Balance
- **Stop-and-Go Cushion**: Too little space = stress. Too much space = others might cut in. Find a middle ground.
- **Rolling Slowly**: Instead of lurching forward then braking, keep a gentle roll if traffic's inching along.

Pro Tip: 3-Second Rule (At Minimum)
Even at slower speeds, aim for at least 3 seconds of following distance. Count "one-thousand-one, one-thousand-two, one-thousand-three" behind a reference point—if you pass it too soon, ease off the gas.

LANE MANAGEMENT & POSITIONING

Pick a Lane & Stick With It
- **Lane-Weaving Doesn't Help**: Constant lane-changing might net you one or two cars' advantage, but at the cost of repeated merges (and potential scrapes).
- **Signal, Mirror, Shoulder Check**: If you must switch lanes (e.g., for an upcoming turn), do it early with clear signals.

Merging Cars & On-Ramps
- **Anticipate & Adjust**: If traffic merges from a side ramp, adjust your speed slightly or shift lanes, if possible, to let them in. Smooth merges reduce congestion.
- **No "Panic Merge"**: If you miss your exit in gridlock, it's safer to loop around at the next opportunity than attempt a last-second lane dive.

Common Mistake: Late Lane Jump
Rushing across multiple lanes to catch your exit invites honks and collisions. Plan your approach well before the off-ramp appears.

HANDLING AGGRESSIVE OR IMPATIENT DRIVERS

Don't Engage
- **Let Them Pass**: If someone tailgates or weaves behind you, let them go—no need to escalate.
- **Stay Predictable**: Resist brake-checking or swerving—it spikes hostility and risk.

Communication & Courtesy
- **Signals & Eye Contact**: Subtle cues let others know your intentions or that you see them. A friendly wave can defuse tension.
- **Avoid Reacting**: A honk or rude gesture might feel tempting but rarely helps.

Pro Tip: Use Calm, Decisive Moves
In bumper-to-bumper conditions, small, consistent steering and speed changes reassure others that you're in control.

DEFENSIVE DRIVING IN CONGESTION

Expect the Unexpected
- **Abrupt Brakes & Lane Swaps**: People get impatient in traffic. Always be mentally prepared for sudden stops or random merges.
- **Watch Blind Spots**: In slow traffic, motorcycles or bikes can slip between lanes. Check mirrors carefully before lane changes.

Keep an Escape Route
- **Position Tactics**: Don't box yourself in. If the lane on your side stops abruptly, you want room to maneuver.
- **Look Two or Three Cars Ahead**: Spot brake lights early; it gives you extra reaction time.

Common Mistake: Zero-Alert Complacency
Slow speeds trick you into thinking it's safe to check your phone or zone out. Collisions in slow traffic can still cause whiplash or damage.

CITY DRIVING VS. HIGHWAY JAMS

City Streets & Gridlock
- **Pedestrians & Bikes**: People darting between cars, crossing mid-block. Be extra aware around parked cars and sidewalk edges.
- **Keep Crosswalks & Intersections Clear**: Don't "block the box." If traffic doesn't let you clear the intersection, wait.

Highway Traffic Jams
- **Speed Variations**: The "fast" lane might stall, while the right lane flows—avoid constant lane flips in search of the magical faster route.
- **Merging Zones**: Watch for on-ramps, especially if you're in the right lane. Slow or shift lanes early to help merging cars.

INTERSECTIONS & TRAFFIC LIGHTS

Don't Clog the Intersection
- **Green Light, But No Space**: If you can't get through before it goes red or traffic ahead is at a standstill, stay put. Blocking cross-traffic is a major cause of jam escalation.
- **Yellow Light, Slow or Go?**: In heavy traffic, approach with caution—flooring it to "beat the yellow" when everything's gridlocked is risky.

Right on Red & Left Turns
- **Courtesy for Crosswalks**: Pedestrians might be crossing even if your path seems open. Look thoroughly before turning.
- **Multiple Turn Lanes**: On wide intersections, ensure you're in the correct lane. No last-second corner cuts across lanes.

Common Mistake: Blocking Pedestrians
If you inch too far forward on a red, you might trap or startle pedestrians crossing in front. Keep behind the stop line.

PUBLIC TRANSPORT & SHARED LANES

Buses & Taxis
- **Frequent Stops**: Buses may swerve in/out of stops; taxis might pull over abruptly. Stay vigilant for brake lights and signals.
- **Bus-Only Lanes**: If your city has dedicated lanes, avoid them unless turning or local rules permit short merges.

Pedestrians & Cyclists
- **Extra Caution**: People walking might appear between stopped cars. Cyclists might squeeze through jammed lanes.
- **Signal and Shoulder Check**: Each time you change lanes or open a door (in the driver's seat), confirm no two-wheeled traveler is lane-splitting beside you.

COMMON MISTAKES & HOW TO AVOID THEM

Braking Too Late
- **Chain Reaction Collisions**: If you constantly stop last-minute, the car behind may not react quickly enough.
- **Smooth Deceleration**: Keep your brake lights as a consistent communication—don't stamp or release repeatedly.

Blocking Merging Lanes

- **Let One In**: Being polite usually pays off—fighting merges slows everyone.
- **Maintain Momentum**: A quick wave or slight slowdown can keep the flow steady.

Not Checking Blind Spots in Stop-and-Go

- **Slow Lane Shuffling**: If you're creeping left or right in heavy traffic, always check your mirrors and do a quick shoulder glance—another driver might be making the same move.

Common Mistake: Distractions

Heavy traffic seems slow, so drivers often text or rummage in the glove box, but abrupt stops or lane shifts can still happen. Keep your phone away—stay alert.

FINAL TIPS FOR BUSY TRAFFIC

Patience & Relaxation

- **Music or Airflow**: Calm tunes and a comfortable temperature can reduce tension.
- **Plan Extra Time**: Accept that peak hours mean slower travel. Stress shrinks when you're not racing the clock.

Mindful Driving

- **Look Ahead**: Two or three cars forward to anticipate brake lights or lane changes.
- **Avoid Over-Reacting**: Small, gentle steering and braking inputs are safer.

Pro Tip: Practice Makes Calm

If busy traffic intimidates you, try mild rush-hour routes or practice in moderate congestion. Building comfort gradually helps you handle bigger jams confidently.

Yes, the roads can fill up with cars, horns, and stop-and-go frustration, but **dense traffic** doesn't have to be an ordeal. By **keeping your distance**, **resisting the urge to weave**, and **staying aware of merges, bikes, and pedestrians**, you'll transform gridlock from a stress-fest into a manageable, if slow, journey. Put your blinkers on earlier than usual, keep a margin of safety around you, and remember: a relaxed approach is the best approach. After all, traffic moves a lot like a crowded concert—some chaos, but if everyone cooperates, the show goes on smoothly.

37. NIGHT DRIVING: NOT SO SCARY WHEN YOU KNOW WHAT YOU'RE DOING

Night driving can feel like venturing into a realm where everything's hidden in shadows and road signs blend into the darkness. It's also prime time for dazzling headlights, unexpected wildlife crossings, and that sleepy lull that can sneak up on you. But fear not—by **using your beams wisely**, **keeping your eyes peeled for nocturnal hazards**, and **managing your fatigue**, you'll handle nighttime roads with a steady grip and calm mind. In this chapter, we'll show you how to handle **reduced visibility, oncoming glare**, and even **midnight wildlife** with confidence.

WHY NIGHT DRIVING FEELS DIFFERENT

Darkness Shrinks Your World
- **Reduced Visibility**: At night, peripheral vision narrows and shadows distort depth perception.
- **Glare & Flicker**: Oncoming headlights can cause sudden whiteouts; neon signs can distract you from the road.

Natural Fatigue
- **Body Clock**: Our systems wind down after sunset, so night driving often amplifies tiredness.
- **Combat Drowsiness**: Opening a window or playing upbeat music can help, but if you're truly tired, take a break.

Common Mistake: Assuming You're Fully Awake
Even if you "feel okay," micro-sleeps can happen. At the first signs of heavy eyelids, stop for coffee or pull over for a nap.

HEADLIGHTS & BEAM USAGE

Low Beams vs. High Beams
- **Low Beams**: Default for most night driving—directed downward to avoid blinding oncoming cars.
- **High Beams**: Use them on empty roads with no opposing traffic. Turn them off quickly when you see headlights or taillights ahead.

Keeping Them Clean & Aligned
- **Dirt & Foggy Lenses**: Over time, headlight covers can haze over.

185

A quick polish or cleaning kit can restore brightness.
- **Proper Alignment**: If your beams illuminate tree branches or the opposite lane, get them checked; misaligned headlights limit your view.

Pro Tip: The "Overdriving Your Headlights" Concept
If you drive too fast at night, you can't stop within the distance you see illuminated. Slow down so you can react to hazards in time.

REDUCING GLARE & DEALING WITH ONCOMING LIGHTS

Look to the Right Edge
- **Glare-Busting Trick**: If an oncoming driver doesn't dim the high beams, shift your gaze to the right shoulder or lane marker to avoid direct eye contact with their lights.
- **Dim Rearview Mirror**: Flip your mirror's night mode if a car behind you blasts bright lights.

Keep Your Dashboard in Check
- **Lower Brightness**: A glaringly bright dashboard can ruin your night vision. Adjust interior light settings to a comfortable low glow.
- **Avoid Reflections**: Items on the dash (like glossy paper) can reflect headlights or streetlights into your eyes.

Common Mistake: Staring into High Beams
The natural reaction is to look at the source of brightness. Fight it. Focus on your lane's edge if you're momentarily blinded.

MANAGING FATIGUE & ALERTNESS

Body Clock Realities
- **Late Hours**: Adrenaline might keep you awake early in the drive, but after an hour or two, weariness can creep in.
- **Signs You're Tired**: Frequent yawning, difficulty focusing, or missing exits.

Anti-Drowsy Strategies
- **Take Breaks**: Every couple of hours, stretch your legs, grab water or coffee.
- **Engage Your Senses**: Play moderate-volume music or chat with a passenger. Cracking a window helps fresh air keep you alert.

Pro Tip: Travel with a Buddy

If possible, share the driving load. Another set of eyes helps spot hazards and keeps conversation flowing.

NIGHTTIME SPEED & SPACING

Slower Pace
- **Limited Reaction Time**: Darkness hides subtle hazards—give yourself more time to react by easing off the accelerator.
- **Avoid Tailgating**: If the driver ahead brakes for something you can't see yet, you need enough space to stop safely.

Extra Following Distance
- **Keep the Cushion**: Boost your usual 3-second gap to 4 seconds or more at night.
- **Mid-Lane Positioning**: In multi-lane situations, pick a lane that grants you optimal sight lines, if it's safe and not too congested.

Common Mistake: Overconfidence on Familiar Roads

Even on your daily route, night illusions or unexpected obstacles can surprise you. Don't speed just because you "know" the road.

OBSERVING ROADSIDE HAZARDS & WILDLIFE

Pedestrians & Cyclists
- **Hard to Spot**: Dark clothes, broken streetlights—sometimes you only see them at the last moment. Slow down in areas with foot traffic.
- **Reflective Gear**: Not everyone wears it, so keep scanning shoulders and sidewalks.

Wildlife
- **Deer & Animals**: Rural roads might see deer or other critters crossing unexpectedly at night. Look for glowing eyes reflecting your headlights.
- **Slow if You See One**: Where there's one deer, more may follow. If an animal darts out, brake firmly—swerving can be more dangerous if you spin out or hit oncoming traffic.

Common Mistake: Relying on Horn

Honking might spook wildlife or they might freeze. Slowing down is your best bet.

NIGHTTIME PASSING DANGERS

Limited Visibility for Overtaking
- **Harder to Judge Speeds**: Headlights can mask how far away oncoming cars really are.
- **Consider If It's Worth It**: On two-lane roads, passing at night can be extra risky—only pass if you're absolutely sure there's ample distance.

Slow or Wait
- **Reduce Risk**: If you're not certain, stay put. Waiting until a clearer stretch or an upcoming passing zone might be safer.
- **Double Blind**: Oncoming lights can hide multiple cars behind them—err on the side of caution.

Pro Tip: Communicate with Headlights
A brief flash to let a car know you're passing might help in remote areas, but remain cautious—some drivers don't interpret or react properly.

NIGHT DRIVING IN TOWNS & CITIES

The Bright City Glow
- **False Security**: Streetlights can trick you into forgetting high beams or ignoring your speed. Remain vigilant, as not all areas are equally lit.
- **Parked Cars & Pedestrians**: Watch for people stepping off the curb between cars, or opening doors in poorly lit streets.

Distractions & Navigation
- **Neon Signs & Billboards**: Flashy lights can draw your eyes from the road. Keep your focus ahead.
- **GPS Use**: If you rely on navigation, minimize screen brightness or switch to a night theme to avoid glare.

Common Mistake: Assuming City = Safe
Urban areas have more streetlamps, but also more crosswalks, cyclists, and unpredictable night activity.

COMMON MISTAKES & SMART SOLUTIONS

Overdriving Headlights
- **What It Means**: If you drive too fast, you can't stop within your illuminated path.

- **Solution**: Match your speed so you can brake in time if something appears suddenly.

Distracted or Tired
- **Fight the Lull**: A warm car plus dark skies can lull you into complacency. Keep alert—no phone fiddling or rummaging in the back seat.
- **Plan Trips**: If you know you'll be drowsy, schedule a rest stop before your eyelids droop.

Misjudging Oncoming Speed
- **Night Illusion**: Headlights can seem closer or further than reality. Double-check if turning left or passing.
- **Be Conservative**: If you're unsure, wait. Another 10 seconds is better than risking a head-on collision.

Common Mistake: Ignoring Reflectors
Road reflectors, guardrails, or signpost reflections can signal a curve or hazard—if you notice them shifting oddly, slow down.

FINAL TIPS FOR SAFE NIGHT DRIVING

Prepare Your Car
- **Clean Windshield**: Smudges and streaks amplify glare from lights.
- **Check Lights**: Make sure all bulbs work, from headlights to brake lights.

Calm & Cautious Attitude
- **Give Yourself Extra Time**: Night drives can be slower. Rushing leads to reckless maneuvers.
- **Stay Aware**: Even on familiar roads, nighttime alters perception—remain engaged.

Night driving can feel like stepping into a different world, one where headlights carve tunnels through darkness and every stray movement in the shadows could be a hazard. Yet with **well-maintained headlights, correct beam usage, extra caution in speed and following distance**, and **awareness of wildlife** or **unpredictable pedestrians**, you'll steer through the darkness without stumbling. Remember: keep your eyes forward (not on bright oncoming lights), slow down if unsure, and don't let fatigue sneak up on you. Soon enough, you'll see nighttime roads as a peaceful drive rather than a lurking menace.

38. WIND WOBBLES:
DON'T GET BLOWN OFF COURSE

Imagine you're cruising along a scenic highway when a sudden gust slams your car sideways—your knuckles whiten, and your heart does a mini flop. **High winds** can ambush drivers in open plains, over bridges, and even on seemingly ordinary roads. But with the right **steering approach**, **speed adjustments**, and **extra caution** around big trucks, you'll keep your car's wheels firmly planted on the ground. In this chapter, we'll explore why heavy winds matter, how to handle them, and how to prevent your commute from turning into a battle with nature's invisible push.

WHY HIGH WINDS MATTER

A Push in the Wrong Direction
- **Reduced Vehicle Stability**: Strong crosswinds can nudge your car off course—particularly smaller, lighter cars or vehicles towing trailers.
- **Less Reaction Time**: Sudden blasts might require instant steering corrections, and you need to be alert for them at all times.

Amplified Risk
- **Lane Drifting**: Even a slight nudge in the wheel can cause you to drift if you overcorrect.
- **Flying Debris**: Gusts can launch lightweight objects—tree branches, trash, or construction materials—straight onto your path.

Common Mistake: Ignoring Wind Advisories
Some regions issue wind warnings for a reason. If you hear one and your route is susceptible to gusts, plan extra travel time or consider waiting it out.

PREPARATION & AWARENESS

Check Forecasts
- **Stay Informed**: A quick glance at weather apps or local news can warn you about wind speeds or gusty conditions.
- **Route Planning**: If you know a high bridge or open plains are part of your drive, be prepared for more intense crosswinds there.

Secure Loose Items
- **Rooftop Cargo**: Wind can rip off poorly tied boxes or bikes, turning them into roadside hazards.
- **Truck Beds & Trailers**: Anything that can flap around or fly out should be tightly strapped or stowed inside.

Pro Tip: Minimize Wind Profile
Removing unnecessary racks or attachments from your car can reduce buffeting. If you don't need that cargo box in high wind, take it off.

STEERING CORRECTIONS & CONTROLLING YOUR CAR

Two Hands on the Wheel
- **Firm but Flexible Grip**: Keep your hands at 9 and 3 (or a similar balanced hold), so you're ready for sudden gusts without overreacting.
- **Smooth Inputs**: Resist the urge to jerk the wheel—small, consistent corrections help maintain your lane position.

Gentle Counter-Steer
- **Feel the Gust**: When you sense the car drifting, counter-steer just enough to stay centered—no abrupt yanks.
- **Maintain Course**: If the wind is steady from one side, you may need a slight constant steering angle into the wind.

Common Mistake: Overcorrection
Sharp or exaggerated wheel turns can send you swerving into adjacent lanes. Keep calm and correct gradually.

ADAPTING SPEED & FOLLOWING DISTANCE

Slow Down
- **Reduced Traction**: High wind can unbalance your tires' grip—easing off the accelerator helps maintain stability.
- **Reaction Window**: Lower speeds allow more time to respond to debris or sudden swerves.

Larger Gaps
- **Following Distance**: Back off a bit more than usual—vehicles ahead might brake unexpectedly if they're hit by a gust or spot debris.
- **Escape Space**: If something blows onto the road, you'll need room to maneuver or brake.

Pro Tip: Err on the Side of Caution
If the wind is especially fierce, don't be shy about traveling a few mph under the speed limit. Your safety—and sanity—are worth it.

BEWARE AROUND LARGE VEHICLES

Tractor Trailers, Buses & RVs
- **Greater Wind Surface**: They act like sails, so sudden gusts can push them into adjacent lanes. Keep a safe distance when passing.
- **Watching for Swing**: Trailers in particular can swing or wobble if a big gust hits them—so pass quickly (but not recklessly) to reduce time in their blind spot.
- **Avoid Prolonged Side-by-Side**: Gusty crosswinds plus a large truck's own turbulence can make handling tough for both vehicles. Plan your pass smoothly and maintain a firm grip on the wheel— don't hover next to them hoping the wind will die down.
- **Watch for Lane Changes**: A big rig may need to shift lanes suddenly to combat gusts. Stay alert for any drift in their lane position, and give them enough space in case they overcorrect.

Common Mistake: Lingering in Blind Spots
If you remain alongside a big rig while both of you battle crosswinds, the driver might not see you. Keep passing efficient—never loiter next to them.

PASSING IN HIGH WINDS

Extra Vigilance
- **Wind Amplifies Lane Drift**: You and the car you're overtaking can both sway if a gust hits at the wrong moment.
- **Signal & Commit**: Use your blinker, check mirrors/shoulder, and pass steadily without hesitation.

Minimize Side-by-Side Time
- **Swift but Safe**: Don't floor it beyond control, but avoid hanging out in the passing lane.
- **Return Smoothly**: Once you see the vehicle's headlights in your rearview mirror, signal back, gently merge over—still prepared for a gust mid-lane change.

Pro Tip: Monitor Oncoming Traffic
On two-lane roads, passing can be riskier in high winds—especially if dust or swirling debris reduces visibility. If unsure, wait.

SPECIAL CONSIDERATIONS

Bridges & Elevated Terrain
- **Open Crosswinds**: Bridges and overpasses are prime spots for extreme gusts—be ready for an extra steering fight.
- **Caution Signs**: Some states post wind advisories for certain bridges. If it's too strong, officials may even close the route.

Common Mistake: Ignoring Weight
Light cars or empty trucks are more easily tossed around by gusts than heavier ones. Adjust your handling if your vehicle's not weighed down.

COMMON HAZARDS & HOW TO REACT

Debris on the Road
- **Fallen Tree Limbs**: Watch for scattered branches after big gusts.
- **Blown Items**: Construction cones, trash cans, or signs can roll into your path—scan far ahead so you can dodge or brake safely.

Fatigue & Stress
- **Mentally Draining**: Constant wheel corrections tire you out faster than normal driving.
- **Take Breaks**: If you're driving long distances in windy conditions, pause occasionally to rest.

Slippery Surfaces
- **Wind + Rain/Snow**: If weather is also wet or snowy, traction is further compromised. Double down on slow speeds and big following gaps.

Common Mistake: Panic at the First Gust
Jerking the wheel or slamming brakes at the initial big wind can create more trouble. Stay composed and make measured corrections.

FINAL TIPS & BEST PRACTICES

Anticipate & Stay Alert
- **Look Ahead**: If you see trees bending or dust swirling in the distance, that's your clue to brace for gusts.
- **Two Hands On**: Always keep both hands on the wheel—this is not the time for one-handed steering.

Adjust & Verify
- **Speed Control**: Lower your speed, keep consistent. If conditions worsen, consider pulling off to a safe spot until gusts subside.
- **Check Cargo**: If traveling with a trailer or rooftop load, ensure it's firmly secured—stop to retighten if you sense shifting.

Pro Tip: Respect Wind Warnings

If authorities advise high-profile vehicles to stay off certain roads, heed that warning. The same caution can apply to all drivers—seek alternative routes if possible.

Pro Tip: Use Landmarks

Watch flags, trees, or tall grass in the distance for cues about wind direction and intensity. Noticing them swaying violently is a heads-up to grip the wheel tighter.

Driving in high winds can turn a routine trip into a white-knuckle adventure, but it doesn't have to. By **reducing speed, keeping firm control of the steering**, and **giving extra room around large vehicles**, you can keep calm in even the gustiest moments. Whether you're dealing with towering tractor trailers or salt-spewing snow plows, a steady hand and mindful driving keep you from being blown off course. Next time you feel a gale trying to play push-and-pull with your car, remember these tips. Remember: when in doubt, slow down!

39. SLIPPERY WHEN WET: TIPS FOR DRIVING WHEN IT POURS

The sky darkens, raindrops scatter across the windshield, and suddenly every puddle seems like a mini lake on the road. **Driving in the rain** doesn't have to feel like a nerve-wracking adventure—though it can if you're unprepared. Slick surfaces mean reduced grip; spraying water kills visibility. But with **proper braking**, **smart speed adjustments**, and **extra care around puddles**, you'll glide through showers without hydroplaning drama or waterfall-like windshield wiper panic. This chapter will help you handle everything from gentle drizzles to torrential downpours.

WHY RAINY ROADS ARE RISKY

Reduced Traction & Invisible Hazards
- **Slippery Layer**: Water + oil residue = slick surfaces, especially early in a storm when built-up grime floats.
- **Tires vs. Water**: Deep puddles or standing water can lift your tires off the pavement momentarily (hydroplaning).

Poor Visibility
- **Rain & Mist**: Hard rain or spray from vehicles can obscure your forward view—and side mirrors.
- **Reflection & Glare**: Wet pavement at night can reflect headlights in a dazzling way that compromises vision.
- **Markings in the Dark**: Heavy rain can dull reflective paint and cause non-reflective stripes to vanish under glare, making it harder to judge lanes and boundaries.

Common Mistake: Underestimating a "Light Shower"
Even mild rain after a long dry spell can create a slippery film on the road—don't ignore that possibility.

SLOWING DOWN & INCREASING FOLLOWING DISTANCE

Adjust Speed
- **Lower Speeds**: Your car can't stop or turn as effectively on wet roads, so ease off the gas and brake earlier.
- **Cushion Space**: Leave extra distance between you and the vehicle ahead. If it stops abruptly, you need more room to respond.

Tailgating: The Big "No"

- **Spray & Visibility**: Riding close behind a car or a truck in heavy rain means your windshield wipers fight constant splatter.
- **Avoid Collisions**: Wet roads + short following distance = rear-end collisions waiting to happen.

Pro Tip: Use the 4-Second Rule
In rainy conditions, extend the usual 3-second following gap to 4 seconds or more for a safer margin.

TIRES & VEHICLE PREP

Check Your Treads

- **Grip vs. Water**: Tires need enough depth to channel water out. Bald tires can't push water aside, increasing hydroplane risks.
- **Regular Rotation/Replacement**: Don't wait until they're nearly slick—it's cheaper (and safer) to replace them early.

Wipers & Lights

- **Wiper Condition**: If they streak or squeak, they might be worn out. Replace them regularly for a clear view.
- **Lights On**: In many places, headlights must be on when wipers are in use—turn them on even if it's daytime, so others see you better.

Common Mistake: Forgetting to Flick on Headlights
Daytime running lights might not illuminate your rear lights. Manual headlights help others spot your car from behind.

HYDROPLANING & HOW TO HANDLE IT

Recognizing Hydroplaning

- **Floating Sensation**: Steering feels light, as if your tires aren't gripping. The car may drift sideways.
- **Common in Puddles**: Higher speeds + deeper water = higher chance of losing traction.

Regaining Control

- **Ease Off the Gas**: Sudden braking or accelerating can worsen the skid. Gently reduce speed.
- **Steer Where You Want to Go**: If you feel a slide, look and steer in that direction—avoid overcorrection.

Pro Tip: Avoid Large Puddles if Possible

If you see a deep puddle, steer around it or slow down significantly. You don't know the potholes or depths lurking under there.

BRAKING & STEERING TECHNIQUES

Gentle Inputs
- **Smooth, Gradual**: Any abrupt pedal push or steering yank can break your tires' limited wet-road grip.
- **Anti-Lock Brakes (ABS)**: If your car has ABS, hold firm pressure on the brake in an emergency stop—don't pump. ABS pulses to prevent lockup.

Avoid Sudden Lane Changes
- **Potential Slip**: Quick lateral movements can trigger skids. Signal early, check mirrors, and move slowly across lanes.

Common Mistake: Slamming Brakes

If you panic-stop on a wet road, you'll skid further. Anticipate and brake earlier with moderate, consistent pressure.

VISIBILITY & WINDOW FOGGING

Defogging Your Windshield
- **AC + Heat**: Warm, humid air inside + cool window surface = fog. Switch on your AC with a bit of heat to dry out the air.
- **Wiper & Defroster**: Many cars have a dedicated defrost setting that focuses airflow on the windshield.

Side Mirrors
- **Keep Them Clear**: Water droplets can distort the view—sometimes a quick cloth wipe or special anti-fog spray helps.

Pro Tip: Crack a Window

Allowing a little fresh air can help balance humidity, especially if you have multiple passengers breathing in a confined space.

PASSING & SPLASHING

Check Mirrors & Blind Spots
- **Spray Alert**: Trucks or cars with big tires throw up rooster tails of water, making passing risky. Prepare for near-zero visibility.
- **Steady Acceleration**: Don't floor it; keep traction under control.

Minimize Splash Impact
- **Avoid Big Puddles While Passing**: Hydroplaning mid-lane change is extra dangerous. Pick a spot where water buildup seems minimal.
- **Courtesy**: Splashing pedestrians or cyclists isn't just rude—some regions have fines for drenching sidewalk-users.

Common Mistake: Pass and Immediately Cut In
Not only do you risk sideswiping, but if you swerve back on a slick surface, you might fishtail or hamper your passing momentum.

PUDDLES & STANDING WATER

Puddle Dangers
- **Unknown Depth**: A small-looking puddle could hide a crater or cause your tires to sink.
- **Slow, Steady**: If unavoidable, enter slowly—water can splash into your engine bay or your brakes, reducing their effectiveness.

Post-Puddle Checks
- **Test Brakes**: Gently tap them after crossing water to ensure they're still responsive.
- **Water in Engine**: If the car runs oddly after a deep puddle, pull over in a safe spot to check or call for assistance.

Common Mistake: Gunning Through
Racing through water can lead to hydroplaning or water damage under the hood. If you see a giant splash, you might be too fast.

COMMON RAIN-DRIVING PITFALLS

First 10-20 Minutes of Rain
- **Extra Slippery**: That's when oils lift off the asphalt. Keep your speed noticeably lower.
- **Sudden Skids**: If you feel the car losing grip, gently ease off the accelerator—no wild steering moves.

Distraction or Complacency
- **Phone or Tunes**: Raindrops and wiper noise might lull you into letting your guard down. Focus is key, especially in heavy downpours.
- **Fewer Landmarks**: Rain can obscure road signs; double-check your route if visibility is poor.

Overconfidence
- **All-Wheel Drive Isn't Magic**: It helps traction, but it won't compensate fully for watery roads.
- **ABS & Traction Control**: Great aids, but they can't beat the laws of physics when hydroplaning at high speed.

Common Mistake: "It's Just a Little Rain" Attitude
Even a slight drizzle can lead to slippery roads—treat all wet conditions with respect. A careless minute can lead to a skid or rear-end crash.

FINAL TIPS FOR RAINY ROAD CONFIDENCE

Stay Prepared
- **Regular Maintenance**: Good tire treads, fresh wiper blades, working lights.
- **Route Knowledge**: If an area floods easily or forms big puddles, plan an alternate path or be extra cautious.

Drive Defensively
- **Slow & Steady**: No abrupt moves—treat every turn, stop, or lane change gently.
- **Read Road Spray**: If you see huge splashes up ahead, that's a sign of deeper water—adjust accordingly.

Pro Tip: Use AC for Defogging
Even in colder weather, the A/C setting helps dry the air inside the cabin quickly, preventing foggy windows so you can see clearly.

A rainy-day drive may feel like nature's obstacle course, with **slippery roads, fogging windows**, and **sprays of water** from vehicles around you. But armed with the knowledge of **how to control hydroplaning, maintain extra space**, and **use your wipers and lights effectively**, you'll see that a little drizzle (or even a torrential downpour) can be navigated safely. Slow down, watch for puddles, and keep your eyes on the horizon. After all, what's a little water when you're ready to handle it?

40. DON'T VANISH IN THE MIST: HOW TO SEE AND BE SEEN

Picture this: you're on a peaceful road, and suddenly the world becomes a giant cloud. Buildings, trees, and cars vanish into a pale haze. **Driving in fog** can feel like an eerie magic trick—poof! Visibility gone. But no need to let the misty gloom spook you. By **using the right lights**, **slowing down**, and **paying attention to road markers**, you can stay on track and out of trouble. In this chapter, we'll show you how to handle fog like a seasoned driver who never loses sight of the important stuff—even when you can barely see a few yards ahead.

WHY FOG IS SO TRICKY

Reduced Visibility & Illusions
- **Shortened Sight Lines**: Thick fog can cut your view to mere feet—making it tough to see that curve, oncoming car, or even a stray pedestrian.
- **Depth Distortions**: Fog plays tricks on your perception. Cars might appear farther (or closer) than reality, and brake lights can be harder to spot.

Slow Reaction Times
- **Less Time to Brake**: If you only see an obstacle when you're almost on top of it, your window to react shrinks drastically.
- **Psychological Pressure**: The eerie feel can make you tense or second-guess your steering, leading to overcorrections.

Common Mistake: Overconfidence on Familiar Roads
Even if you know the route by heart, fog changes everything. That usual bend can sneak up on you if it's hidden in the mist.

CHOOSE THE RIGHT LIGHTING

Low Beams, Not High Beams
- **Why Low Beams?**: High beams bounce light off the fog, shining it back into your eyes like a bright white wall. Low beams aim downward, illuminating the road without glare.
- **Fog Lights**: If your car has them, use them. They're specifically designed to slice through fog at a lower angle.

Avoid the "Blinding" Mistake

- **No Overkill**: Combining high beams and fog lights intensifies glare. Stick to low beams + fog lights (if available).
- **Clean & Functional**: Check your headlight covers for grime—fog plus dirty lenses is a double visibility whammy.

Pro Tip: Dim the Dash

Bright dashboard lights can ruin your night vision. Turn them down so your eyes adapt better to the murk outside.

SLOW DOWN & EXTEND FOLLOWING DISTANCE

Slower Pace

- **No Need to Rush**: Fog is the ultimate reason to drop your speed. If you can't see far, you can't safely maintain high speeds.
- **Adjust to Density**: Thicker fog = more significant speed reduction. If visibility drops near zero, pull off the road until it clears—just remember to use your hazard lights while stopped.

Give More Room

- **Double the Usual Gap**: Instead of a 3-second rule, aim for 5-6 seconds. You need that extra buffer if the driver ahead brakes suddenly.

Common Mistake: Keeping Same Speed as Clear Weather

Mist leads to illusions of calmness—until you find an unexpected obstacle. Slowing is always the safer bet.

LANE POSITION & ROAD MARKINGS

Use the Right Edge

- **Find a Reference**: In dense fog, following the center line can be risky if oncoming traffic does the same. Use the right lane marking or road edge to guide you.
- **Stay in Your Lane**: Fog can hide lane lines if they're faded—be extra vigilant to avoid drifting.

Reflective Markers & Studs

- **Built-In Clues**: Many roads have reflectors or cat's eyes. They bounce your headlights back, giving you glimpses of the lane path.
- **Curves & Turns**: Watch for changes in these markers indicating a bend ahead.

Pro Tip: Minimal Lane Changing

Changing lanes in fog can be dicey—oncoming or parallel traffic might appear out of nowhere. Only shift if truly necessary.

COMMUNICATION & WARNING SIGNALS
Gentle Brake Taps
- **Signal Your Intent**: In low visibility, trailing drivers can't see subtle slow-downs. Tap your brakes lightly to flash brake lights, warning them you're reducing speed.
- **Hazards When Stopped**: If forced to stop (e.g., breakdown), use hazard lights so others realize you're stationary.

Don't Overdo Hazards
- **Active Movement**: Driving with hazards on while moving can confuse people. Use them only if you're going extremely slowly or are forced to move well under normal speeds.
- **Lights for Lane Changes**: If you must turn or merge, use your blinkers as usual—no skipping signals just because you can't see well.

Common Mistake: No Signal

Fog or not, other drivers need to know your intentions. Turn signals remain crucial.

AVOID UNNECESSARY PASSING

Risky Overtakes
- **Blind Spot**: In thick fog, you have minimal clues about oncoming vehicles. Passing on a two-lane road is especially dangerous.
- **Patience Pays**: Unless you're sure there's a clear stretch, wait. A little delay is better than a head-on collision.

On Multi-Lane Highways
- **Still Exercise Caution**: Cars might linger in a lane or drift. Keep your head on a swivel, checking mirrors thoroughly.
- **Commit Quickly**: If you must pass, do it at a modest speed without lingering next to the other driver's blind spot.

Pro Tip: Wait for a Patch of Clearer Visibility

Sometimes fog thins momentarily or breaks in patches. Use that window if you need to overtake—but only if it's truly safe.

PULLING OVER OR STOPPING

Finding a Safe Spot
- **Avoid Road Shoulders**: Stopping half-on the shoulder is risky in fog—approaching cars may not see you until last second.
- **Look for Parking Lots or Rest Areas**: If visibility is almost zero, exiting the road entirely is best.

Stay Visible
- **Hazards On**: If you must stop on the roadside, use hazard lights, reflective triangles, or flares if available.
- **Don't Rely on Just Tail Lights**: A car behind might interpret your tail lights as moving traffic—hazards clarify you're stationary.

Common Mistake: Stopping in the Lane
If you panic and halt in the lane, you become an obstacle. Always try to exit the flow—finding a wide shoulder or an off-road safe zone.

COMMON FOG DRIVING PITFALLS

Overconfidence
- **Familiar Routes**: It's easy to think you know the road, but hidden hazards are doubly hidden in fog.
- **Speeding**: Even mild speeding in fog is a top cause of collisions—especially chain-reaction pileups on highways.

Late Reactions
- **Tailgating**: A car's brake lights might only be visible at close range, giving you zero time to stop. Keep that buffer zone!
- **Distractions**: Fog requires full attention—no phone use or messing with the radio. You need your eyes front and center.

Oncoming Traffic Illusions
- **Headlight Halos**: A single bright glow can mask multiple vehicles behind it. Wait if you're unsure.
- **Curve Deceptions**: Fog in curves can hide the entire opposite lane until you're face-to-face with oncoming lights.

Common Mistake: Ignoring the 'Low Beam Only' Rule
High beams cause intense reflection in fog, giving you a white-out view. Stick to low beams for clarity.

STAY ALERT, STAY SAFE

Check Weather Updates
- **Ever-Changing Fog**: It can roll in or lift unexpectedly—monitor local forecasts if you plan a long drive.
- **Plan Extra Time**: Foggy journeys naturally take longer—reduce stress by leaving earlier.

See and Be Seen
- **Drive Your Own Speed**: If traffic behind you wants to go faster, let them pass, but keep your safe pace.
- **Don't Be Invisible**: Use all available lights—low beams, fog lights (front and rear)—and keep them in good repair.

Pro Tip: Practice Night Fog Drills
If you live where fog is common, pick a less busy route and drive carefully to familiarize yourself with the feeling of limited visibility. Building comfort in mild conditions helps you stay calmer when it's denser.

Common Mistake: Hurrying in Dense Fog
Rushing a trip in thick fog endangers everyone. Embrace the slow pace—it's your shield against unseen obstacles and sudden stops.

Fog can transform your drive into a hazy guessing game—especially on winding roads or highways at night. But that milky-white cloak can be managed with **smart lighting** (low beams/fog lights), **slower speeds**, and **extra scanning** of the road edges. Keep passing minimal, maintain that following cushion, and if the soup's too thick, pull over safely until conditions improve. You might not see more than a few car lengths ahead, but with the right moves, you'll still reach your destination safe, sound, and with zero "where did that come from?" moments.

41. BABY, IT'S COLD OUTSIDE: TIPS FOR DRIVING IN FROSTY WEATHER

Winter's knocking on your windshield, and you might notice your car feeling a bit… sluggish. The battery groans, tires seem flatter, and your fuel gauge seems to drop faster than your desire to leave a warm bed. **Cold weather driving** poses unique challenges—yes, even when there's no snow or ice in sight. From tire pressure drops to thicker engine oil, understanding how lower temperatures affect your vehicle is crucial for a smoother, safer drive. In this chapter, we'll explore how to keep both you and your car cozy in the chill.

COLD WEATHER & YOUR CAR: A CHILLY RELATIONSHIP

Batteries Struggle in the Cold
- **Chemical Slowdown**: When temps plummet, battery power output takes a hit. A battery that was "just fine" in summer might deliver a pitiful click on a frosty morning.
- **Proactive Testing**: If your battery is older than three years, get it tested or replaced before winter sets in. A simple test can save you from a frigid tow-truck wait.

Fluids Become Thick & Sluggish
- **Engine Oil & Coolant**: These liquids become more viscous in the cold, so your engine works harder initially.
- **Longer Heater Warm-Up**: Since heater systems draw warmth from engine coolant, your cabin heat might take a while.
- **Common Mistake**: Idling for ages to "warm up" your car. Instead, start up, wait about a minute, then drive gently to let everything warm naturally.

Tire Pressure Drops Like a Rock
- **PSI & Temperature**: Expect to lose about 1 PSI for every 10°F drop. Underinflated tires = poor traction and lower MPG.
- **Stay Ahead**: Check pressure weekly in winter to avoid that "skating-on-ice" sensation.

Pro Tip: Monitor and Maintain Proper Tire Pressure Regularly
Keep a small compressor or tire gauge in your trunk—handy when the temperature dips.

WARMING UP YOUR CAR: MYTHS & REALITY

Do Modern Cars Need a Long Warm-Up?
- **Short Answer? No.** Modern, fuel-injected engines typically need just **30 seconds** of idle time—excessive idling is mostly wasted fuel.
- **Exception**: Subzero conditions. A brief warm-up (1–2 minutes) can help loosen super-thick oil and fluids.

Best Way to Warm Up
- **Start, Wait, Then Go**: Turn on the engine, give it half a minute to circulate oil, then drive gently. This warms your car faster.
- **Avoid Revving**: Cold oil can't lubricate as quickly, so big revs stress your engine unnecessarily.

Cabin Heat Delays
- **Slow to Heat**: The heater pulls warmth from engine coolant—if the engine is cold, so is your blower. Be patient.

Pro Tip: Heater Trouble Signs
If the heater never warms up, check your coolant level or thermostat—could be a sign of a bigger issue.

SEEING CLEARLY: DEFOGGING & DEFROSTING

Clearing Foggy Windows Fast
- **Use AC, Even in Winter**: AC dehumidifies the air, quickly defogging your windshield.
- **Defrost Mode**: A dedicated defrost setting directs airflow to the windshield—letting the magic happen.

De-Icing Your Windshield
- **Ice Scraper + De-Icer**: Your best combo for removing frosty buildup quickly.
- **No Hot Water Trick**: Rapid temperature changes can crack your windshield. Don't do it!

Prevent Frost Buildup
- **Windshield Covers**: Put one on overnight to avoid a morning scraping marathon.
- **Park Facing East**: Let morning sunlight help melt that layer of frost while you sip coffee.

COLD ROADS: SNEAKY HAZARDS WITHOUT SNOW

Longer Braking Distances
- **Cold Pavement**: Tires take time to warm up, reducing traction. Keep more space between you and the car ahead.
- **Easy Does It**: Hard braking on chilly roads can lead to minor slides.

Cold Tires = Less Grip
- **Warm-Up Period**: Your tires won't grip at their best until friction heats them a bit. Drive cautiously for the first few minutes.
- **Careful on Turns**: Sudden cornering might break traction if the rubber stays cold.

Bridges & Overpasses Freeze First
- **Lack of Ground Insulation**: They can develop black ice even when the main roads seem okay.

Pro Tip: Gentle Inputs
Approach bridges with gentle throttle—no abrupt braking or lane changes if you suspect a slick patch.

COLD WEATHER & FUEL ECONOMY

Lower MPG in the Cold
- **Longer Warm-Ups**: The engine runs richer to heat up, burning extra fuel.
- **Short Trips**: Each cold start is an inefficient cycle—bad for MPG if you do multiple short errands in freezing temps.

Keep the Tank Half Full
- **Condensation Concerns**: Moisture in an empty space can freeze in the fuel lines—don't let your tank run low in cold weather.
- **Emergency Reserve**: If you're stuck in traffic or roadside in the cold, you'll want enough gas to keep the heater going.

COLD WEATHER DRIVING TIPS & TRICKS

Watch for Sudden Temperature Drops
- **Early Mornings & Evenings**: Prime time for black ice, especially if the sun sets and pavement cools fast.
- **Morning Dew + Cold = Thin Ice**: Don't be fooled by a "dry" look— it might be a slick glaze.

Sun Glare on Cold Mornings
- **Low Sun Angles**: The morning or late afternoon sun can be blinding.
- **Clean Windshield + Sunglasses**: A quick wipe of glass plus tinted shades helps big time.

Don't Rely Too Much on AWD/4WD
- **Acceleration vs. Braking**: AWD may help you accelerate on slick roads, but it won't magically fix the braking difficulties you'll face on cold pavement.
- **Black Ice = Everyone's Problem**: Even 4WD can slip and slide. Gentle, defensive driving is key.

Snow Tires vs. All-Season Tires
- **Tread & Rubber**: Snow tires have softer rubber and deeper tread for superior grip on icy or snowy roads; all-season tires handle mild winters but lose some traction in extreme cold.
- **Which Is Better?**: If you regularly deal with freezing temps and snow, snow tires are safer. In milder climates with only occasional cold, all-season tires may be fine – no seasonal swap needed.

EMERGENCY READINESS: STAYING SAFE IN THE COLD

Pack a Cold-Weather Kit
- **Blanket, Gloves, Hat**: If you get stranded, keep warm until help arrives.
- **Phone Charger**: Cold temps drain phone batteries—carry a spare power source.
- **Snacks & Water**: If you're stuck for hours, you'll thank yourself for that granola bar stash.

Stuck in the Cold? What to Do
- **Stay With Your Car**: Wandering off in freezing temps is dangerous.
- **Short Engine Runs**: Every so often, run the heater to preserve fuel. Ensure the exhaust pipe isn't blocked by snow.
- **Crack a Window**: Prevent carbon monoxide buildup if you're idling for heat.

Pro Tip: A Clean Windshield is a Clear Win
Stash a microfiber cloth in your car to wipe away unexpected fog. A single swipe makes the difference between confusion and clarity.

Common Mistake: Ignoring Tire Pressure Until It's Too Late

Low pressure = worse traction, worse mileage, and a bumpier ride. Keep that gauge handy and check weekly in winter.

Cold weather might make your car grumble and your tires sink, but with a few tweaks—regular battery checks, short warm-ups, mindful tire pressure, and an emergency kit at the ready—you'll be set for a safer, smoother drive. Don't forget to keep your windows clear, your seat warm (if you're lucky enough to have heated seats!), and your pace cautious on chilly roads. Bundle up, stay vigilant, and show that winter who's boss!

42. SNOW WAY YOU'RE LOSING CONTROL: HOW TO DRIVE IN A WINTER WONDERLAND

Fresh snow might conjure images of holiday postcards and ski trips, but once you're behind the wheel, it's less about sipping cocoa and more about dodging icy patches, hidden potholes, and spraying snow from plows. Don't let the winter scenery fool you—**snowy roads** can be treacherous if you're unprepared. In this chapter, we'll walk through **car prep**, **driving techniques**, and **plow etiquette** to ensure your ride through this winter wonderland remains a safe, stress-free adventure. Let's dig into the essentials for a secure ride through winter's fluffiest obstacle course.

WHY SNOW DEMANDS SPECIAL CAUTION

Reduced Traction & Concealed Dangers
- **Slippery Surface**: Snow, slush, or ice beneath drastically reduce tire grip.
- **Hidden Hazards**: Fresh snow can bury potholes, speed bumps, and road markings—always assume surprises lurk below.

Longer Stops & Skid Risks
- **Braking Distance**: Wheels lock up more easily on snow, so stops take longer.
- **Gentle, Predictable Moves**: Harsh inputs = your car gliding like a figure skater—beautiful in a rink, not so much on a highway.

Common Mistake: Treating Snow Like Rain
Snow can reduce traction more than rain or slush, so drop speeds and up your caution level a notch.

GETTING YOUR CAR WINTER-READY

Winter Tires
- **Specialized Tread & Rubber**: Snow tires grip cold roads and ice better than all-seasons.
- **When to Switch**: If you see substantial snowfall each year, swapping to dedicated winter tires is a game-changer. When temperatures drop below 46°F, it's a good time to swap to winter tires.

Clearing Off Snow & Ice
- **Windows, Lights & Roof**: Clear all snow from your car to maintain full visibility and safe driving. Avoid driving with a thick layer of snow on your roof—it can slide down your windshield or fly off onto other cars.
- **Wipers & Washer Fluid**: Keep them in good shape, using winter-grade fluid that won't freeze on contact.

Defrosters & Cabin Warmth
- **Fog & Frost**: Cold, moist air can fog windows—turn on AC or defrost mode to clear glass faster.
- **Brush or Scraper**: A quick manual scrape often beats waiting for the heater alone.

SPEED & FOLLOWING DISTANCE

Slow Down
- **Traction Basics**: Even with snow tires, your stopping power isn't the same as on dry pavement. Adjust speed to conditions.
- **Plan Extra Time**: Rushing on snowy roads is a recipe for spin-outs or rear-enders.

Increase the Gap
- **Double the Usual Buffer**: If you normally keep a 3-second gap, consider 6 seconds in snowy or slushy roads.
- **Anticipate Early**: Begin braking sooner than usual—sliding is easy if you jam the brakes last minute.

Pro Tip: Plan for Extra Travel Time
Winter driving is naturally slower; building in a time buffer helps you stay calm and safe.

BRAKING & STEERING TECHNIQUES

Smooth Inputs
- **Avoid Jerks**: Gentle braking and gradual steering keep tires at the edge of grip.
- **ABS & Steady Pressure**: If you have anti-lock brakes, press firmly and let the system do its pulsing job—no pedal pumping needed.

Anticipate Stops and Turns
- **Look Farther Ahead**: Spot traffic lights or signs well in advance so you can begin slowing without slamming the brakes.

- **Turn Gently**: Slow down **before** the corner—accelerating or braking mid-turn is an easy way to skid. Accelerate gently out of it—no sudden pedal stomps.

Common Mistake: Panic-Breaking in a Skid
Jamming the brake can lock wheels on slippery surfaces, making skids worse. Ease off and steer calmly.

SKID RECOVERY & TRACTION CONTROL

Handling a Slide
- **Front-Wheel**: If the front tires plow straight despite your turn, lift off the brake or gas, and steer gently to regain direction.
- **Rear-Wheel**: If the back end slides out, steer into the skid until you realign—avoid a frantic overcorrection.

Traction Aids
- **Stability Control**: Modern cars limit wheelspin automatically and help correct minor fishtails, but can't defy physics.
- **AWD Doesn't Equal Invincibility**: Helps you accelerate, yes, but stops just as clumsily as any other car on ice.

HILLS & INCLINES

Uphill Approach
- **Build Momentum**: Get rolling before the hill—stopping mid-slope can leave you spinning in place.
- **Steady Throttle**: Avoid big accelerations or your wheels might spin and lose traction. Keep it smooth.

Going Downhill
- **Use Lower Gears**: Engine braking helps maintain control without overusing brakes, which can lock on slick surfaces.
- **Don't Ride the Brakes**: Overheating them can reduce effectiveness—gentle, intermittent braking is best.

VISIBILITY & FLYING SNOW

Headlights On (Day or Night)
- **Be Seen**: Heavy snowfall can dim daylight—low beams help others spot you.
- **Watch for Snow Buildup**: Periodically clear off your headlights and taillights; caked-on snow kills visibility.

Passing & Visibility

- **Passing Big Vehicles**: Trucks fling slush onto your windshield, temporarily blinding you. Pass quickly (but carefully) to dodge the white-out.
- **Wiper Vigilance**: Keep fluid topped off. Salty slush can form a smudge that blocks your view in seconds.
- **Flying Ice Sheets:** Large trucks can shed sheets of ice that turn into airborne hazards. Keep a safe distance and wait for a clear opportunity to pass before that "frozen frisbee" comes your way.

Common Mistake: Not Clearing the Roof
Leaving a snow "cap" on top can blow off onto following cars—or slide forward onto your windshield when you brake.

DRIVING AROUND SNOWPLOWS

Snowplow Etiquette

- **Give Them Space**: Snowplows often move slower and make frequent stops or lane shifts. Maintain a safe following distance to avoid flying salt or chunks of ice.
- **Passing with Caution**: If you must overtake, do it carefully—plows are wide, may have extended blades, and can throw up snow clouds that blind you momentarily.
- **No Tailgating**: Apart from risking damage from flying debris, stopping distances behind a plow can be shorter than you think if they brake or pivot suddenly.

DRIVING ON PACKED/FROZEN ROADS

Packed & Frozen Surfaces

- **Ice Under the Snow**: Hard-packed snow can hide a glassy sheet of ice. Keep speeds moderate—tires can lose grip instantly if you brake hard.
- **Packed Ice Potholes:** When packed ice begins to melt, hidden craters can appear overnight. Slow down, keep a firm grip on the wheel, and steer gently around them when possible.
- **Concealed Potholes**: Potholes hidden under snow or ice can jolt your suspension or even cause tire damage. Slow down and keep an eye on the road texture—odd lumps or dips might hint at a sneaky hole.
- **Tread Cautiously**: On glazed surfaces, gentle acceleration and light braking are crucial. Jerky moves can set your tires spinning or cause a sideways slide.

COMMON MISTAKES & EXTRA TIPS

Overconfidence in AWD/4WD

- **Soft Pedal:** Even with AWD, stomping the gas on ice means wheelspin.
- **Acceleration vs. Braking:** All-wheel drive helps you go, but it doesn't magically shorten your stopping distance. Keep speeds modest.

Minimal Lane Changes

- **Slush Ridges:** Changing lanes across a ridge of slush can jerk your wheels sideways. Signal early, change lanes gradually (only if necessary), and keep an eye on your speed throughout the maneuver.
- **Check Mirrors:** Visibility can be poor in swirling snow—ensure the next lane is clear.

Emergency Kit & Smarts

- **Blanket, Shovel, Kitty Litter:** Helps if you're stuck—shovel out snow, sprinkle litter for traction.
- **Stay in the Car:** If you're stranded, wandering off in a snowstorm can be dangerous. Keep a window cracked if you run the engine for heat.

Common Mistake: Tailgating in Snow

Following too closely leaves no margin if the car ahead stops or spins out. Double or triple your usual gap.

Pro Tip: Know When to Stay Off the Roads

If a storm is fierce or the plows haven't cleared major routes, consider postponing non-essential trips. Sometimes waiting it out is the safest call. Also, stay updated on any potential driving bans or restrictions.

Snow-capped roads may look like a holiday card, but they present hidden ice, low traction, and can transform driving into an unplanned ski adventure. By properly **equipping your car** (winter tires, defrost gear), **slowing down, allowing big safety gaps**, and **taking caution around snowplows**, you'll master the winter wonderland behind the wheel. Whether you're facing powder, slush, or frozen grooves, stay smooth with your inputs, keep your view clear, and have your emergency kit ready. Embrace the frosty challenge with confidence—because when it comes to snowy roads, slow and steady truly wins the race.

43. DON'T GET CAR SICK:
TACKLING TWISTY MOUNTAIN ROADS

Imagine the crisp mountain air, winding roads hugging steep cliffs, and breathtaking views around every bend. It's all very enchanting—until you realize a sharp hairpin turn is coming up, and your passengers are already gripping the door handles. Navigating **hilly terrain** can be a thrill but also a challenge if you're not prepared. In this chapter, we'll show you how to **get your car (and yourself) ready, tackle those twisting climbs and descents**, and **prevent any of your passengers from going green in the face**. Let's conquer those scenic switchbacks—without the queasy aftermath!

PREPARATION BEFORE THE DRIVE

Car Health Check
- **Brakes & Tires**: Steep inclines demand reliable stopping power, and twisty roads need decent tread for grip. Check both thoroughly—worn brake pads or bald tires won't cut it.
- **Cooling System**: Engines can heat up on climbs. Top off coolant and confirm the radiator's in good shape—overheating mid-mountain is a buzzkill.
- **Passengers Prone to Motion Sickness**: Suggest anti-nausea meds, wristbands, or frequent stops. A front seat vantage helps some folks.

Know Your Route
- **Elevation & Weather**: Mountain microclimates can turn sunny skies into fog and drizzle fast. Research altitudes, closures, or typical weather patterns.
- **Maps & Signals**: Cell reception might fade in remote areas— offline maps or a paper backup come in handy.

Common Mistake: Ignoring Minor Issues
A squeaky brake or slight coolant drip might seem trivial, but mountain stress multiplies small problems fast.

Pro Tip: Offline Maps
Before you head into the mountains or any off-the-grid spot, download offline maps. That way, if your signal drops, your sense of direction doesn't.

DRIVING TECHNIQUES FOR WINDING ROADS

Speed Control
- **Slower Is Smarter**: Zipping around blind bends is reckless—keep it moderate. For descents, downshifting (for manuals; or automatic low gear) helps manage speed without frying the brakes.
- **Smooth Inputs**: Hard jerks on the wheel or pedals jostle passengers and unbalance the car. Steady arcs, gentle accelerations, and early braking make for a calmer ride.

Look Ahead
- **Eyes on the Next Turn**: Let your sight lead the way, scanning further up the road to anticipate curves, oncoming traffic, or wandering wildlife.
- **Open vs. Tight Bends**: For an open bend with good visibility, you can keep a steady speed. Tight hairpins need earlier braking and possible downshifts.

Pro Tip: Listen to the Engine
If you're pressing hard on the gas in a high gear while climbing, consider downshifting—better torque, less strain.

CRESTING HILLS & DEALING WITH DESCENTS

Blind Crests
- **Ease Off the Gas**: You never know if there's a sharp turn, slow car, or animal crossing just over that rise.
- **Be Ready to Brake**: Keep a safe following distance and pay attention to your mirrors if you reduce speed near a crest.

Engine Braking on Downhills
- **Avoid Riding the Brakes**: Excessive brake use can lead to brake fade—where heat buildup reduces stopping power.
- **Stop often**: During long, steep descents, you'll often find flat pull-offs—stop there to let your brakes cool while enjoying the scenery.
- **Shift Down**: In a manual, pick a lower gear; in automatics, use "L" or downshift modes. This helps the engine hold you back gently.

Common Mistake: Excessive Braking
If you smell hot brakes or feel them go spongy, pull over and let them cool. Heat is their enemy on steep descents.

HANDLING SWITCHBACKS & HAIRPINS

Wide Entry, Smooth Apex
- **Racing Line, But Safely**: Approaching a hairpin from the outer lane side, turning in smoothly, and exiting can reduce sudden steering changes.
- **Beware Opposite Traffic**: On tight curves, some drivers cross the center line—give yourself an "escape" margin just in case.

Watch for Over-the-Line Drivers
- **Stay in Your Lane**: Especially if the road is narrow, hugging the inside might get you clipped by an oncoming car if they're sloppy.
- **Use Turnouts**: If you're slower and notice a queue behind, let them pass when it's safe to keep traffic flowing.

Pro Tip: Patience Pays
Don't accelerate into a blind switchback. It's safer to gently roll through, then pick up speed once your sightline opens.

WEATHER & MOUNTAIN MICROCLIMATES

Fog & Sudden Temperature Changes
- **Headlights & Defrosters**: Fog can appear with little warning at higher altitudes; low-beams or fog lights help you and others see.
- **Layer Up**: If you're planning a quick stop to take in the scenic view, keep in mind that mountain weather can shift fast—bring an extra jacket just in case.

Rain, Snow & Slippery Surfaces
- **Leafy or Gravelly Roads**: Wet leaves or loose gravel can be just as slippery as ice. Reduce speed and avoid abrupt moves.
- **Snow Chains**: In some mountainous areas, they're mandatory during certain seasons. Practice putting them on before you're freezing at the roadside.

Common Mistake: Overconfidence in 4WD/AWD
Having extra drive wheels boosts traction, but it won't help you stop on a dime. When grip is questionable, ease up on the speed.

Pro Tip: Check the Weather
Tune into local weather updates or road condition apps – mountain storms, hail, or sudden wind gusts can appear with little warning, and staying informed lets you adjust your driving plan swiftly.

BRAKES, OVERHEATING & SAFETY

Brake Fade
- **Symptoms**: Pedal feels soft, or you must push it further to slow down.
- **Cause**: Excessive brake heat leads to pad off-gassing, which disrupts their proper contact with the rotor.
- **Solution**: Shift to a lower gear, let the engine help manage speed, and pull over if necessary.

Safe Pull-Overs
- **Cool Down**: If you suspect overheated brakes, find a turnout, let them rest for a few minutes.
- **Check for Smoke/Odors**: The "burning brake" smell is a hint to ease up on pedal mashing.

Common Mistake: Ignoring Warning Signs
Hearing squeals, smelling burning, or feeling spongy brakes? Act immediately to prevent a bigger hazard.

PASSENGER COMFORT & AVOIDING CAR SICKNESS

Fresh Air & Ventilation
- **Open Windows or A/C**: Prevents stale cabin air that triggers nausea.
- **Front Seat = Less Nausea**: Passengers prone to motion sickness usually fare better up front.

Frequent Breaks
- **Scenic Stops**: Mountains are beautiful—take advantage and let everyone stretch their legs.
- **Snacks & Sips**: Light, bland snacks can calm unsettled stomachs. Avoid heavy, greasy meals mid-ride.

Smooth Driving Style
- **Gentle Movements**: Hard turns and quick acceleration cycles can make passengers queasy.
- **Focus on the Road**: For those prone to sickness, looking out the windshield, not burying heads in phones, helps orientation.

Pro Tip: Ginger Chews or Candy
Some folks swear by ginger's anti-nausea properties—worth a try if motion sickness is a repeat offender.

Pro Tip: Anti-motion-sickness Bracelets
They work wonders by gently pressing a specific acupressure point on the wrist. It's a simple, drug-free way to ease queasy stomachs on twisty roads – and if it keeps your passengers from turning green, it's totally worth a shot!

RESPECT MOUNTAIN RULES & SIGNS

Yield to Uphill Traffic
- **Common Courtesy**: On narrow roads, vehicles going uphill often get priority, since restarting on a slope is harder.
- **Watch for "Pull-Out" Spots**: Use them to let oncoming traffic pass if needed.

Passing Lanes
- **For Passing Only**: Don't treat these as bonus cruising lanes—use them only if you're overtaking, then merge back right to keep faster traffic flowing.

Wildlife & Falling Rocks
- **Keep Eyes Peeled**: Deer, sheep, mountain goats, or even bears might appear without warning.
- **Rockslides**: Look for "Falling Rock" signs—if you see debris, slow down or swerve gently.

Common Mistake: Speeding Past Warning Signs
Mountain signs exist for a reason; ignoring them can get you into serious trouble fast.

COMMON MISTAKES & TIPS

Hugging the Center
- **Stay in Your Lane**: Cutting corners can be tempting, but on blind bends it's dangerous.
- **Prepare to React**: Some oncoming drivers may wander—give a margin to avoid last-second swerves.

Ignoring Fast Cars Behind
- **Pull Over**: If you're enjoying a leisurely drive but collecting a line of impatient motorists, use turnouts. Everyone benefits.
- **No Pressure**: Don't let tailgaters force you into risky speeds—maintain your comfort zone.

Tip: Ease into It
- **Practice Smaller Hills**: Before tackling a giant mountain pass, get used to moderate slopes and curves.
- **Listen to Seasoned Locals**: Forums or local driver communities often share route-specific advice.

Pro Tip: Fun Factor
Mountain roads can be a blast if handled safely. Enjoy the scenery, plan scenic photo ops, and savor that crisp air.

Common Mistake: Treating Mountains Like Normal Roads
Their unique challenges—steep grades, blind curves, shifting climates—demand a different driving approach. Respect that, and you'll stay safe.

Twisty mountain roads don't have to be intimidating. By **checking your car's health**, **going easy on speed and brakes**, and **treating your passengers gently**, you'll conquer those switchbacks without queasy complaints. Embrace the breathtaking views between corners, master downhill engine braking, and remember: the key to not getting car sick (or scaring everyone else) is driving smoothly. So, keep your eyes forward, and let the mountains show you how rewarding winding roads can be—motion sickness not included.

PART III:

WHAT EXPERIENCED DRIVERS KNOW AND YOU DON'T

44. DODGE THE DANGER:
HOW TO SPOT AND AVOID ROAD HAZARDS

Picture cruising along when suddenly you spot… something up ahead: a rogue tire tread, a hunk of metal, or an empty box in the middle of your lane. **Road hazards** can appear out of nowhere, forcing you to decide whether to swerve, brake, or hope it's small enough to straddle. But not all hazards are so obvious—potholes might hide around a curve, or unexpected wildlife could dart across after dark. In this chapter, we'll explore **how to spot** these potential pitfalls, **how to respond** calmly (instead of panicking), and **how to ensure** you and your car emerge unscathed from whatever the asphalt throws your way.

IDENTIFYING COMMON HAZARDS

Debris & Litter
- **Fallen Cargo**: Maybe a loose sofa cushion, tire scraps, or even a lost mattress—any of which can cause a wreck if you slam into them.
- **Tree Branches & Trash**: After a storm, branches can drop onto the road, and strong gusts might blow garbage (or trash bins!) from the shoulder into your lane.

Potholes & Cracks
- **Wheel Busters**: Deep potholes can bend rims, pop tires, and damage suspension.
- **Hidden by Water**: Sometimes a puddle conceals a crater—watch for odd ripples or dips if you suspect trouble beneath the surface.

Animals & Wildlife
- **Darting Squirrels to Wandering Moose**: Depending on where you live, road-crossing critters come in all sizes.
- **Slow or Swerve?**: The appropriate action depends on your speed, the animal's size, and traffic around you. If you're traveling at low speeds and have room to stop safely, slowing down is the best choice.

Common Mistake: Tunnel Vision
Only staring at the car directly in front of you might mean not spotting a hazard early enough. Develop a habit of scanning the road far ahead.

SCANNING & EARLY RECOGNITION

Look Far Ahead
- **Aim High**: Keep your gaze several cars up the road—if you see brake lights or swerves, there might be a hazard.
- **Peripheral Checks**: Periodically glance at the shoulder or center median for debris or animals edging into the road.

Use Mirrors & Head Checks
- **Situational Awareness**: Know what's behind and to your sides, so you're ready for a quick lane shift if needed.
- **Blind Spot Glance**: If you must swerve or change lanes suddenly, ensure you're not merging into someone else's path.

Pro Tip: "Sweep" the Road
Every few seconds, do a quick visual sweep: far ahead, mid-range, rearview mirror, side mirrors. This helps spot hazards early.

LANE POSITION & MANEUVERING

Subtle Lane Adjustments
- **Mini-Shift**: Often, a small move within your lane can avoid smaller debris like cardboard boxes or trash. No need for a big swerve—just a safe "drift" if there's space.
- **Holding Your Line**: If the hazard is minor and stable, sometimes staying put might be safer than veering and risking a collision with another vehicle.

Safe Evasive Moves
- **Check Mirrors First**: Never jerk the wheel blindly—someone might be in the next lane.
- **Signal if Possible**: Even a quick blink can alert other drivers, though hazards sometimes force split-second decisions.

Common Mistake: Oversteering
A massive swerve to dodge a small item can cause rollovers or multi-car collisions. Weigh the risk of hitting the object vs. a severe lane change.

SPEED & FOLLOWING DISTANCE

Reaction Time Is King
- **More Distance = More Time**: A comfortable following gap helps you notice hazards early and react calmly.

- **Adapting to Traffic**: If vehicles around you are closely packed, you might have nowhere to go if debris appears. Adjust speed to avoid tailgating.

Slow Down When Unsure
- **Curves or Hills**: Blind corners and rolling terrain hide surprises—ease off the gas so you can manage last-second obstacles.
- **Poor Lighting**: In low visibility, extra speed is your enemy. Less illumination means more caution.

Pro Tip: 4-Second Rule
If conditions are iffy (nighttime, fog, heavy traffic), bump your usual 3-second gap up to 4 or more. You'll have a bigger margin for maneuvering or stopping.

NIGHT & LOW VISIBILITY CONDITIONS

Use Proper Headlights
- **Low Beams in Fog**: High beams bounce light back, hiding obstacles behind glare.
- **Dim for Oncoming Traffic**: Don't blind others, or they could miss hazards themselves.

Glare & Reflection
- **Adjust Mirrors**: Reduce rearview glare by flipping your mirror to night mode if possible.
- **Dash Lights**: Dim them if they reflect on the windshield, making spotting debris tougher.

Common Mistake: Overlooking Reflective Markers
Reflectors can hint at an obstacle's position—like a missing chunk of guardrail or a sideways barrier. Keep an eye out for unusual reflections or missing ones.

APPROACH & AVOID STRATEGIES

Weighing Risks
- **Small Debris**: Sometimes driving over a small cardboard box is safer than an aggressive swerve at high speed.
- **Do Not Oversteer**: Quick lane changes can be more dangerous than hitting a lightweight object.

If You Must Swerve
- **Check Surroundings**: Mirrors, blind spots—make sure your new path is clear.
- **Smooth Steering**: A gentle arc is better than a sudden yank. Keep both hands on the wheel for control.

Common Mistake: "Must Avoid at All Costs" Mindset
Not all road debris justifies a swerve. If it's small and not likely to cause major damage, hitting it might be safer than risking a multi-lane collision.

REPORTING HAZARDS

Who to Call
- **Highway Patrol or City Hotline**: Non-emergency lines often handle debris removals. If it's an immediate threat, call 911.
- **Pull Over Safely**: Don't attempt to call or text while driving—stop in a safe area first.

Safety First
- **Don't Become a Hazard**: Trying to remove debris yourself on a busy highway can be deadly. Let professionals handle it if traffic is heavy.
- **Details Count**: Note mile markers or cross streets to direct authorities accurately.

AFTER ENCOUNTER: VEHICLE CHECK

Listen & Feel
- **Strange Noises or Pulling**: If you bump or roll over debris, pay attention to new rattles, vibrations, or steering pulls that could mean a damaged tire or undercarriage.
- **Tire Check**: If you sense a wobble, find a safe spot to inspect for punctures or bent rims.

Pull Over if Needed
- **Better Safe than Sorry**: Catching a slow leak or a lodged metal piece early beats a blowout on the highway.
- **Visual Inspection**: A quick look under the car can reveal fluid leaks or dangling parts if the debris was large.

Common Mistake: Ignoring Minor Damage
A small scrape or rattle could be a sign of bigger issues. Don't wait until it worsens—handle it promptly for safety and lower repair costs.

Pro Tip: Develop an "Escape Route" Mindset

Always have a "Plan B" lane or shoulder space in mind—knowing where you can move if something pops up gives you a vital edge.

From stray boxes to dreaded potholes, road hazards can sneak up on even the most alert driver. **Scanning far ahead, maintaining a safe following distance,** and **using controlled evasive moves** are your best defenses against sudden obstacles. Don't forget to adjust for **nighttime glare** or **poor weather**—and remember that sometimes the lesser evil is gently rolling over a small object if swerving poses greater danger.

45. EXCUSE THE MESS:
CONSTRUCTION ZONES MADE LESS CONFUSING

Orange cones, flashing signs, and hi-vis overalls—welcome to the labyrinth of **road construction**! It might feel like traffic's worst enemy, but remember: these zones improve our roads and keep them from turning into pothole jungles. With the right mindset—and a little patience—you can navigate **lane shifts**, **reduced speeds**, **merges**, and even the dreaded **mile-long backups** without losing your cool (or your car's paint job). In this chapter, we'll unveil the secret to conquering construction chaos—safely and politely—while respecting the hardworking crews out there.

RECOGNIZING CONSTRUCTION ZONES

Signs & Warnings
- **Bright Orange Everywhere**: Diamond-shaped signs, barrels, and cones practically shout "Caution!" from a distance.
- **Flashing Arrows & Digital Boards**: Indicate closed lanes, detours, or reduced speeds. Pay attention, even if traffic looks normal at first glance.

Lower Speed Limits & Doubled Fines
- **Reduced Speed**: Many work zones impose limits 10-15 mph below the usual. It might feel slow, but it's for everyone's safety.
- **Hefty Tickets**: Some regions double or triple fines for violations, meaning that 15-over ticket can cost a fortune if it's in a work zone.

Common Mistake: Ignoring Early Signs
Those "Road Work Ahead" warnings aren't optional reading. They exist so you're prepared before the orange cones strangle your lane options.

SAFETY & COURTESY

Watch for Workers
- **Close to Traffic**: Construction workers are often just feet away from live traffic—so give them plenty of room, and stay alert to avoid any sudden swerves or close calls.
- **Obey Flaggers**: If a flagger waves you to stop or slow, do it—those directions override standard road signs and signals.

Keep Traffic Flowing (Within Reason)
- **No Tailgating**: Even if it's slow, maintain safe following distances. Sudden lane shifts or stops happen often in these zones.
- **Minimize Lane Weaving**: Cones often narrow lanes. Signal clearly and merge smoothly if needed—everyone's working with limited space.

Pro Tip: Patience Pays
Frustration might boil when speeds drop, but an extra minute behind the wheel is better than risking a collision with a concrete truck or the crew.

LANE SHIFTS & NARROWED LANES

Sudden Changes
- **Sharp Shifts**: Sometimes your lane veers left or right abruptly to accommodate construction. Stay alert for signage.
- **Concrete Barriers**: These might appear in place of cones. Extra caution—scraping a barrier is more damaging than knocking over a flimsy cone.

Avoid Last-Second Swerves
- **Signal Early**: If your lane's ending, indicate your move in advance.
- **Keep Calm**: Everyone is in the same boat—cutting off other drivers only fuels tension and potential fender-benders.

Common Mistake: Rushing Past Cones
Racing to the front, then merging abruptly is not only rude but risky in tight work zones.

MASTERING THE ZIPPER MERGE

The Zipper Technique Explained
- **Stay in Both Lanes**: Contrary to what many think, you don't need to merge a mile early. Use the open lane until the merge point.
- **Alternate Turns**: At the merge point, each lane's drivers take turns—one car from the left, one from the right, forming a neat "zip."

Why Merging Early Can Be Bad
- **Extended Backups**: If folks merge too soon, one lane ends up crawling while the other remains underused.
- **Smoother Traffic**: Filling up both lanes fully, then merging at the pinch point, keeps flow steady and shortens the tailback.

Pro Tip: Stay Courteous at the Merge
If you're in the open lane, don't race to cut everyone off—get in line properly. If you're in the main lane, don't block the open lane—zipper style is proven to reduce congestion.

MAINTAINING TRAFFIC FLOW

No Tailgating
- **Frequent Stops**: Work zones can bring abrupt halts—an excavator crossing the lane or crane repositioning overhead. Keep bigger gaps so you can stop calmly.
- **Scan Far Ahead**: Spot slow moving equipment or brake lights early to give yourself time to react safely.

Using Turnouts (If Available)
- **Some Work Zones**: Offer pull-off areas for breakdowns or letting traffic pass. Great for reducing bottlenecks if you must pause.
- **Be Swift**: Pull over quickly but safely—don't linger in partial lanes or half-blocked shoulders.

Common Mistake: Distracted Driving
Tempted to check your phone in slow traffic? Resist. Cones and shifting lanes demand your concentration.

RESPECT THE LOWER LIMITS & FINES

Double Penalties
- **Costly Mistake**: Getting clocked at even moderate speeds over the limit can yield shocking fines.
- **Worker Safety**: Speed limits aren't arbitrary—debris, equipment, and closeness to workers factor in.

Nighttime Work
- **Off-Peak Surprises**: You might expect empty roads late at night, but many crews prefer cooler temps or fewer cars.
- **Follow the Cones**: Drowsy driving is extra risky when lanes shift quickly in low visibility.

Pro Tip: Budget for Fines? No Thanks
Any thoughts of rushing through a work zone disappear fast when you factor in double or even triple fines—plus the serious safety risks.

STAYING AWARE OF EQUIPMENT & DEBRIS

Construction Vehicles
- **Unpredictable Movements**: Dump trucks, bulldozers, or backhoes might roll into or out of lanes slowly.
- **Watch Your Mirrors**: If you see large machinery edging forward, give them room to maneuver.

Loose Materials
- **Gravel & Dirt**: Patches of loose gravel or uneven pavement can reduce tire traction—slow gently.
- **Metal Plates**: Temporary covers over open trenches might be slick when wet.

Common Mistake: Ignoring "Bump" or "Uneven Lane" Signs
Hitting an unmarked transition at high speed jolts your suspension—and your nerves.

COMMON MISTAKES & TIPS

Ignoring Warnings
- **Missing Early Signs**: If "Lane Ends 1 Mile" is posted, start planning your merge or preparing for the zipper technique.

Distractions
- **Rubbernecking Equipment**: Cool excavators? Sure. But not worth rear-ending someone while gawking.

Pro Tip: Alternate Routes
If a main route is under heavy construction, take a detour or adjust your schedule—fewer delays and fewer headaches.

Construction zones may feature endless orange cones, hi-vis vests, and confusing lane shifts, but they're not a signal to panic—just **slow down, stay alert**, and **respect** the crew and signage. Adopting the **zipper-merge** approach, **giving heavy equipment lots of room**, and **maintaining a polite, patient attitude** helps everyone navigate work zones safely. Sure, it might delay your commute slightly, but the improved roads at the end of the project are worth it.

46. PULLING OVER:
WHEN, WHERE, AND HOW TO STOP SAFELY

Whether it's a sudden "Check Engine" light, a looming bladder emergency, or a persistent squeak that demands investigation, sometimes you simply **need to pull over**. But stopping in the wrong place or at the wrong time can turn a simple pause into a dangerous road hazard. In this chapter, we'll show you **when** to pull over, **how** to do it safely, and **what** to watch out for as you merge back into traffic—ensuring your quick stop doesn't become someone else's next close call.

KNOWING WHEN TO PULL OVER

Emergencies & Sudden Issues
- **Warning Lights & Strange Noises**: If your dashboard lights up or your car makes an alarming clank, it's time to find a safe spot to investigate.
- **Health or Driver Fatigue**: Feeling unwell or drowsy? Better to pull over and rest for a few minutes than risk dozing off at the wheel.

Routine Stops
- **Calls & Texts**: If you absolutely must check your phone, do it off the roadway. Pull over safely—no texting at traffic lights, please.
- **GPS & Directions**: Take a moment to set your navigation or confirm your route without rolling slowly and risking a traffic jam behind you.

Common Mistake: Stopping Mid-Lane
Never come to a complete stop in an active lane if you can help it. Always make it onto the shoulder or a parking area.

CHOOSING A SAFE SPOT

Shoulders & Designated Areas
- **Wide Shoulder**: Look for a decent gap between your car and traffic; narrow shoulders can be scary if vehicles zoom by inches away.
- **Rest Stops & Parking Lots**: If possible, exit the highway or find a nearby lot. You'll feel safer off the main flow of traffic.

Visibility & Lighting
- **Avoid Blind Curves**: Drivers whipping around a bend won't anticipate your parked car.
- **Nighttime Considerations**: Under dim conditions, choose a well-lit spot if you can—makes you and your vehicle easier to see.

Pro Tip: Ramp Shoulders = Safer Stops

When you must stop on a highway, using the shoulder of an **on-ramp** or **off-ramp** can offer extra protection from fast-moving traffic in the main lanes. Just be sure to watch for merging or exiting vehicles—signal early, check your mirrors, and keep hazards on to stay visible.

SIGNALING & SLOWING DOWN

Advance Warning
- **Blinkers or Hazards**: Let others know you're about to reduce speed. A quick turn signal or blinking hazard lights can alert them in time.
- **Mirrors & Blind Spots**: Always glance over your shoulder—someone might be trying to overtake as you veer right.

Smooth Deceleration
- **No Sharp Braking**: In high-speed zones, slamming brakes can trigger chain reactions behind you.
- **Blend Into the Shoulder**: Aim for a gentle curve onto the shoulder or stopping area—abrupt angles confuse trailing traffic.

Common Mistake: Forgetting to Check Rearview

You see a perfect pull-off, but the driver behind might not. A mirror check ensures you don't cut them off or cause panic braking.

HAZARD LIGHTS & SAFETY MEASURES

When Hazards Are Helpful
- **Temporary Roadside Stop**: Switch on hazard lights to indicate you're not moving—especially crucial in poor visibility.
- **Poor Weather**: If fog or heavy rain is involved, hazards provide extra warning to passing vehicles.

Reflective Triangles & Flares
- **Extended Stops**: If you'll be there a while (e.g., waiting for a tow truck), placing reflective triangles or flares a few yards behind your car adds a safety buffer.

- **Night or Low-Light**: These items become literal lifesavers if drivers can't see your parked car soon enough.

Pro Tip: Stay Aware

Don't get too relaxed—keep an eye on traffic. Some drivers might drift onto the shoulder or not notice you until the last moment.

EXITING & REJOINING TRAFFIC

Exiting the Vehicle
- **Away from Traffic**: If possible, step out on the side away from moving vehicles.
- **Keep an Ear Open**: Watch for approaching cars—sound can help if you don't see them.

Merging Back In
- **Signal, Mirror, Shoulder Check**: Treat re-entry like a normal lane change—give traffic time to spot your intention.
- **Match Speed**: Accelerate smoothly on the shoulder (if safe) before merging, reducing the speed difference with main-lane cars.

Common Mistake: Opening the Driver's Door into Traffic

Always check side mirrors—on a busy road, a driver's-door fling can lead to a collision or door rip-off.

HANDLING BREAKDOWNS & EMERGENCIES

Quick Assessment
- **Engine Trouble or Blowout**: If your car suddenly loses power or a tire blows, aim for the nearest safe pull-over.
- **Overheating**: If steam rises, shut the engine off once you're safe, and let it cool down before popping the hood.

Call for Help
- **Roadside Assistance**: Have a contact number or app ready for towing or mechanical assistance.
- **Stay in the Vehicle If Unsure**: If it's a narrow shoulder or fast traffic zone, remain inside, seatbelt on, hazard lights blinking.

Pro Tip: Keep An Emergency Kit

Stash a flashlight, reflective vest, phone charger, and some basic tools— handy if you're stranded after dark or in a remote area.

LEGAL & POLITE ETIQUETTE

Avoid Blocking
- **Driveways & Hydrants**: Even for a quick break, ensure you're not obstructing private entrances or fire safety equipment.
- **Bus Stops & Bike Lanes**: If possible, find an alternative place to park so you're not forcing cyclists into traffic or blocking public transport.

No Random Mid-Lane Halts
- **Pull Over Properly**: Drifting halfway onto a shoulder or curb confuses everyone. A partial stop is still a road hazard.
- **Obey Signs**: Some highways have restrictions on where you can stop. Check for "No Stopping" markers.

Pro Tip: Plan Your Pit Stops
If you anticipate a phone call or suspect your car's acting up, decide on a likely pull-over spot before it becomes urgent.

Pulling over might sound straightforward, but if done carelessly, it can create hazards or disrupt traffic. **Choosing a safe, visible spot, signaling clearly, and using hazard lights properly** can make all the difference. Whether it's a quick break or an unexpected issue, planning both your stop and your return to traffic ensures a smooth and safe roadside pause.

47. MANAGE YOUR CARPOOL: TIPS FOR DRIVING WITH PASSENGERS

Driving alone can be peaceful, but toss in a few friends, family members, or kids, and suddenly your cabin feels like a mini circus on wheels. While having company helps beat boredom, it also brings **extra noise, requests**, and **even peer pressure** that can distract you from your primary job—**safe driving**. This chapter shows you how to handle those lively (sometimes chaotic) passenger dynamics, from setting boundaries on gossip and music requests to dealing with laws restricting how many people you can carry when you're a new driver.

UNDERSTANDING PASSENGER DYNAMICS

Extra Distractions
- **Noise Factor**: Conversations can ramp up, and next thing you know, you're glancing in the rearview to join the fun instead of focusing on the road.
- **Handling & Braking Changes**: More passengers add extra weight. Your car might accelerate slower and require a longer distance to stop.

Weight & Space Considerations
- **Heavier Load**: Braking distances lengthen, and you might feel the car leaning more on tight turns.
- **Tight Quarters**: Overfilled back seats can block your rear window or hamper your side mirror usage.

Common Mistake: Treating Passengers Like Invisible Cargo
People move around, talk, and distract—unlike a trunk of groceries. Recognize their effect on your awareness and driving style.

SETTING BOUNDARIES & GROUND RULES

Focus on Driving
- **Polite Reminders**: Before rolling out, kindly ask for lower volume levels when navigating heavy traffic or complex turns.
- **Designated Co-Pilot**: If a passenger can manage the GPS or watch for turn signs, let them take over to minimize distractions and keep your focus on the road.

Avoiding Backseat Chaos
- **No "Hold My Food"**: Juggling your friend's fast-food meal while steering is a recipe for greasy, distracted driving.
- **Music & Chat**: Let passengers choose tunes or chat—just remind them you might need quiet during tricky merges or inclement weather.

Pro Tip: Create a "Silent Zone"
When approaching a busy intersection or highway ramp, announce "silent zone!" so everyone knows to tone it down briefly while you focus.

STATE LAWS & RESTRICTIONS FOR NEW DRIVERS

Passenger Limits
- **Many Regions Have Rules**: Some states restrict the number of under-21 passengers a novice driver can have to help minimize distractions and peer pressure.
- **Curfew Laws**: Late-night driving often carries extra restrictions for teens. Check your local regulations if you're a fresh license-holder.

Consequences of Breaking Rules
- **Tickets & Insurance Woes**: Violating passenger restrictions could lead to fines or even license suspension.
- **Safety Rationale**: Younger drivers are more prone to accidents when the car is packed with energetic peers.

Rear Seat Belt Laws
- **Legal Consequences:** Many states require all passengers, including those in the back seat, to wear seat belts. Ignoring this could result in fines or even points on your license.
- **Increased Injury Risk:** Unbuckled rear passengers face a higher risk of severe injuries in a crash, as they lack airbag protection and can be slammed into the car's interior or even ejected.

COMMUNICATION & DISTRACTION MANAGEMENT

Responsibility Talk
- **Set the Tone**: A quick "Hey, I need you guys to keep it cool when we're on the highway" can curb chaos.
- **High-Pressure Conditions**: Heavy traffic, night driving, or bad weather? Let them know you'll need extra calm.

Tech & Music Delegation
- **Phone Co-Pilot**: If directions or playlists are needed, a passenger can handle it—no need for you to multi-task.
- **Volume Checks**: Deafening bass might be fun, but not when you miss an ambulance siren or squealing brakes behind you.

Pro Tip: "Guys, I'm Driving" Card
Politely but firmly remind them you're responsible for everyone's safety. A bit of seriousness can reduce the background buzz.

DRIVING WITH CHILDREN

Car Seats & Restraints
- **Follow Age/Size Guidelines**: Properly install seats for toddlers or boosters for older kids. The wrong setup can be life-threatening in a crash.
- **Lock the Doors**: Child locks and window locks prevent curious hands from fiddling with doors mid-drive.

Soothing the Ride
- **Frequent Stops**: Children may need breaks to burn off energy, use the restroom, or avoid car sickness.
- **Minimal Distraction**: Keep an eye out in the rearview, but don't let tantrums or constant questions break your focus.

Common Mistake: Turning Around Mid-Drive
If a child is crying or fussing, pull over to assist rather than twisting in your seat. Swerving while your eyes are off the road is a huge hazard.

PEER PRESSURE & RISKY BEHAVIORS

Encouraging Reckless Driving
- **Speed Dares**: Buddies may tease you to "floor it," but it's not worth the ticket, or worse, the accident risk.
- **Distracting Challenges**: Some might want you to check memes or selfies while driving—no thanks!

Handling Intoxicated Passengers
- **No Tolerance**: If friends are intoxicated, they might behave unpredictably or distract you. Keep your focus and, if necessary, pull over if they become uncontrollable.
- **Don't Let Them Drive**: If you're the sober one, ensure nobody tries to operate another vehicle after a party.

Pro Tip: "Driver's Orders"
You're the captain of the car—if passengers push for stunts or speeds, politely but firmly decline. Safety outranks social pressure.

DRIVER FATIGUE & OVERLOADING

Long Trips
- **Passenger Rotation**: If someone else is licensed and insured, consider swapping drivers. Otherwise, plan rest stops or ask a passenger to keep you engaged.
- **Avoid Overcrowding**: More than your seat capacity is illegal and dangerous—lack of seatbelts or crammed space can hamper control.

Adjusting Mirrors & Visibility
- **Heads Blocking Rearview**: With a full back seat, check if you can still see the rear window. Adjust side mirrors if your direct rear view is compromised.
- **Weight Distribution**: A heavily loaded trunk plus a full car can affect handling—take corners and braking more gently.
- **Headlight Aim**: When the back of your car is heavily loaded, the front may lift slightly, angling your headlights higher. Adjust them if possible (or reduce load) so you're not blinding oncoming vehicles—even on low beams.

Common Mistake: Forgetting to Re-Adjust Mirrors
Passengers can shift around or lean, so do a mirror check, especially if you're used to seeing more out your back window.

EXITING & ENTERING SAFELY

Opening Doors in Traffic
- **Mirror Check**: Passengers should confirm no cyclists, pedestrians, or cars are alongside before flinging open a door.
- **Use the Curb Side**: Whenever possible, let them exit from the side not facing moving traffic.

Stop for Drop-Offs
- **Avoid Busy Lanes**: Pull into a safe spot or parking area for letting folks out—don't block traffic or cause abrupt stops behind you.
- **Hazards On if Brief**: If it's a quick curbside drop-off, turning on hazard lights alerts others, but make sure you're truly out of the traffic lane.

Common Mistake: Sudden Mid-Lane Drop-Offs
Trying to drop a friend in the middle of a busy street is an invitation for rear-end collisions or door-swipe accidents. Always find a safe pull-over point.

Pro Tip: "Quiet Zone" on Demand
Politely request silence or low chatter in high-risk situations (merging, dense traffic, or tricky weather). Your passengers should appreciate that safety comes first.

Driving with passengers doesn't need to turn your car into a bumper-car chaos zone. By **establishing simple ground rules**, **delegating tasks** like music or GPS, and **staying firm against peer pressure**, you can enjoy sociable rides without losing focus. Remember, extra weight and chatter mean you'll need to adapt your speed, watch your mirrors, and ensure everyone's safely strapped in. Whether it's a car full of chatty friends or restless kiddos, a little organization and clear communication can keep the ride fun and accident-free.

BONUS: DRIVING WITH PETS

Keeping Pets Safe
- **Legal or Not:** A growing number of states have laws that require pets to be properly restrained while in a moving vehicle.
- **Use a Crate or Harness:** A crash-tested pet harness, seatbelt clip, or secured crate in the back seat keeps both you and your furry passenger safe.
- **No Front Seat, No Lap Rides:** Airbags can seriously injure pets. Keep them in the back, ideally with a barrier if they're larger.

What Could Go Wrong
- **Distraction Danger:** Pets that roam freely may bark, jump, or panic during the ride—just as you're trying to merge, turn, or park.
- **Crash Risk & Injury:** In a sudden stop, even a small pet can be thrown forward at high speed. Unrestrained animals can also prevent EMTs from safely assisting passengers in an emergency.

Pro Tip: Plan Ahead
Bring water, a leash, and waste bags. If it's a longer trip, factor in breaks for your pet to stretch and relieve themselves. Never leave a pet alone in a parked car—even with the windows cracked.

48. DISTRACTIONS:
THE #1 REASON SMART PEOPLE CRASH

You're cruising along, singing to your favorite song, or maybe glancing at that *ding* on your phone. Suddenly, the car ahead brakes sharply, and you scramble to slam on yours. Was that half-second glance worth it? **Distractions** are no joke—they're the sneaky culprits that yank your attention off the road and can spark a chain reaction of near misses, fender benders, or worse. In this chapter, we'll show you **how distractions creep in, why they're so perilous**, and **practical ways** to keep your eyes (and brain) firmly on the road.

DEFINING DISTRACTIONS

Types of Distractions
- **Visual**: Anything that pulls your eyes from the road—like looking at texts, rummaging for a dropped item, or gawking at roadside attractions.
- **Manual**: Taking your hands off the wheel to adjust the radio, eat a burger, or swipe on your phone.
- **Cognitive**: Daydreaming, intense conversations, or emotional stress that hijacks your mental bandwidth.

Everyday Distraction Traps
- **Phone Fixation**: That "quick check" of a message or social feed is the top distraction culprit.
- **In-Car Shenanigans**: Rowdy passengers, fiddling with GPS, or a meltdown from kids in the back seat.
- **Food & Drink**: Juggling coffee cups, dipping fries in ketchup—every moment your hands are not on the wheel increases the risk of an accident.

Common Mistake: "I'm Just Peeking Quickly"
A quick one-second glance at 60 mph means covering nearly 90 feet—more than enough distance for danger to appear.

WHY DISTRACTIONS ARE SO DANGEROUS

Reduced Reaction Time
- **Blink-and-Miss**: While your mind drifts or your eyes wander, the

road doesn't pause—hazards can appear in an instant, and by the time you react, it might be too late.

- **Stats & Real Stories**: Distracted driving consistently ranks among top causes of collisions—each year, tragedies occur that a second of attention could have prevented.

Compound Effects

- **Chain Reactions**: One distracted driver slams brakes late, the next is tailgating... results in a multi-car pileup.
- **Confidence vs. Complacency**: Believing you're "skilled enough" to multitask leads to riskier choices, especially on busy roads.

Pro Tip: Imagine Blindfolded Driving

Taking your eyes off the road is like driving blindfolded for that period—would you do that intentionally?

TECH-RELATED DISTRACTIONS

Phones & Texting

- **A Leading Culprit**: Texting while driving is illegal in many places for a reason—it's a triple threat: visual, manual, and cognitive.
- **App Overload**: Scrolling social media or checking notifications means your focus is anywhere but the road.

GPS & Entertainment Systems

- **Pre-Set Your Route**: Punch in addresses before moving. If plans change mid-drive, pull over or ask a passenger to handle it.
- **Touchscreens & Built-In Menus**: Even built-in car systems can be distracting if you're hunting for that perfect playlist or route change.

Common Mistake: The "One-Handed" Approach

Some assume holding a phone in one hand is safe—nope! You're visually, mentally, and physically distracted all at once.

OTHER EVERYDAY DISTRACTIONS

Eating & Drinking

- **Fast Food Frenzy**: Balancing a sauce-laden burger while steering? Unwise. A sudden slip and you're panicked, not paying attention.
- **Spills & Burns**: Hot coffee or soup can cause knee-jerk reactions if spilled, leading to abrupt swerves.

Passengers & Conversation

- **Friendly Chatter**: A lively debate about last night's game can pull your mind off merging traffic.
- **Rowdy Backseat**: Kids or pets can create chaos—pull over to handle tantrums or barking fits safely.

Glancing at "Interesting Stuff" Outside

- **Rubbernecking**: Slowing down to look at a roadside crash or exotic car can cause new accidents.
- **Billboards & Scenery**: Stunning views deserve appreciation—maybe park at a scenic overlook rather than weaving within your lane.

Pro Tip: Snack Smart

If you absolutely must eat, choose simple, mess-free snacks that don't require both hands or your eyes off the road. Better yet, pull over to enjoy your meal.

DEFENSIVE STRATEGIES TO MINIMIZE DISTRACTIONS

Pre-Drive Prep

- **Plan Your Entertainment**: Cue up music or podcasts, set climate controls. Then buckle in and stay focused.
- **Secure Loose Items**: Keep everything within easy reach so you're not twisting around to grab something in the back seat.

Hands-Free & "Do Not Disturb"

- **Phone Settings**: Activate driving modes that silence notifications and auto-reply to texts.
- **Delegate**: Let a passenger handle navigation or incoming calls if necessary.

Pull Over if Necessary

- **Out of Traffic**: If something absolutely needs your attention (urgent text, meltdown in the back), find a safe shoulder or parking lot.
- **Hazards On**: Alert others you're stopping and do so well off the travel lane.

Common Mistake: Thinking You Can Wing It

You may get away with a quick phone check—until you don't. Consistent safe habits beat playing distraction roulette.

LEGAL & SAFETY CONSEQUENCES

Fines & Penalties
- **Hefty Tickets**: Handheld phone use can cost hundreds in fines, plus possible license points.
- **Insurance Impact**: Distracted driving citations may spike your insurance rates, sometimes drastically.

Ethical Considerations
- **Life & Liability**: A collision caused by a text or fiddling with GPS can injure or kill innocent people.
- **Moral Responsibility**: We share the road—everyone's safety depends on every driver's full attention.

Pro Tip: Keep It Real
That text or social feed will still be there when you arrive. A lifetime of guilt is a heavy price for a momentary distraction.

COMMON MISTAKES & TIPS

"I'm Just Checking Quick"
- **Reality Check**: Even glancing at a phone for two seconds at 50 mph covers nearly half a football field.
- **Safer Solutions**: Let calls go to voicemail or texts to auto-reply. You'll handle them once parked.

Radio, AC & Car Systems Overload
- **Too Many Buttons**: Constantly changing stations or blasting the AC can eat up precious focus.
- **One & Done**: Set a station or temperature, then let it ride—no need for endless tweaking.

Kids & Pets
- **Contain the Chaos**: Properly restrain pets and use child seats or seat belts for kids.
- **Pull Over**: If a meltdown occurs, park somewhere safe to address it—no turning around mid-lane.

Common Mistake: Trivializing "Small" Distractions
Even minor tasks—like rummaging in a bag—steal your attention. A second can be life-altering on the road.

Common Mistake: "It Won't Happen to Me"

Accidents from distracted driving happen daily. Don't gamble—commit to staying present and engaged every time you drive.

Distractions might seem harmless—until a split second of inattention changes everything. By **setting up your car** (music, mirrors, climate) in advance, **banning phone use** behind the wheel, and **managing** any potential chaos (be it from kids, passengers, or messy fast food), you'll keep your drive distraction-free. Remember, no text or snack is worth more than someone's safety. With your eyes on the road, hands on the wheel, and mind focused on the task, you're not just a better driver—you're a safer one for everyone else too.

49. PEER PRESSURE SURVIVAL: HOW TO STEER CLEAR OF DUMB DARES

Ever had a buddy call you a "chicken" for not speeding, or tease you when you refuse to race at a green light? **Peer pressure** behind the wheel is real, and it can make you feel like you're caught between being a "chicken" or a "rooster" showing off. But letting others push you into risky moves can lead to serious accidents, license trouble, and lasting regret. In this chapter, we'll explore **how to recognize** these pressures, **why it's vital** to resist them, and **practical tips** for staying cool when friends want you to act reckless.

UNDERSTANDING PEER PRESSURE ON THE ROAD

What It Looks Like
- **Direct Dares**: "Come on, floor it!" or "Don't be a baby—take that shortcut!"
- **Mocking & Teasing**: Laughing if you slow at a yellow light or refusing to run a stop sign. Sometimes the jokes push you harder than direct demands.
- **Hidden Competition**: Subtle remarks like "We made it in 10 minutes last time" that suggest speeding is expected.

The Social Factor
- **Group-Think**: If your friends peer pressure you, it's tough to be the lone voice of caution.
- **Status & Image**: Some might see fast driving or dangerous maneuvers as "cool," making you feel like you need to prove yourself.

Common Mistake: Believing "They Won't Like Me"
Real friends respect your cautious stance. If they only approve of you when you take risks, that's peer pressure you don't need.

WHY GIVING IN IS RISKY

Safety vs. Showing Off
- **Physical Danger**: Speeding, weaving through traffic, or ignoring signals can lead to collisions, injuries, or worse.

- **Guilt & Blame**: If your passengers (or another motorist) get hurt because you caved to pressure, the weight of that regret is enormous.

Legal & Ethical Concerns
- **Tickets, Fines, & Insurance Pain**: A single reckless driving charge can dent your wallet and your driving record.
- **Moral Responsibility**: You're in control of a moving vehicle—decisions affect not just you, but everyone on the road.

Pro Tip: Visualize the Consequences
Before you rev that engine at a dare, picture a police siren behind you or a crashed car. Reality checks can deflate peer hype fast.

IDENTIFYING TRIGGERS & TACTICS

Spotting the Pressure Cues
- **"Don't Be a Chicken"**: Classic name-calling or sarcasm.
- **"Everyone Else Does It"**: Suggesting it's normal to speed or show off, so you should too.
- **Competition Vibes**: Friends bragging about times or speeds they "achieved" last drive.

Subtle Manipulation
- **Rolling Eyes or Sighs**: Friends might not verbally push you but show disdain if you're careful.
- **Emotional Appeals**: "We'll be late if you don't hurry!" or "The party's starting without us!"

Common Mistake: Ignoring the Build-Up
Often, the push starts small—someone cracks a joke about your slow pace—then escalates. Catch it early and steer the conversation.

BUILDING CONFIDENCE & SAYING "NO"

Stay True to Your Limits
- **Gut Check**: If your instincts scream "unsafe," trust them. You know your driving skills and comfort zones best.
- **Respect the Law**: Speed limits and traffic rules aren't suggestions—they're there to protect everyone, including your passengers.

Firm, Polite Responses
- **Practice a One-Liner**: Something like "No, thanks. I'm not risking our safety," or "Sorry, I'd rather keep my license, guys."
- **Re-Direct**: If they want excitement, suggest turning up the music or picking a safe spot to do something fun off the road.

Common Mistake: Over-Explaining
You don't owe a lengthy justification. A brief, confident "I'm not comfortable with that" often ends the debate faster.

TEAMWORK VS. PRESSURE

Positive Passenger Roles
- **Helpful Co-Pilot**: A friend who handles GPS, phone calls, or eyes the blind spots is an ally, not a distraction.
- **Encouraging the Safe Choice**: Real friends commend your caution when conditions are dicey—like heavy traffic or tricky intersections.

Leading by Example
- **Model Safe Driving**: Once your passengers see it's possible to have a chill, enjoyable ride without stunts, they might follow suit in their own cars.
- **Set the Tone**: If you're calm and confident, peer pressure usually fizzles.

Pro Tip: Rewarding the Right Behavior
Praise friends who appreciate your safety over speed. Positive feedback fosters a safer group dynamic.

LEGAL & SAFETY CONSEQUENCES

Tickets & Accidents
- **Big Fines, Big Insurance Hikes**: A reckless driving conviction can send your insurance rates soaring or even cost you your license.
- **Crashes**: Risking your car and your friends' well-being for a moment of bravado? Not worth it.

Emotional Fallout
- **Guilt**: Injuring someone because you gave in to a dare is a lifelong regret.
- **Strained Relationships**: Friends (or their families) might blame you if an accident happens under peer pressure influence.

Common Mistake: Underestimating the Fallout
One speeding ticket or at-fault crash can follow you for years, financially and psychologically.

PRACTICAL TIPS TO RESIST

Plan Your Reaction
- **Mentally Rehearse**: Before you pick up friends, decide how you'll respond to demands like "Faster!" or "C'mon, pass that car!"
- **Short & Direct**: A simple "Nope, not happening" can carry more weight than rambling excuses.

Blame the Rules or Circumstances
- **Deflect**: "Sorry, I can't afford a ticket" or "My insurance would kill me."
- **Use Car Tech**: If your ride's speed limiter or safety systems beep, it underscores why you're not going any faster.

Rehearse Gentle but Firm Lines
- **"I'm Responsible for Everyone"**: People sometimes forget you hold that responsibility—reminding them can quiet the pressure.
- **"We'll Arrive in One Piece"**: Stress the bigger picture: better safe than being a roadside statistic.

Pro Tip: Humor Works
If pressed, you can joke: "Hey, I like having my license—losing it isn't on my to-do list," or "I'm no rooster—I'm the wise owl!" Lighthearted deflection can ease tension.

Peer pressure can make you feel like a "chicken" if you won't show off behind the wheel, but letting them push you into speeding or risky maneuvers can end in tickets, wrecks, or worse. **Staying firm** with a simple "no," **focusing on safe, lawful driving**, and **keeping your confidence intact** is how you truly prove your worth. The real bravery? Standing up to the crowd and saying, "I won't put us at risk." You're not a chicken for being cautious—you're a smart and responsible driver, and that's something to be proud of.

The next time your friends try to pressure you into something risky or reckless (because let's be real, it's a matter of "when", not "if"), make a promise to yourself now that you'll remember what you learned in this chapter—and stick to it.

50. YOUR HORN ISN'T ROAD RAGE THERAPY: KEEPING CALM BEHIND THE WHEEL

You're cruising along, minding your own business, when someone cuts you off—or honks the second a light turns green. Your pulse spikes, and for a brief moment, you imagine slamming the gas to "teach them a lesson." **That's road rage in a nutshell**—a surge of anger that can spiral out of control faster than you think. Whether you're an experienced driver or just starting out, losing your cool behind the wheel puts everyone at risk. And remember: **other drivers don't know you're still learning**; they may assume your hesitations are insults or challenges. Younger drivers, in particular, are more prone to emotional outbursts, making it all the more important to keep a level head. But it doesn't have to go that way. In this chapter, we'll break down **what triggers road rage, why it happens, how to recognize it in yourself**, and—most importantly—**how to stay calm** when faced with aggressive drivers.

WHAT IS ROAD RAGE?

More Than Just Annoyance
- **Aggressive or Violent Behavior**: Road rage isn't just mild irritation; it's tailgating out of anger, brake-checking someone, or rolling down your window to hurl insults.
- **Escalating Emotions**: A minor frustration can balloon into loud honks, gestures, or even physical clashes if anger takes the wheel.

Levels of Rage
- **Mild**: Yelling inside your car or honking excessively when you're annoyed.
- **Moderate**: Deliberate tailgating, lane-blocking, or swerving at another driver.
- **Severe**: Threatening someone physically or using your car as a weapon—yes, it can get that bad.

The Age Factor
- **Younger Drivers:** Studies suggest they're often more susceptible to emotional swings and peer pressure, hence quicker to anger.
- **New Driver Label:** Others on the road might not realize you're still perfecting your skills, interpreting your cautious moves as road rage triggers or "incompetence."

Common Mistake: Believing an Anger Burst Will "Teach Them a Lesson"
Harsh reality: you risk a crash or confrontation, and the other driver rarely learns anything except that you're reckless.

WHY ROAD RAGE HAPPENS

Triggers & Pressures
- **Stress, Fatigue & Being Late**: The more strained you feel, the easier it is for small annoyances (like a slow driver) to set you off.
- **Heavy Traffic**: Bumper-to-bumper situations test patience; every minor delay can feel personal.
- **Feeling Disrespected**: Getting cut off or honked at might sting worse if you're insecure in your driving skills.

Sense of Embarrassment vs. Overconfidence
- **New Driver Awkwardness:** Taking turns slowly or hesitating at merges can cause tailgaters or honkers to "blame" you, fueling your resentment or insecurity.
- **Entitlement & Overconfidence:** Some drivers think they own the road and view cautious driving as a nuisance, heightening conflicts.

Pro Tip: Don't Let Shyness Turn to Anger
If you hesitate at a turn because you're unsure, that's okay. Don't let honks or gestures push you into retaliation—focus on completing your maneuver safely.

Pro Tip: Own Your Learning Curve
If you're still polishing your driving skills, accept that you might be slower or more cautious. That's safer than letting impatience or shame push you into risky moves.

RECOGNIZING ROAD RAGE IN YOURSELF

Early Warning Signs
- **Tight Grip:** White knuckles on the wheel as frustration builds.
- **Heated Thoughts:** Mentally cursing or fantasizing about "teaching someone a lesson."
- **Vengeful Moves:** Speeding up to tailgate, brake-checking, or weaving around the other driver.

Emotional Indicators
- **Racing Heart**: Stress hormones spike, you start breathing faster.

- **Tunnel Vision**: Obsessing over what "that jerk" did, ignoring your surroundings.

Common Mistake: Dismissing Mild Anger as Harmless
Small outbursts can escalate fast—recognize them early so you can reset before it snowballs.

HOW TO KEEP CALM

Before Anger Strikes
- **Give Extra Time:** If you know traffic might be bad, leaving earlier cuts the stress of running late.
- **Relaxing Atmosphere:** Play soothing tunes or a lighthearted podcast—avoid super-aggressive music if you're already on edge.

In the Heat of the Moment
- **Pause & Breathe**: A deep inhale-exhale cycle can drop your pulse and give you a second to think.
- **Loosen Up**: Unclench your jaw, relax your shoulders. Physical relaxation helps mental calm.
- **Count to Ten**: Avoid an impulsive horn blast or swerve by giving yourself a quick mental break.

Pro Tip: Humor Over Heat
Imagine the "offending driver" is a funny cartoon character—hard to stay mad when you're picturing them as a goofy figure.

HANDLING AGGRESSIVE DRIVERS

Defusing Their Hostility
- **Don't Engage:** No eye contact, no gestures, no horn blasts.
- **Let Them Pass**: If someone's tailgating or weaving, give them space—don't feed their anger with brake taps or blocking.

Avoiding Escalation
- **Stay Predictable:** Maintain steady speed or lane; random moves might provoke them more.
- **Move to Safety:** If they keep harassing, drive to a public place (gas station or parking lot). Call 911 if you feel threatened.

Common Mistake: 'I Must Show Them!'
Trying to prove something on the road rarely ends well—someone usually ends up with a ticket, an accident, or a big regret.

WHEN ROAD RAGE TURNS DANGEROUS

Recognizing Extreme Behavior
- **Persistent Following**: If they're tailing you for miles, that's more than momentary frustration.
- **Physical Threats**: If they're yelling outside your window or trying to box you in, it's time to get help.

Protecting Yourself
- **Stay in Public View**: Drive to a well-lit, populated area, like a gas station.
- **Lock Doors**: Never leave the vehicle or confront them on foot.
- **Call 911**: Provide details and your location if you fear for your safety.

REMINDERS FOR NEW DRIVERS

Acknowledge Inexperience
- **Apologize or Gesture Politely:** If you make a mistake (like slow merges), a wave of apology can defuse some tension.
- **Don't Let Shame Turn to Anger:** If someone honks, it's not personal—learn from the slip and move on calmly.

Peer Pressure & Dares
- **Friends in the Car:** They might dare you to "show them." Resist. Safe driving is cooler than any short-lived thrill.
- **Learning Takes Time:** Mistakes happen. Don't channel frustration into aggression—breathe, reset, keep practicing.

Common Mistake: Assuming Others "Get" Your Hesitation
They won't. A little courtesy wave or a quick signal often diffuses tension far better than speeding up in a panic.

STRATEGIES TO REDUCE ROAD RAGE

Polite Habits
- **Signal Your Intentions**: Use turn signals well before lane changes—sudden moves invite anger.
- **Keep Right**: If you're slower, move right so faster cars can pass.
- **Avoid Unnecessary Honks**: A gentle toot can alert another driver, but a blaring horn fuels rage.

Mindset for New & Young Drivers
- **Accept You're Learning**: You might stall, fumble a merge, or brake too soon—shrug off onlookers' rudeness.
- **Stay Calm If Criticized**: Not everyone gets that you're new. Let them go if they're impatient. **Your** safety is more important than their opinion.

Spreading Calm
- **Be a Good Example**: If a friend or passenger starts mocking other drivers or encouraging aggression, politely shut it down.
- **Gratitude & Waves**: A small thank-you wave can defuse tension, whether you made a mistake or the other driver let you in.

Common Mistake: Forgetting That Calm Is Contagious
Politeness on the road can inspire others to mirror your chill attitude, but aggression tends to spark more aggression.

Pro Tip: Playlist Power
Keep a playlist of chill or upbeat tunes. Hard to stay mad when bopping to your happy jams.

Road rage isn't just shouting—it's a danger that can escalate into real harm, both physical and legal. **Keeping your temper in check** and **not engaging** with aggressive drivers is crucial, especially for new or younger drivers who might already feel anxious or insecure. If someone else wants to blow their stack, let them. You'll cruise on safely and avoid the fallout of a heated clash. By **building calm habits**, **giving yourself leeway**, and **staying mindful of your emotions**, you become a steady, confident driver—proof that the real "tough guy" on the road is the one who doesn't let anger drive the car.

51. TRAFFIC VIOLATIONS:
FINES, POINTS, AND REGRET

Imagine you're rushing, frustrated by a "ridiculously low" speed limit, and thinking, "Just this once…" when suddenly you spot flashing lights in your rearview mirror. **Traffic violations** aren't just minor slip-ups—they can bring hefty fines, insurance nightmares, and even jail time for severe offenses. Whether you're a well-traveled driver or still finding your lane, grasping **what qualifies as a violation, why it matters**, and **how to avoid those dreaded tickets** will keep your driving record clean and your license firmly in your pocket.

WHAT ARE TRAFFIC VIOLATIONS?

Definition & Scope
- **Any Rule Break on the Road**: From speeding to running stop signs, ignoring yield signs, using a phone while driving, or even bigger no-no's like DUI—these all fall under traffic violations.
- **Minor vs. Major**: Some are infractions (like drifting a bit over the speed limit), while others can be serious crimes (hit-and-run, reckless driving).

Why They're No Joke
- **Endangering Lives**: A "quick text" could cause a pileup; a "brief red-light run" might lead to a T-bone crash.
- **Ripple Effects**: Tickets lead to fines, fines lead to insurance hikes, and major convictions could mean suspended licenses or even jail time.

Common Mistake: Thinking Minor Infractions Don't Add Up
Points accumulate, and each "tiny" ticket can eat away at your clean record—risking bigger consequences down the line.

COMMON OFFENSES & THEIR CONSEQUENCES

Speeding
- **The Most Common Ticket**: Going 10 over in a 25-mph zone might seem harmless until the sirens start wailing.
- **Penalties**: Fines, license points, potential license suspension after repeat violations. Insurance rates might spike, too.

Red Light & Stop Sign Violations
- **Danger to Others**: One reckless dash through red can cause a severe collision.
- **Costs**: Hefty fines, added penalty points, possible traffic school. Some cities use cameras, meaning even if you don't see an officer, a ticket could appear in the mail.

Distracted Driving
- **Phone Use**: Many areas ban handheld phones; fines can be steep, especially for repeat offenders.
- **Other Distractions**: Eating, grooming, or messing with the radio—accidents often follow. Laws are cracking down more each year.

DUI / DWI
- **Serious Offense**: Driving under influence of alcohol or drugs can result in arrests, license revocation, jail time, and a criminal record.
- **Zero Tolerance**: Particularly for underage drivers. One misstep might lead to losing your license before fully enjoying it.

Pro Tip: Think of Your Future
One moment of "just a bit over the line" can cause problems at college admissions, jobs requiring a clean record, or your insurance rates.

IMPACT ON DRIVING RECORD & INSURANCE

Points & Suspensions
- **Accumulated Points**: Each violation typically carries points; rack up enough, and you face license suspension.
- **Serious Penalties**: Some states put new drivers on probation—violations can swiftly lead to losing driving privileges.

Insurance Troubles
- **Rate Hikes**: Even minor speeding tickets often trigger premium bumps—multiple tickets can skyrocket them.
- **Major Offenses**: DUIs or reckless driving can prompt insurers to drop you or classify you as high risk, costing big.

Common Mistake: Underestimating the Long-Term Effects
That single ticket might vanish from your memory, but it can remain on your record or insurance calculations for years.

HOW TO AVOID VIOLATIONS

Know the Limits & Local Laws
- **Speed Limits**: They're not suggestions—exceeding them is a straightforward ticket risk. Pay special attention in school/work zones where fines double.
- **Phone & Distracted Driving Bans**: Many places are adopting strict "hands-free" rules—obey them or face big fines.

Stay Vigilant
- **Road Signs & Signals**: Notice changes in speed zones, yield signs, or posted rules. Overlooking a yield sign can lead to pricy tickets or collisions.
- **Defensive Driving**: Expect mistakes from others; be prepared to slow or stop without slamming the brakes last minute.

Practice Mindfulness
- **No "Just This Once"**: That short gamble might end in a cop's radar or, worse, a crash.
- **Keep Calm**: Anger can push you to speed or run lights—don't let frustration sabotage your legal, safe driving.

Pro Tip: Refresh Regularly
Laws evolve. If you move states or after a few years, glance through local driving codes or official updates to avoid inadvertent violations.

LEGAL PROCEEDINGS & YOUR RIGHTS

Tickets & Court
- **Citation Options**: Usually, you can pay the fine, attend traffic school (if eligible), or dispute in court.
- **Pros & Cons**: Sometimes fighting a ticket can help if you suspect errors—like faulty radar or unclear signs. But it demands time and potential legal fees.

Hiring a Lawyer
- **Serious Offenses**: DUI, reckless driving, or repeated violations might warrant legal counsel to minimize jail time or reduce penalties.
- **Plea Bargains**: Lawyers can negotiate lesser charges or fewer points if the evidence allows.

Common Mistake: Ignoring the Ticket
Failing to address a citation can lead to increased fines, license suspensions, or even arrest warrants in extreme cases.

YOUNG & NEW DRIVERS: EXTRA CAUTION

Probationary Period
- **Stricter Enforcement**: Many regions keep a closer watch on new drivers. One or two tickets might instantly suspend your license.
- **Passenger & Curfew Laws**: Breaking these added newbie rules piles up serious penalties fast.

Future Impact
- **College & Employment**: Some applications might ask about driving records—keep it clean for better opportunities.
- **Developing Good Habits**: Early safe driving sets a foundation—repeated violations now can shape unsafe habits for life.

Pro Tip: Treat Rules Like Life Lessons
Respecting them from the start saves you from hassle and potential financial strain down the road.

CULTURAL & LOCAL VARIATIONS

Different Areas, Different Rules
- **State/Province Lines**: Speed camera laws, phone restrictions, seatbelt mandates can differ widely.
- **Zero Tolerance Zones**: School or construction zones might enforce doubled fines for infractions.

Educate Yourself if Traveling
- **Research**: If road-tripping across states, quickly check key local driving laws to dodge surprise tickets.
- **City vs. Rural**: Urban areas often use cameras or heavy enforcement; rural roads might see fewer officers but can still catch speeders.

Common Mistake: Assuming Uniform Rules Everywhere
A legal left turn on red in one state might be illegal in another—ignorance won't exempt you from a citation.

COMMON MISTAKES & TIPS

"Everybody Speeds"
- **Reality**: Everybody might do 5 mph over, but officers can and will ticket you for even slight excess if they choose—especially in targeted areas.
- **Tip**: Stick close to posted limits; get used to scanning your speedometer regularly.

Documents Renewal
- **Expiring License or Registration**: Overlook these, and you're effectively driving illegally.
- **Calendar Check**: Mark renewal dates or set phone reminders— simple but crucial.

Handling Officer Encounters
- **Pull Over Calmly**: Slow down, use blinkers, and keep hands visible. Composure can influence how the officer treats you.
- **Respect & Communication**: Arguing at roadside rarely helps— save disputes for court if needed. We'll dive deeper into handling traffic stops in a later chapter.

Pro Tip: Better to Arrive Late Than Ticketed
Resist the temptation to speed when pressed for time—one citation can cost far more than the extra minutes you'd have saved.

Common Mistake: Betting on Luck
A run of luck eventually ends. Consistent, rule-abiding driving is the sure bet to avoid violations entirely. Stay safe and ticket-free!

Traffic violations aren't just random checkmarks on your record—they can drain your bank account, double your insurance, or even cost you your license. **Whether it's speeding, ignoring signals, or texting at the wheel**, the law won't let "just one time" slide without consequences. Especially for **younger** or **brand-new drivers**, the margin for error is slim—probation periods and stricter rules can escalate infractions into major repercussions. Remember: staying vigilant, respecting the road, and brushing up on your local laws is the easiest way to keep your wallet, license, and peace of mind intact.

52. DRIVING DRUNK OR HIGH: JUST DON'T. EVER.

Imagine you're at a party—someone offers you a drink, or a friend hands you an edible, insisting it's mild. You think, "I feel fine, I can totally drive." But once you're on the road, your reflexes lag, your judgment's off, and you can't gauge that stop sign's distance. **Alcohol and drugs**—even so-called "harmless" amounts—can distort your abilities in ways you might not notice until it's too late. This chapter dives into **why impairment** is so hazardous, **how the law sees it**, and **practical ways** to keep yourself (and others) out of harm's path. Spoiler alert: no hangover or short-lived high is worth risking lives—or your license.

WHY IMPAIRMENT IS DANGEROUS

Slowed Reaction & Reduced Coordination
- **Visual & Motor Skills**: Alcohol blurs your vision, drugs can muddle your coordination. Whether you're weaving or missing the brake, you're risking a crash.
- **Judgment Fog**: Impairment leads to overconfidence—like thinking you can handle a tight turn at higher speeds. Spoiler: you can't.

High Risk of Accidents
- **Statistics**: DUIs contribute heavily to fatal collisions worldwide. Even "buzzed" driving causes thousands of accidents annually.
- **Young & New Drivers**: Inexperience plus lowered inhibitions can be lethal. If you're still mastering the road sober, adding any substance is a recipe for disaster.

Common Mistake: Thinking "I Don't Feel Drunk (or Stoned)"
You may not feel impaired, but your reaction times and reflexes say otherwise. You'll only know for sure once your car's in a ditch—or worse.

LEGAL LIMITS & ZERO TOLERANCE

BAC (Blood Alcohol Concentration)
- **Limits**: For adults, the DUI threshold is 0.08% (0.05% in Utah). Some states also enforce DWAI laws, which target drivers showing signs of impairment even when their BAC is below the DUI limit.

- **Underage?**: All 50 states enforce Zero Tolerance Laws for drivers under 21—any trace of alcohol is grounds for heavy penalties.

Drug Impairment Laws
- **It's All Impairment**: Legal or not, cannabis, edibles, or prescription meds that affect driving can lead to a DUI.
- **Testing & Scrutiny**: Officers can use field tests or specialized drug tests if they suspect you're high.

Pro Tip: Edibles Count, Too
Marijuana isn't only about smoking—a "simple brownie" can alter your reaction times. Don't assume edibles are safer for driving—they're not.

PRESCRIPTION & OVER-THE-COUNTER MEDS

Labels Are Crucial
- **Drowsiness Warnings**: Antihistamines, cold meds, or certain painkillers might make you sleepy or reduce alertness.
- **Talk to a Pharmacist**: If you're uncertain, consult a professional to ensure your medication won't impair your ability to drive.

Legal Meds, Real DUIs
- **Any Impairment Counts**: Even if your prescription is legit, if it impairs your senses, you're at risk for a DUI.
- **Combining Substances**: Mixing alcohol with certain pills magnifies effects, making driving even more hazardous.

Common Mistake: Prescribed Doesn't Mean Risk-Free
Just because a doctor prescribed it doesn't mean it's safe for driving. Side effects vary, so read the label—don't rely on a friend's experience.

MYTHS & MISCONCEPTIONS

"I'm Okay After One Drink"
- **Individual Factors**: Body size, metabolism, and tolerance differ wildly. One "small" drink can impair some more than others.
- **No Guaranteed Threshold**: Even below legal BAC, you might be too fuzzy for complex driving tasks.

"Coffee & Cold Showers Sober You Up"
- **Masks Fatigue**: Caffeine might wake you, but it doesn't reduce your BAC or reverse drug effects. You're still impaired—just jittery.

"Edibles Are Milder Than Smoking"
- **Delayed Effects**: Edibles can take longer to hit, leading people to consume more. Once it kicks in, your reaction time can plummet without you realizing it.

Pro Tip: Buzzed Driving Is Drunk Driving
Any impairment—alcohol, weed, meds—lowers reaction times. The law doesn't see "buzzed" as safer than "drunk."

PLAN AHEAD STRATEGIES

Designated Driver
- **Sober Buddy**: No brainer—if you plan to drink or consume weed/edibles, line up a friend who sticks to water or soda.
- **Rotate Responsibility**: Share the burden among your group so no one always ends up the driver.

Rideshare & Public Transit
- **Cheaper Than a DUI**: An Uber or bus fare is a fraction of the cost of legal fees, fines, and insurance hikes.
- **No Car Worries**: You avoid searching for parking or retrieving your car later if you can't drive.

Crash on a Couch
- **Stay Over**: Stay at a friend's place if the night runs long—"sleeping it off" might just save your life.
- **Avoid Next-Morning Surprise**: Keep in mind, you might still be impaired at sunrise, especially with potent edibles.

Common Mistake: Gambling on "I'll Be Fine Later"
Impairment can last longer than you think. If you're unsure whether you're fully sober, stay off the road.

REFUSAL & PEER PRESSURE

Handling Persuasion
- **Friends' Approval**: They might insist you're "okay" to drive—they don't face the consequences if you crash.
- **Stay Firm**: A short "No thanks, I'm not risking it" can outlast the loudest peer pressure.

Better to Be Awkward than Regretful
- **A Tiny Embarrassment**: Yes, refusing to drive or leaving your car might feel weird, but jail, injury, or guilt is far worse.
- **Safer Exits**: If pressured, hand over your keys to someone sober, or hide them if you must.

Pro Tip: Blame "Parental Rules"
If you're underage, say, "My folks would kill me if I tried that," or "My insurance is strict." Shifting blame can defuse peer pressure.

IMPACT ON YOUR RECORD & FUTURE

Criminal Record & License
- **DUI Convictions**: These can linger for years, affecting job hunts and college admissions.
- **License Suspension**: Even a first offense might yank your driving privileges.

Financial Fallout
- **Fines & Fees**: Court costs, mandatory classes, possibly installing ignition interlocks.
- **Insurance Premiums**: Skyrocketing rates—some providers might drop you entirely.

Emotional & Moral Weight
- **Living with Harm**: Injuring or killing someone because of impaired driving is a burden no one wants.
- **Rebuilding Trust**: Parents, employers, or friends might doubt your responsibility for a long time.

Common Mistake: Underestimating DUI Consequences
A single misstep can derail big life plans—don't bet your future on "I probably won't get caught."

YOUNG & NEW DRIVERS

Lower BAC Limits
- **Zero Tolerance**: Often under-21 drivers can't have any alcohol in their system—it's a license suspension waiting to happen.
- **Stricter Penalties**: New drivers on probation can lose driving rights after just one slip-up.

Building Safe Habits
- **Start with a Clean Approach**: If you're still learning the mechanics of driving, adding booze or marijuana is doubling your risk.
- **Show Maturity**: Proving you can say "no" to peer pressure or temptation underscores real driving confidence.

Pro Tip: Don't Let "Cool" Ruin Your Future
The coolest driver is the one who arrives safely—and keeps that license free of DUIs.

Pro Tip: Think Long-Term
A short buzz or high isn't worth the massive risk. Protect your future: stay sober behind the wheel, or hand those keys to someone who is.

Whether it's **a single beer, a strong edible,** or **a drowsy cold med,** anything that clouds your judgment, delays your reaction, or compromises focus is bad news behind the wheel. Laws on impairment aren't mere suggestions; they protect you, your passengers, and everyone else on the road. For new and young drivers, the stakes are even higher—one mistake can echo for years in legal, financial, and emotional costs. So plan ahead, stand firm against peer pressure, and keep your wits about you. Because truly, **you need your head for driving**—and you don't want it spinning from substances when a split second can decide everything.

53. BEING PULLED OVER:
THE RIGHT WAY TO HANDLE A TRAFFIC STOP

You're driving along, humming to your favorite song, when suddenly—**flashing lights** in your rearview mirror. Uh-oh… Whether it's for a minor mistake or for speeding, being pulled over can spike your adrenaline faster than you can say, "License and registration, please." But take a deep breath: a traffic stop doesn't have to be a nightmare. **Staying calm, knowing your rights, and cooperating** can make the difference between a quick warning and a stressful showdown. This chapter shows you how to **safely pull over, communicate with the officer**, and **handle whatever comes next**—so you can drive away with dignity (and hopefully no ticket).

PULLING OVER SAFELY

Spot the Patrol Car Early
- **Check Your Mirrors**: If you see a police car behind you with lights or hear a siren, confirm it's directed at you.
- **Don't Panic**: Resist the urge to speed up or ignore it. Officers can track you easily—fleeing is never the right move.

Find a Safe Stopping Spot
- **Signal ASAP**: Turn on your blinker to show you're cooperating.
- **Choose Visibility**: Avoid stopping around intersections, blind curves or narrow shoulders. If it's dark, aim for a well-lit area, like a parking lot or gas station.

Park and Prepare
- **What to do**: Shift to Park, turn off the engine, and roll down your window enough to talk.
- **Hands on the Wheel**: Keep them visible. Don't rummage around for your documents until instructed—let the officer see you're not hiding anything.

Common Mistake: Grabbing Documents Too Soon
Wait until you're asked before diving into your glove box, or you risk making the officer nervous.

INTERACTING WITH THE OFFICER

Stay Calm and Polite
- **Friendly Greeting**: A simple "Hello, Officer" sets a cooperative tone. No snarky remarks or side-eye, please.
- **Avoid Sudden Moves**: If you need to reach for something (like license/registration), mention it first, then do it slowly.

Handling the Basics
- **Driver's License, Registration, Insurance**: Typically requested. If you're missing anything, say so upfront—panicking or making excuses can look suspicious.
- **Answering Questions**: Keep responses short and polite. If you're unsure about answering something, you have the right to remain silent.

If You Receive a Ticket
- **Signing Isn't Admission of Guilt**: Signing acknowledges you received it. You can always challenge it later.
- **Court Date or Payment**: Check the ticket for instructions on contesting or paying.

Pro Tip: Think of Them as Doing Their Job
The officer isn't out to ruin your day; they're enforcing rules that keep roads safer. If you feel nervous, take a deep breath before responding to questions.

COMMON REASONS FOR BEING PULLED OVER

Speeding
- **Caught on Radar**: Claiming "I didn't see the sign" rarely helps. Radar doesn't lie.
- **Keeping Up with Traffic**: Officers can pick any speeder among a pack—unfair maybe, but that's how it goes.

Equipment Issues
- **Broken Lights / Expired Tags**: An out-of-date registration sticker or a burned-out taillight can prompt a stop.
- **Loud Exhaust or Tinted Windows**: Some state laws ban heavily tinted glass, loud exhaust systems, or even certain aftermarket modifications.

Distracted or Reckless Driving
- **Phone Use or Swerving**: Easy to spot, high on an officer's watch-list.
- **Aggressive Moves**: Tailgating, weaving, or brake-checking is a magnet for police attention.

Routine Stops & Checkpoints
- **DUI & Registration Checks:** Some states permit sobriety checkpoints or random vehicle inspections.
- **Fair Application:** These stops are legal as long as they apply equally to all drivers.

Common Mistake: I Drive Carefully

Thinking you're immune to getting pulled over because you "drive carefully." Officers can pull you over for any violation, even minor ones.

Common Mistake: "It's Just a Small Violation"

Sometimes smaller infractions lead to bigger discoveries (like expired registration). Best to keep your car in compliance.

KNOWING YOUR RIGHTS

Answering Questions
- **Basic Info Required:** You must provide your name, license, and registration.
- **Right to Remain Silent:** Beyond that, you're not obligated to answer further questions.

Recording the Interaction
- **Yes, You Usually Can**: Most states allow you to film, but do so responsibly—don't wave your phone at the officer's face.
- **Keep Your Hands Visible**: If filming, mount or hold your device calmly, clarifying that's what you're doing.

Search Requests
- **Probable Cause**: An officer needs a valid reason (smell of drugs, visible contraband) to search.
- **Consent**: If they ask permission, you can decline unless they have a warrant or cause.

If You Disagree
- **Debate in Court**: Don't argue on the roadside—it rarely changes the outcome and can escalate tension.

- **Stay Respectful**: A calm "I prefer not to answer further" works better than yelling.

Common Mistake: Losing Temper
Heated arguments invite suspicion. Remain cool, gather facts, handle disputes later in court.

HANDLING SPECIFIC SITUATIONS

Night Stops
- **Interior Lights On**: Helps the officer see inside, reassuring them you're not up to mischief.
- **Listen for Instructions**: Some officers prefer you to keep your hands on the wheel until they approach.

Isolated Areas
- **Hazards & Lower Speed**: If you feel uneasy, slow down, flash hazards, and drive to a populated, well-lit spot.
- **Call 911**: If you suspect it's not a legitimate officer, confirm with dispatch.

If You Have Passengers
- **Remind Them**: Stay quiet and keep hands visible. No sudden moves, no rummaging for gum or phone at the wrong moment. Keep the atmosphere calm.
- **Kids or Pets**: If they're restless, politely explain to the officer if you need extra time.

Common Mistake: Trying to Argue or Drive Off
Don't. Either action worsens the situation—stay put, stay polite, let the process run its course.

AFTER THE STOP: NEXT STEPS

If You Get a Warning
- **Whew!**: A verbal or written warning means no ticket—learn from it, though. You might not be so lucky next time.

If You Get a Ticket
- **Court or Payment**: The citation has details. Pay by the due date or appear in court to contest it.
- **Insurance Impact**: Tickets can raise premiums—drive safer to avoid repeats.

If You're Arrested
- **Stay Composed**: Don't resist. You'll have your day in court if needed.
- **Call Legal Help**: Once in custody, you can exercise your right to an attorney.

Common Mistake: Ignoring the Ticket
Skipping payments or court dates can escalate fines or lead to a license suspension. Don't procrastinate.

Pro Tip: Officer Safety
Officers don't know your story—small gestures to ease their concerns (like turning on cabin lights) can foster a smoother interaction.

Being stopped by the police can rattle anyone, but it doesn't have to be a disaster. **Pull over safely**, **show respect**, **know your rights**, and if you do end up with a citation, handle it responsibly. The best way to avoid stops? **Follow the rules**—simple but effective. If that's not feasible (hey, mistakes happen), then at least show you're a courteous, level-headed driver who's willing to learn. After all, it's better to drive away with a warning than ride away in the back of a patrol car.

54. NOT JUST YOU OUT THERE: DRIVING WITH EVERYONE ELSE IN MIND

Ever feel like you own the road? Guess what—**you don't**. It's shared real estate: drivers, cyclists, pedestrians, electric scooters, delivery vans, garbage trucks, and more, all have a stake. Your job is to give everyone space to breathe and time to move. In this chapter, we'll explore how to **recognize and respect** each type of road user, ensure you're **not hogging** the space, and keep the traffic flow peaceful rather than a chaotic, selfish madness.

WHY SHARING THE ROAD MATTERS

Safety & Harmony
- **Fewer Collisions**: When you account for cyclists, e-scooters, and pedestrians, you're less likely to crash into them.
- **Legal Obligations**: Many regions have laws granting right-of-way to pedestrians, specifying safe distances for passing bikes, etc.

The "Shellfish" Mentality
- **Rushing & Resentment**: Acting like the road is yours alone often triggers honking, near-misses, or worse.
- **Attentive Drivers**: A quick mirror check or yield prevents potential accidents and fosters a friendlier commute.

Common Mistake: Seeing Others as Obstacles
People out there—on bikes, in cars, or walking—aren't annoyances. Treat them as fellow travelers, not traffic cones.

RESPECTING PEDESTRIANS

Right-of-Way at Crosswalks
- **Slow & Scan**: Pedestrians have priority at crosswalks, even if they move slowly or wander mid-block.
- **School Zones**: Extra caution—kids might dart into the street without checking.

Spotting Joggers & Kids
- **Between Parked Cars**: Stay alert for pedestrians unexpectedly stepping into the road, especially in bustling city areas.

- **Night Visibility**: Pedestrians in dark clothing can be hard to see—keep your headlights and focus sharp.

Pro Tip: Eye Contact
Making eye contact with a pedestrian clarifies intentions and helps avoid confusion about who moves first.

BIKES & E-SCOOTERS

Safe Passing Distance
- **Give Them Room**: Some areas require at least three feet; others specify more. Move over safely rather than zooming by, inches away.
- **Don't Crowd**: Even if a cyclist or scooter user is slow, riding their tail is risky. If traffic allows, pass carefully.

Unpredictable Moves
- **Two-Wheel Instability**: A cyclist might swerve to avoid a pothole; e-scooters may turn abruptly. Watch for sudden moves.
- **Lane Sharing**: If local laws allow bikes to ride in full lanes, respect that—no honking or nudging them to the curb.

Common Mistake: Honking to Speed Them Up
It startles and endangers them. A calm, wide pass is safer than blasting your horn for a quick fix.

Pro Tip: Always Look Both Ways
While turning from a side road, it's natural to focus on traffic from your left. Still, make a quick check to the right—bicycles or pedestrians could be crossing just as you pull out.

MOTORCYCLES & BIGGER WHEELS

Motorcycles & Their Hidden Spots
- **Small Profile**: They vanish in side or rear mirrors easily—double-check before lane changes or turns.
- **Don't Assume**: Motorcycles can accelerate quickly or slow abruptly. Give them a little extra cushion.

Large Vehicles (Trucks, Buses, etc.)
- **Wide Turns & Blind Spots**: Trucks need more turning radius; never hang out alongside their trailer.

- **Stopping Distance**: Heavy vehicles can't brake on a dime—avoid cutting them off.
- **Give 'Em Room**: If a bus or truck signals, let them merge without drama.

Pro Tip: Pass Swiftly, Not Aggressively
For big rigs or motorcycles, spend as little time as possible in their blind spots—accelerate past safely (without tailgating first).

STOPPED VEHICLES & DELIVERY VANS

Stopped Vehicles on the Highway Shoulders
- **Unpredictable Circumstances:** Drivers might be handling an emergency, phone call, or flat tire, so anticipate someone stepping out or opening a door.
- **Move over:** Shift lanes if possible, or slow down to pass safely – passing too closely at highway speeds puts both you and the stopped driver at risk.

Delivery & Garbage Trucks
- **Frequent Stops**: They stop often, sometimes double-parking or in awkward spots.
- **Pass With Care**: Check for oncoming traffic or someone stepping out from behind the truck.

Livery Cars & Taxis
- **Sudden Pullovers**: Rideshare drivers might swerve to pick up or drop off passengers.
- **Door Danger**: Watch for passengers flinging doors open into traffic.

Electric Scooters & Mopeds (in the Bike Lane)
- **Unexpected Moves**: E-scooters might hop onto sidewalks or crosswalks unpredictably.
- **Overtake Gently**: If they're in a shared lane, a quick swerve to pass can be hazardous—plan your pass with turn signals and mirror checks.

Common Mistake: Whipping Around a Parked Van
Delivery drivers might step out any second—take an extra second to be sure no one's popping out into your path.

Pro Tip: Passing Stopped Delivery Vans
Keep in mind that oncoming traffic has the right of way—wait behind the stopped delivery van until it's safe to pass. Keep an eye on the driver— they could be stepping out of the van or just getting back in.

BUSES & SCHOOL ZONES

Stopping for School Buses
- **Flashing Red Lights**: You must stop—kids might be crossing. Wait until the bus moves or lights stop flashing.
- **No Passing**: Passing a school bus with flashing red lights, whether from behind or the opposite lane, is illegal. Be alert for flashing amber lights as well—they signal that the bus is about to stop.

Transit Buses
- **Merging After Stops**: If a city bus signals to merge from a stop, slow or yield to let it back into the traffic flow.
- **Keep Patience**: They might pause longer to pick up passengers, but it's the law to let them do so safely. So stay patient if you find yourself waiting behind a stopped bus.

Pro Tip: Think of the Kids
Any area near a bus with flashing lights is a kids' zone—stay vigilant and respect the bus signals to protect them.

EMERGENCY VEHICLES

Yield & Pull Over
- **Immediate Response**: Sirens or flashing lights behind you mean move aside to let them pass—no hesitation.
- **No Tag-Along**: Don't follow closely for a "free lane" advantage. That's illegal and dangerous.

Let Them Do Their Job
- **Intersections**: If an ambulance or fire truck approaches, stop even on green if it helps them through.
- **Awareness**: Check mirrors regularly—you might hear the sirens before seeing the vehicle.

Common Mistake: Freeway Confusion
On highways, carefully move to the right lanes, slow or stop if necessary—but don't slam your brakes abruptly when you see flashing lights behind you.

DRIVING IN CONSTRUCTION AREAS

Expect Delays & Lane Shifts
- **Reduced Lanes**: Construction zones often squeeze traffic into fewer lanes or shift them unexpectedly. Stay alert for signs and cones.
- **Sudden Slowdowns**: Be ready for abrupt stops as vehicles merge or workers step near the roadway.
- **Stay Alert**: In both city streets and highways under construction, watch for temporary markers, lane dividers, and workers directing traffic.

Respect Workers & Reduced Speeds
- **Safety First**: Speed limits can drop significantly in work zones; slow down to protect roadside crews and yourself.
- **Fines & Penalties**: Many regions impose doubled or tripled fines for violations in construction areas.
- **Cooperation**: Yield to any flaggers or official signals; they're coordinating traffic flow to prevent chaos and collisions.

DEFENSIVE DRIVING & COURTESY

Anticipate Mistakes
- **People Are Unpredictable**: Bikers might swerve, pedestrians might jaywalk—always be ready.
- **Scanning**: A quick left-right mirror glance helps you see e-scooters or a cyclist creeping up.

Model Good Behavior
- **Friendly Waves**: A quick thanks or apology wave can defuse tension if you must edge around a cyclist or pass a slow walker.
- **"After You" Mindset**: Taking a few seconds to yield won't disrupt your day, but it could keep someone else safe.

Pro Tip: Smile and Nod
A simple acknowledgment can create mutual respect, turning the road into a shared space rather than a battleground.

LOCAL LAWS & VARIATIONS

Cycling Lanes & Scooters
- **No Driving in Bike Lanes**: It's illegal and endangers cyclists or e-scooter riders. Some places have distinct scooter lanes, too.

- **Shared vs. Protected Lanes**: Know the difference—protected lanes often have physical barriers, and crossing them can land you fines.

Pedestrian Priority
- **Right-of-Way**: In many areas, pedestrians have the right of way at crosswalks—even unmarked ones.
- **Jaywalking Laws**: Some places penalize pedestrians crossing mid-block, but that's not an excuse to ignore them with your car.

Common Mistake: Assuming Universal Rules
Laws can vary drastically. If you travel across states, do a quick check of local road-sharing regulations.

Pro Tip: Treat Others How You'd Want to Be Treated
If you were on a bike or scooter, you'd appreciate drivers being cautious. Let that empathy guide your actions.

Sharing the road is more than just a slogan—it's a mindset that keeps everyone safer. By **giving space** to pedestrians, cyclists, e-scooters, and other vehicles (big and small), you're showing courtesy while reducing your risk of collisions or conflicts. And yes, it might mean waiting an extra second behind a bus or gently passing a wobbly cyclist. But that brief patience is worth far more than the hassle of an accident or a confrontation. So be a courteous and responsible road user: **wave politely, maintain safe distances,** and let everyone navigate the roads safely.

55. SO YOU CRASHED: WHAT TO DO AFTER AN ACCIDENT

You're cruising down the road, maybe tapping along to your favorite song, when **CRUNCH**—it happens. Whether it's a fender-bender or a more serious smash, being in an accident can feel surreal and terrifying. But it doesn't have to be pure chaos. A calm, **step-by-step** approach helps keep everyone safe, clarify details for insurance, and get you back on the road faster. This chapter tackles everything from **immediate safety checks** to **collecting evidence** and **coping with those post-crash jitters**.

IMMEDIATE SAFETY CHECKS

Stop & Assess
- **Don't Drive Off**: Fleeing the scene isn't just unethical—it's also illegal.
- **Hazards On**: Flip those emergency flashers to alert oncoming drivers.
- **Scan for Injuries**: Check if you or your passengers are hurt. If so, call **911** straight away.

Move to a Safe Spot
- **Shoulder Time**: If possible, carefully move your car out of traffic flow—avoid backing into lanes blindly, though.
- **Stay Visible**: If it's dark or foggy, find a well-lit area or set up reflective triangles if you have them.

Common Mistake: Arguing on the Road
Heated debates or blame-shifting can wait. First priority: make sure no one else piles into your stationary vehicle.

SECURING THE SCENE

Prevent Further Collisions
- **Flares or Triangles**: A minute spent placing them behind your car can prevent secondary crashes.
- **Keep Yourself Safe**: Don't stand in the middle of the road waving arms. Instead, direct traffic from a safe distance if absolutely needed.

Stay Calm
- **Check Emotions**: Adrenaline spikes after an accident—breathe, keep your voice steady, and focus on tasks.
- **No Panic**: Even if damage looks severe, handle each step methodically.

Pro Tip: Steady Yourself
A few deep breaths help you think straight—especially vital if you need to call for help or coordinate with others quickly.

CHECKING FOR INJURIES & OFFERING AID

Look After Yourself & Passengers
- **Any Pain?**: Even if no one's bleeding, watch for dizziness or shock. Some injuries show up as "I'm just sore" initially.
- **Call 911 if Uncertain**: Better safe than sorry. EMS can evaluate everyone properly.

Helping Others
- **Within Your Skill Level**: If another driver or passenger is hurt, call **911**. Provide basic first aid only if you know how—moving someone with a neck injury can worsen it.
- **Clear the Danger Zone**: If cars are in a risky spot (like a blind curve), try to move them or wait in a safer area until help arrives.

Common Mistake: Self-Diagnosing Injuries
You might think you're fine, but some neck/back issues appear hours later. Seek medical advice if you're in doubt.

CONTACTING AUTHORITIES & INSURANCE

When to Call the Police
- **Injuries or Major Damage**: Most places require a police report if anyone's hurt or property damage is beyond a certain dollar amount.
- **Disputed Fault**: Having an officer's official notes can protect you if stories differ later.

Insurance Notifications
- **Report Promptly**: Some insurers want to know within 24 hours.
- **Honest Info**: Provide accurate details, but don't guess if you're unsure—say "I'm not certain."

If police arrive, note their badge number and any report number. This info helps your insurance or lawyer track the case.

EXCHANGING INFORMATION

Drivers Involved
- **Names, Numbers, Plates**: Collect the other driver's full name, phone, license plate, driver's license details, and insurance info.
- **Stay Civil**: Even if the other driver is upset, calmly gather details. Resist arguments—they won't fix your bumper.

Witnesses
- **Bystanders or Passengers**: Grab their contact info, too. Third-party accounts can be crucial if there's a dispute.
- **Business Cards**: If a local store owner or resident saw it, ask for a quick note or phone number.

Common Mistake: Forgetting to Record the Scene
Don't rely on memory alone. People can change their story—photos and witness details keep facts straight.

EVIDENCE COLLECTION

Photos & Videos
- **Snap Damage**: Capture all angles of vehicles, license plates, street signs, skid marks, and road conditions.
- **Environment**: Road layout, lighting, weather—for example, was it raining or was the intersection under construction?

Notes on Details
- **Time & Location**: The date, time, intersection or highway mile marker.
- **Initial Impressions**: Any offhand comments from the other driver like "I didn't see you" or "My brakes failed" can be telling.

Pro Tip: Use Your Phone's Voice Notes
If writing is tough amid stress, record a quick voice memo about what happened—fresh details now beat fuzzy recalls later.

Pro Tip: Better Prepared Than Sorry
Keep an accident checklist in your glove box—simple reminders for a stressful moment can save you from confusion.

DEALING WITH EMOTIONS & NEXT STEPS

Shock & Stress
- **Adrenaline Crash**: After everything settles, you might feel shaky, upset, or even tearful—that's normal.
- **Talk It Out**: Friends, family, or a counselor can help process the scare if you feel anxious about driving again.

Follow-Up Actions
- **Keep Receipts**: Towing bills, repairs, medical expenses—document them for insurance claims.
- **Insurance Claim**: An adjuster may inspect the car; be available and honest about what transpired.

Common Mistake: Skipping a Medical Check
Some injuries surface days later. If you feel odd or in pain, see a doctor.

POTENTIAL LEGAL & MEDICAL CONSIDERATIONS

Ongoing Injuries
- **Delayed Pain**: Soft tissue injuries might develop soreness after you "feel fine" initially.
- **Doctor's Records**: If you suspect an injury, a medical paper trail helps if an insurance or legal dispute arises.

Liability & Legal Advice
- **Major Damage or Disputed Fault**: Consider consulting an attorney—especially if big claims or lawsuits loom.
- **Watch Your Statements**: Don't admit fault prematurely. Let the investigation decide. Sometimes multiple factors are at play.

Pro Tip: Be Careful on Social Media
Posting "I'm fine" after an accident could complicate claims if you develop symptoms later. Stick to official reports and direct communication with insurers or lawyers.

Accidents can rattle the calmest driver—but with a methodical approach, **life can go on** with minimal hassle. Prioritizing safety (yours and others'), **documenting the scene**, and **following up properly** sets you up for a smoother recovery—whether it's from a slight fender-bender or a bigger crash. Emotions may run high, but staying level-headed helps you handle immediate threats, gather crucial info, and navigate insurance or legal steps.

PART IV:

SOME ADVICE FOR THE ROAD

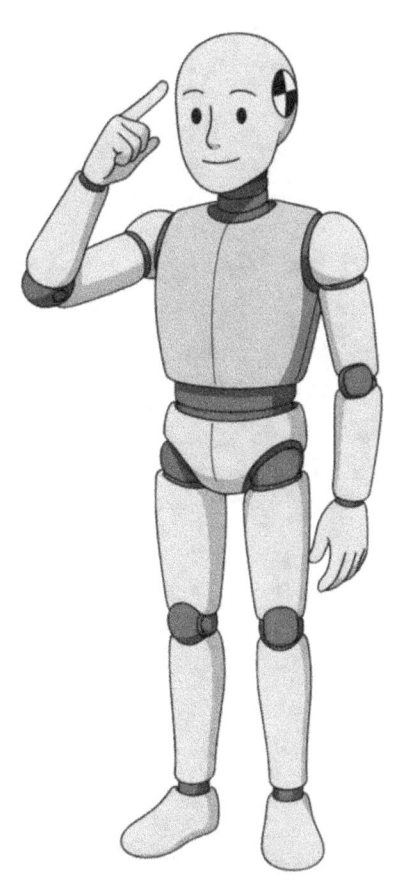

56. FIRST AID KITS:
WHAT TO KEEP IN YOUR CAR AND WHY

Picture this: You're on a road trip, someone nicks a finger or takes a tumble. It's no hospital-level emergency, but you suddenly notice—you don't have a single bandage in the car. That's when you realize how handy a **well-stocked first aid kit** could be. An **emergency first aid kit** is like having a dependable friend riding along—a friend you hope you never truly need. But when trouble strikes, you'll be thanking yourself you packed it. In this chapter, we'll explore **what to include in your kit**, **how to store it**, and **how to use it effectively**—even if your biggest medical skill is slapping on a Band-Aid.

WHY AN EMERGENCY FIRST AID KIT MATTERS

Immediate Response, Less Panic
- **Accidents Happen**: A passenger cuts themselves on a seatbelt buckle or you scrape your arm while changing a tire—it's easier to treat quickly if you have the right supplies.
- **Peace of Mind**: Just knowing you're prepared keeps stress lower during minor road mishaps.

Beyond Big Emergencies
- **Minor Fixes**: Splinters, blisters, or a mildly twisted ankle don't always need the ER, but do need some TLC.
- **Complement Your Other Prep**: A first aid kit pairs beautifully with your roadside emergency gear (jack, flashlight, jumper cables, etc.).

Pro Tip: A Little Preparedness Goes a Long Way
Just a few basic supplies and know-how can save precious minutes—and a lot of worry—until professional help arrives.

WHAT TO INCLUDE IN A BASIC KIT

Bandages & Gauze
- **Variety Matters**: Different sizes for small cuts or deeper wounds.
- **Adhesive Tape**: For securing gauze—and tackling quick fixes when needed.

Antiseptics
- **Alcohol Wipes**: Quick disinfectant for minor scrapes.
- **Antibiotic Ointment**: Keeps cuts from getting infected.

Gloves & CPR Mask
- **Disposable Gloves**: Essential for hygiene when assisting someone else's injury.
- **Breathing Barrier**: A face shield or CPR mask if you end up needing to give life-saving breaths.

Pain Relievers & Basic Meds
- **OTC Painkillers**: Like ibuprofen or acetaminophen—nothing too fancy, just enough to tide someone over.
- **Allergy Meds**: An antihistamine can be crucial if a passenger gets stung or reacts badly to pollen on a scenic route.

Pro Tip: Customize It

If you have specific health concerns—like migraines or mild asthma—add relevant meds. Keep them labeled and within their expiration dates.

OPTIONAL (BUT HANDY) EXTRAS

Scissors & Tweezers
- **Tiny Yet Mighty**: Perfect for trimming gauze or pulling out splinters/glass shards.
- **Rounded Tips**: Some kits use child-safe scissors to reduce accidental stabs.

Thermal Blanket & Eye Wash
- **Thermal Blanket**: Prevents shock and mild hypothermia.
- **Eye Wash**: A simple saline solution can clear dust, debris, or chemicals (like spilled battery acid in a worst-case scenario).

Personal Comfort Items
- **Contact Lens Backup**: If you wear lenses, a small kit can be priceless if one tears.
- **Inhalers or EpiPens**: If you or frequent passengers have severe allergies or asthma, keep spares in the kit.

Common Mistake: Overstuffing

Unless you're a trained medic, you don't need advanced equipment you don't know how to use. Keep it practical.

PROPER STORAGE & MAINTENANCE

Container Choice
- **Sturdy & Labeled**: A small plastic box or zippered pouch that won't pop open if tossed around.
- **Water-Resistant**: Helps keep bandages and meds dry. Some folks use a waterproof container for extra protection.

Checking Expirations
- **Rotate Stock**: Antibiotic ointments, pain relievers, and antiseptic wipes can expire—mark calendar reminders to replace them.
- **No Mystery Meds**: Don't let pills run loose without labeling; you don't want guesswork in an emergency.

Easy Accessibility
- **Not Buried Under Stuff**: If you have to dig past suitcases, it defeats the purpose. Keep it in the trunk corner or a reachable side compartment.
- **Glove Box Limitations**: If space is tight there, make sure at least a few bandages are in easy reach.

Common Mistake: Using Items and Not Replacing
If you use up the bandages or ointment once, restock promptly—or you'll be empty-handed next time.

BASIC USAGE & TRAINING

Familiarize Yourself
- **Know the Basics**: How to wrap a wound, apply pressure to stop bleeding, use antiseptic wipes, etc.
- **CPR Mask Knowledge**: If you carry one, watch a quick tutorial on correct usage.

Consider First Aid Training
- **Short Courses**: Many community centers offer half-day classes teaching bandaging, CPR, and more.
- **Stay Within Skills**: Don't try advanced procedures you're not trained for. If injuries are serious, call 911 instead of playing doctor.

Pro Tip: Confidence Matters
A little knowledge and calm can turn a scary moment into a manageable blip until pros arrive.

LEGAL CONSIDERATIONS & GOOD SAMARITAN LAWS

Protection for Helpers
- **Good Samaritan Laws**: Often protect well-intentioned responders from lawsuits if they act within reasonable limits.
- **Act in Good Faith**: As long as you're genuinely trying to help, you're typically shielded from legal blame for outcomes you can't control.

Know When to Call Professionals
- **Serious Injuries**: Broken bones, major bleeding, unconsciousness—call 911 right away.
- **Don't Replace EMTs**: Even with a kit, professionals have the training and tools for major trauma.

Common Mistake: Overconfidence
Attempting advanced care you're not trained for can do more harm than good—stabilize the situation and let medical experts handle the rest.

INTEGRATION WITH CAR EMERGENCY SUPPLIES

Pair It with Other Tools
- **Flashlight & Reflective Triangles**: A well-lit environment helps you see wounds and prevent further accidents.
- **Jumper Cables & Basic Toolkit**: Rounding out your trunk stash means you're ready for mechanical and medical mishaps alike.

Climate Considerations
- **Cold Weather**: Adding hand warmers or extra blankets can be a lifesaver in winter.
- **Hot Regions**: Be mindful that extreme heat can degrade medications faster—check expiration more often.

Pro Tip: One-Stop Bag
Some drivers combine everything—first aid kit, flares, essential tools— into a single bag or box for ultimate convenience.

COMMON MISTAKES & TIPS

Forgetting Personal Needs
- **Allergies & Chronic Conditions**: If you or family members have them, keep spare EpiPens, inhalers, or relevant meds.

- **Kids' Items**: Children's versions of pain relievers or bandages might be necessary if you have little passengers often.

Neglecting to Restock
- **Refill After Use**: If you used up all the gauze, don't wait until the next cut to realize you're out.
- **Mark Down Replacements**: If an ointment is close to expiry, set a phone reminder—nobody wants a half-crusty antibiotic tube in an emergency.

Overpacking the Irrelevant
- **Stick to Essentials**: If you're not qualified to use advanced medical supplies (like IV kits), keep them out. They add clutter and confusion.

Pro Tip: Throw in a Small Guide
A mini first aid booklet can help you recall steps under stress. Some kits include it; if not, print one off.

Common Mistake: Thinking "It Won't Happen to Me"
Emergencies are unpredictable by nature, but a well-stocked kit and a steady mindset help you stay prepared.

Accidents or injuries can strike anytime, often where paramedics aren't immediately available. Having a **friend in need**—a first aid kit—by your side ensures you're not scrambling for tissues to patch a bleeding cut. By **stocking sensible items**, **maintaining them**, and **knowing how to use them**, you transform minor roadside mishaps into manageable hiccups. It's one of those car essentials you hope never to use, but when you do, you'll be darn glad it's there.

57. DEFENSIVE DRIVING:
OUTSMARTING DANGER BEFORE IT STRIKES

Ever find yourself gripping the steering wheel and thinking, "If that guy doesn't move over, I'm toast"? **Preventive driving**—or **defensive driving**—is all about staying ahead of trouble, not reacting to it last-minute. By anticipating sudden stops, swerves, and surprises, you keep control of the situation instead of becoming part of the chaos. In this chapter, we'll dive into the mindset of a driver who **spots problems before** they unfold—whether it's reading traffic patterns, adjusting for weather, or navigating tricky merges. Ready to sharpen those psychic driving senses?

WHAT IS PREVENTIVE (DEFENSIVE) DRIVING?

The "Look & Think Ahead" Mindset
- **Seeing Beyond the Bumper**: Don't just trail the car ahead—peek further up the road for braking lights, merging chaos, or any sign of trouble.
- **Assuming the Unexpected**: Even if the car in front has a turn signal on, are they turning at the next street or the one after that? Always have a "what if they brake suddenly?" backup plan.

The Benefits
- **Reduced Collisions**: By acting early, you avoid last-second panic stops or swerves.
- **Less Stress**: You'll be calmer when you feel in control, prepared for unexpected events.

Common Mistake: Driving on "Autopilot"
Zoning out or just following the herd invites surprises. Keep your brain engaged, scanning for changes that could force you to act quickly.

WHY HAVING A "PLAN B" MATTERS

Escape Routes
- **Side Lanes & Shoulders**: Mentally note if the lane to your left or right is open enough to swerve if the driver ahead slams on brakes.
- **Safe Distances**: If you keep a decent following gap, you'll have time to maneuver without rear-ending someone else.

Turning Near-Misses into Non-Issues
- **Early Action**: Spot a driver texting and drifting? Switch lanes before it becomes a close call.
- **Minimizing Surprises**: Proactive moves beat reactive panic. If you wait to see how events unfold, it might be too late.

Pro Tip: Always Ask, "What If?"
If the car ahead stops short or if someone merges unexpectedly, how would you react? Picturing scenarios helps keep reflexes sharp.

KEY ELEMENTS OF PREVENTIVE DRIVING

Safe Following Distance
- **3-Second Rule**: In normal weather, choose a landmark (like a sign) and ensure three seconds pass before you reach it once the car ahead passes it.
- **Weather Adjustments**: In rain, fog, or snow, double it—slippery surfaces demand extra buffer.

Proper Speed Control
- **Match Conditions**: Doing the speed limit isn't always enough. Heavy traffic or poor visibility might need a safer, slower pace.
- **No "Fast Lane" Ego**: If everyone's crawling in a blizzard, a speedster is just begging for trouble. Move over and let them pass.

Lane Positioning
- **"Clean Sight Lines"**: If a giant truck blocks your view, shift slightly to see around it or change lanes if safe.
- **Avoid Blind Spots**: Stay out of zones where bigger vehicles can't see you. Communicate with signals and pass quickly.

Common Mistake: Tailgating = Zero Time to React
Even if you're alert, being too close means no space to brake if the driver ahead stops abruptly.

ADJUSTING FOR CONDITIONS

Weather & Visibility
- **Rain & Fog**: Double your scanning, use low beams in fog (high beams create glare), and maintain a bigger following gap.
- **Snow & Ice**: Slow down more than your gut suggests. Black ice can lurk, and your Plan B might be coasting gently or shifting lanes early.

Night Driving
- **High Beam Savvy**: Use them on dark roads, but dim for oncoming traffic. Don't blind others—friendly road-sharing is part of being a preventive driver.
- **Reflective Hazards**: Look for glints from signs or animal eyes— wildlife can hop out unpredictably.

Pro Tip: Resist Overconfidence
Weather is the ultimate equalizer. Even the best drivers can slide if they push too hard on wet or icy roads. Ease up, keep extra space, and stay in control.

ANTICIPATING OTHER DRIVERS' MISTAKES

Watch for Clues
- **Inconsistent Speeds**: A driver repeatedly speeding up, slowing down, or drifting might be distracted. Plan your pass or create a gap.
- **Turn Signal Confusion**: Some leave signals on forever, others never use them. Don't trust the blinker blindly— observe the car's movement and wheel direction for true intent.

Intersections & Traffic Lights
- **Left-Right-Left**: Even with a green light, check for potential red-light runners.
- **Rolling Stops**: Some folks barely pause at stop signs—be ready for that "they won't fully stop" scenario.

Common Mistake: Assuming Everyone Follows the Rules
Defensive drivers accept that rules get broken. Expect it, and you'll rarely be caught off guard.

INTERSECTION & LANE MERGE STRATEGIES

Head on a Swivel
- **Mirrors & Quick Glances**: Merging traffic can pop from on-ramps at highway speeds. Monitor behind and to the sides.
- **Signal Early**: Communicate your merges or lane changes so others can adapt (or not, but at least you did your part).

Merge Courtesy
- **Space & Timing**: If you see someone merging, adjust speed or lane to reduce conflict.

- **Zipper Method**: Where lanes narrow, letting cars alternate merges can keep traffic flowing—no fights needed.

HANDLING UNPREDICTABLE MOMENTS

Sudden Stops & Debris
- **Keep a Plan B Lane**: A quick flick to the shoulder might spare you from slamming into a stalled car.
- **Scanning Far**: See a brake-light wave up ahead? Start slowing early to avoid a chain-reaction.
- **Stopped Highway Traffic**: If heavy traffic forces a sudden stop on the highway, briefly turn on your hazards. This alerts drivers behind you to slow down or change lanes in time. Give yourself a generous gap between you and the stopped traffic ahead as you slow down, and keep an eye on the cars behind you to ensure they're slowing too.

Swerving Hazards
- **Calm Steering**: If debris or an obstacle appears, a gentle swerve is safer than jerking the wheel, which can lead to losing control.
- **Avoid Overreaction**: Sometimes braking is enough. Decide fast but keep your movements measured.

Common Mistake: Slamming Brakes Without Checking Mirrors
A rear-end collision might happen if you panic-stop and the tailgater behind can't react. Evaluate if it's safer to swerve.

IPDE FRAMEWORK

Identify
- **Observe Your Surroundings**: Scan the road for changes—like a driver inching into your lane or brake lights flickering ahead. Recognize potential hazards early.

Predict
- **Project Possible Outcomes**: If a car is drifting, predict they might swerve or stop abruptly. Consider how weather, traffic flow, or a sudden lane closure might affect your next move.

Decide
- **Choose Your Action**: Once you anticipate a hazard, decide on the safest strategy—brake gently, switch lanes, or reduce speed.

Execute
- **Carry Out Smoothly**: Follow through promptly and cleanly. A calm, well-timed move is safer than a last-second yank on the wheel.

CONSISTENCY & COURTESY

Clear Communication
- **Signals Matter**: Turn them on at least 3 seconds before a lane change or turn—others can't guess your plan.
- **Brake Lights**: Tapping brakes slightly before a big slow-down warns drivers behind to prepare.

No Abrupt Moves
- **Smooth Lane Changes**: Drifting gently and signaling well is a hallmark of a safe driver.
- **Avoid Surprise**: If you do see you're about to miss an exit, it's often safer to go to the next one than yank the wheel dangerously.

Pro Tip: Polite Gestures
A small wave when someone lets you in or a quick courtesy flash of hazards can defuse tension. Good vibes help all parties.

COMMON MISTAKES & TIPS

Tunnel Vision
- **Focusing on One Car**: Keep scanning the entire field—left, right, and far ahead.
- **Ignoring Side Lanes**: A car from a side road could jump in or a motorcycle could come up in your blind spot.

Overconfidence
- **"I'm Good Enough to Handle Anything"**: That pride can blind you to sudden hazards. Stay humble, keep scanning.
- **Fatigue & Boredom**: Long drives breed complacency—switch up the music or take breaks to remain sharp.

Continual "What-If" Drills
- **Practice Scenario Thinking**: "If this car stops abruptly, can I switch lanes or do I brake?" This mental game hones reaction speed.
- **Celebrate Mini-Victories**: Each time you avoid a near-miss through a good Plan B, it's proof you're doing it right.

Pro Tip: Defensive Doesn't Mean Paranoid
It's about readiness, not fear. Staying observant is your best defense on the road.

Preventive driving is about **staying one move ahead**, seeing the road as an ever-changing puzzle. By keeping safe gaps, scanning for potential hazards, and always formulating a Plan B (or even C), you dodge accidents others might bumble into. From slippery roads to reckless drivers, anticipating trouble means you rarely get blindsided. You'll find your drives calmer, your near-misses fewer, and your confidence in handling the unpredictable far higher. So adopt the "preventive driver" mindset—**it's like having a superpower** that transforms chaos into calm escapes.

58. SMART CARS, DUMB MISTAKES: WHAT TO TRUST AND WHAT TO WATCH

Ever had your car gently steer you back into the lane or slow down because it "saw" traffic up ahead? That's not wizardry—it's the rising world of **driver assist technologies**. From basic features like **adaptive cruise control** to autonomous systems that let you take hands off the wheel, we're edging closer to science fiction every day. But as you'll see, this tech still has limits, quirks, and a few legal question marks. Let's explore how your car can practically drive itself, while you're still the boss.

WHAT ARE SELF-DRIVING CARS & DRIVER ASSIST SYSTEMS

Levels of Autonomy

- **From Hands-On to Hands-Off**: Levels range from minimal assistance (like standard cruise control) to higher levels where the car can handle steering, braking, and more. True "no driver needed" autonomy (Level 5) isn't on public roads yet, but we're inching there.
- **Adaptive vs. Autonomous**: Many new cars feature advanced driver assistance systems (ADAS) to reduce driver workload—**not** to replace the driver entirely.

Today's Reality

- **Human Oversight Still Required**: Even the coolest "self-driving" systems on the market ask you to keep your hands on (or near) the wheel and eyes forward.
- **Caution**: Some owners get too comfortable, leading to fiascos when the tech misreads road lines or fails to react to an obstacle.

Common Mistake: Assuming "Auto" Means Hands-Free
In mainstream cars, "semi-autonomous" is marketing lingo—be ready to step in if the system gets confused.

COMMON DRIVER ASSIST FEATURES

Adaptive Cruise Control (ACC)

- **Following Distance**: Adjusts your speed automatically to maintain a set gap behind the car ahead, perfect for highway commutes.

- **Watch for Surprise Stops**: Some systems might hesitate if a lead vehicle slows suddenly or if traffic merges unexpectedly.

Lane Keep Assist (LKA)
- **Gentle Corrections**: Cameras detect lane markings, nudging you back if you drift. Great for drowsy or distracted moments, but not an excuse to ignore the wheel.
- **Don't Rely Blindly**: Faded lines or weird weather can baffle the system—stay alert.

Automatic Emergency Braking (AEB)
- **Life Saver**: If the car senses a looming collision and you don't brake, it'll hit the brakes for you—can prevent or lessen crashes.
- **False Alarms?**: Sometimes the car overreacts to a parked vehicle, bush, or even shadows, so keep your foot ready to override if needed.

Blind Spot Monitoring
- **Indicator Lights**: Small signals on mirrors or the dash let you know someone's lurking where you can't see.
- **Still Shoulder Check**: Technology helps, but never skip that quick glance—hardware can fail or get blocked.

Pro Tip: Treat Them Like Assistants
ADAS is your co-pilot, not your chauffeur. Use them wisely but remain the captain of your ride.

HOW THEY WORK (SIMPLIFIED)

Sensors & Cameras
- **Radar & Lidar**: Measures distance and speed of nearby objects.
- **Ultrasonic**: Short-range detection (like for park assist).
- **Cameras Everywhere**: They keep an eye on lane lines, signs, and potential hazards.

Data Processing & AI
- **Brains of the Operation**: Complex algorithms interpret sensor input, deciding when to brake, steer, or warn you.
- **Constant Updates**: Some systems learn through software improvements—your car might get "smarter" over time with updates.

Car Commands
- **Actuation**: Once the car's logic decides to accelerate, steer, or brake, it sends signals to the respective mechanicals—like invisible puppeteer strings.

Common Mistake: Believing They're Infallible
Sensors can get obstructed (snow, mud) or misread complicated situations. Double-check cameras or rely on your eyes in messy conditions.

BENEFITS & LIMITATIONS

Pros
- **Reduced Collisions**: Human error is a leading cause of crashes— if the car can spot danger earlier, that's fewer accidents.
- **Less Driver Fatigue**: Adaptive cruise and lane assist can ease monotony on long highway treks.
- **Smoother Commutes**: No more "speed up, slow down" jostling; instead, the car can keep consistent spacing.

Cons
- **Complacency**: The better systems get, the more some drivers zone out. Incidents happen when the car can't handle a sudden event.
- **Sensor Struggles**: Heavy snow, poorly painted roads, or bright sunlight can throw off cameras and radar.
- **Regulations Lag**: Laws around usage vary, and reliability testing is ongoing.

Pro Tip: Stay Engaged
Think of it like an airplane autopilot—pilot must stay awake and ready to seize control if something goes wrong.

LEGAL, ETHICAL & LIABILITY ISSUES

Changing Regulations
- **Each Region Differs**: Some places allow advanced self-driving tests on public roads, others are cautious.
- **Driver vs. Manufacturer**: In a crash, is it the system's fault or the human who should've intervened? Courts are still figuring that out.

Insurance & Data
- **Higher Premiums?**: Some insurers see partial autonomy as risk-lowering, others worry about driver complacency.

- **Privacy Concerns**: Cars may log location, speed, and sensor data. Who owns it and how is it used?

Common Mistake: Assuming You're Off the Hook
Even with "auto" functions on, you can be legally responsible if you fail to supervise or react.

FUTURE OUTLOOK

Ongoing Advances
- **Better Sensors & AI**: LiDAR is getting cheaper, machine learning helps the car interpret complex city scenes.
- **Vehicle-to-Everything (V2X)**: Cars chatting with traffic lights, other vehicles, and road infrastructure to predict hazards or sync speed.

Common Mistake: Believing Self-Driving Is Here
True "Level 5 autonomy" that handles every scenario independently isn't yet on the consumer market—even if marketing claims say otherwise.

COMMON MISTAKES & TIPS

Neglecting the Road
- **Overtrust in Tech**: If you start binge-watching your phone, the car might fail to see a construction zone or bizarre obstacle in time.
- **Sudden Interventions**: The system may beep or disengage abruptly—be ready.

Overriding Too Late
- **Smooth Takeover**: If you must brake or steer suddenly, do so early. Jerking the wheel can confuse the system or cause a swerve.
- **Understand Your System**: Some cars have different beep patterns or dash icons for warnings—know them.

Stay in Control
- **Eyes Up**: Even if the system steers, you need to watch for anomalies.
- **Hands Close**: Keep a hand near the wheel—some systems have sensors verifying you're not going hands-free for too long.

Pro Tip: Treat It Like a Co-Pilot
Engage with your ADAS, but never trust it blindly. You're still the pilot in command, so don't kick back and snooze.

Pro Tip: Stay Updated

Software updates can refine your car's ADAS performance. Keep them current—just like your smartphone. You'll likely see small improvements that make a big difference.

Common Mistake: Forgetting You're Still Responsible

No matter how advanced the feature, if a crash occurs, you're still accountable unless laws explicitly say otherwise. Drive with caution, let the car assist, but never relinquish total control!

The world of self-driving cars and driver assists may feel **magical**, but it's firmly rooted in sensors, AI, and a dash of driver responsibility. These features can **reduce crashes, ease commute stress**, and potentially shape an autonomous future. But for now, **you** remain the ultimate decision-maker—staying watchful, adjusting for weather, and taking over whenever the car's logic stumbles. Embrace the convenience, but keep your hands (and mind) near the wheel. Technology can be your best road companion, but the bond only works if you stay attentive behind the scenes.

59. JUST IN CASE: SAFETY STUFF THAT'S WORTH THE TRUNK SPACE

You're cruising down a scenic highway, wind in your hair, music in your ears... then *bam*—a nail in your tire, or a sudden stall. In moments like these, having the right stuff in your car can turn a possible disaster into a mere detour. Think of it like packing a parachute you hope never to deploy – but if you do, you're really glad it's there! In this chapter, we'll explore the **essential safety gear** that can keep unexpected bumps in the road from derailing your day, plus **a few extras** that fit snugly in your trunk (or glove box) to help you handle breakdowns and minor mishaps like a total pro.

WHY CAR SAFETY ITEMS MATTER

Unexpected Emergencies
- **Flat Tires or Dead Batteries**: These can happen anywhere—highway shoulders, remote roads, or city streets—and having tools on hand prevents panic.
- **Peace of Mind**: You won't sweat the possibility of a breakdown when you know you're prepared.

Roadside Saviors
- **Self-Sufficiency**: You don't always need a tow truck if you can handle minor fixes yourself.
- **Less Stress**: Even if help is on the way, items like blankets or snacks keep you comfy while you wait.

Common Mistake: The "It Won't Happen to Me" Mindset
Sooner or later, everyone faces a hiccup. Don't let overconfidence leave you empty-handed when it does.

ESSENTIAL TOOLKIT ITEMS

Spare Tire & Tools
- **The Basics**: A **properly inflated spare**, plus a jack and lug wrench that fit your car's wheel nuts.
- **Check Periodically**: Spare tires can lose air over time; peek at it every few months to avoid a flat spare.

Jumper Cables or Battery Pack
- **Dead Batteries**: Whether you left the headlights on or winter killed your battery, a **jumper cable kit** can revive you.
- **Portable Battery Packs**: Some come with USB ports—bonus if your phone's also low.

Small Fire Extinguisher
- **Engine Bay or Electrical Fires**: Rare but can happen. A compact, **car-friendly extinguisher** can quickly snuff out a small flame.
- **Mounting Matters**: Store it securely so it doesn't roll around—some kits include brackets.

Pro Tip: Learn How to Use Them
Knowing how to change a tire or safely operate an extinguisher is crucial—YouTube tutorials or a quick lesson from a mechanic can help.

EMERGENCY SIGNALING & VISIBILITY

Reflective Triangles or Road Flares
- **Warn Oncoming Traffic**: Place them a short distance behind your car if you're stopped on the shoulder.
- **Night & Day**: Even in daylight, triangles help drivers see your disabled vehicle sooner.

High-Visibility Vest
- **Stay Seen**: If you must exit your car on a busy road or in poor lighting, wearing a reflective vest is safer than hoping drivers notice you.
- **Minimal Space**: They fold up small, so no big storage hassle.

Common Mistake: Relying on Hazard Lights Alone
Hazards help, but a physical warning device on the road gives approaching traffic more time to react.

BASIC REPAIR & MAINTENANCE SUPPLIES

Duct Tape & Zip Ties
- **Temporary Fixes**: From a dangling bumper to a loose hose, these can hold things in place long enough to reach a mechanic.
- **Universal MVPs**: They're lightweight yet invaluable for quick roadside rigging.

Multipurpose Tool
- **Compact Helper**: A small gadget with pliers, knife, and screwdrivers can resolve minor issues—like tightening a loose clamp or cutting away debris.
- **No Overkill**: You don't need a full mechanic's toolbox; just a device you can handle safely.

Car Fluids
- **Engine Oil, Coolant, Windshield Washer**: Top off if levels run low—avoids bigger damage or poor visibility.
- **Small Funnel**: Helps prevent spillage and keeps your hands cleaner.

Pro Tip: Check Shelf Life
Some fluids (like coolant) can degrade or leak if stored long. Inspect them occasionally.

DRIVER & PASSENGER COMFORT

Blanket & Warm Clothing
- **Cold Weather Saviors**: If you're stuck waiting for a tow in winter, a blanket staves off hypothermia.
- **Picnic Bonus**: Doubles as a cozy seat if you're waiting outdoors in milder weather.

Water & Non-Perishable Snacks
- **Long Delays**: Traffic jams or breakdowns can stretch hours—stay hydrated and keep hunger at bay.
- **Energy Boost**: Granola bars or nuts provide quick, mess-free sustenance.

Common Mistake: Forget the Water
In hot climates, dehydration can hit fast if you're stranded. Keep a few sealed bottles in the trunk.

PHONE-RELATED ESSENTIALS

Car Charger or Power Bank
- **Stay Connected**: A dead phone means no call for help, no GPS, no rescue from roadside boredom.
- **Power Bank vs. Charger**: One plugs into your car's 12V socket; the other works if the battery's dead. Both are good backups.

Paper Map
- **Electronics Fail**: If your phone or GPS glitches out, you can still navigate old-school style.
- **Minimal Space**: Folded in a glove box, it's a travel-lifesaver when signal or battery is gone.

Pro Tip: Offline Maps
Download maps for offline use or take a quick screenshot of your route before heading out—so you're not left stranded if your cell signal drops mid-drive.

SEASONAL ADD-ONS

Winter Gear
- **Ice Scraper & Small Shovel**: Clear windshields and dig out of light snowdrifts.
- **Traction Aids**: Sand, kitty litter, or traction mats help you escape icy patches.
- **Hand Warmers**: If you're stuck in frigid temps, these keep fingers functional.

Summer Gear
- **Extra Water**: Critical in scorching heat.
- **Sun Protection**: A reflective windshield shade keeps your car cooler; sunscreen helps if you're stuck outside.

Pro Tip: Rotate Seasonally
Don't lug around a shovel in July or pile blankets in August. Tailor your trunk to the climate.

COMMON MISTAKES & TIPS

Ignoring Maintenance
- **Car Care First**: A trunk full of gear won't help if your car never gets oil changes or tire checks.
- **Synergy**: Proper car maintenance plus a well-stocked roadside kit make the ultimate backup plan.

Overstuffing the Trunk
- **Organization**: A tangled mess of items in your trunk can slow you down in an emergency. Keep your roadside kit in a designated spot.
- **Easy Access**: Use a dedicated bin or bag to keep essential tools neat and within reach.

Regular Checks
- **Perishables & Expirations**: Snacks and car fluids can expire—do a quick refresh every few months.
- **Refill After Use**: If you used up your tape or water supply, restock promptly.

Common Mistake: Forgetting to Practice

Ever tried changing a tire or hooking jumper cables only after you're stranded? A quick practice session helps avoid fumbling in real emergencies.

Pro Tip: Keep It Tidy

A neat trunk isn't just aesthetically pleasing—it ensures you can grab your roadside gear without wrestling luggage or random junk first.

"Just in case" is more than a phrase—it's a lifestyle for savvy drivers. By **loading up on essential safety items**, from a spare tire and a small fire extinguisher to snacks and power banks, you'll cruise with confidence that minor mishaps won't turn catastrophic. Whether it's a dead battery or unexpected snowdrift, a simple stash of the right tools and supplies can turn "Uh-oh!" into "No worries, I've got this." So be that driver everyone's grateful to have around—you might never need to break out that kit, but if you do, you'll be ready to handle anything with a smile (and a fully charged phone).

60. KEEP YOUR CAR IN SHAPE: PERIODIC MAINTENANCE AND CHECK-UPS

Think of your car like an athlete—it performs best when it's fit. Regular check-ups and tune-ups aren't just fussy extras; they keep your vehicle **safe** and **reliable**. Regular **oil changes**, **belt checks**, and **tune-ups** keep performance sharp, and a **well-maintained engine** also helps you breeze through yearly inspections without last-minute scrambling. In this chapter, we'll explore the essentials of periodic maintenance, from fluid checks to tire rotations, plus a quick look at what inspectors typically check. Because giving your car a little TLC now means fewer breakdowns, fewer headaches, and a much happier relationship with the open road.

WHY PERIODIC MAINTENANCE MATTERS

Preventive Health for Your Car
- **Stop Small Problems Early**: A tiny oil leak or worn belt can become a major, budget-busting fix if ignored.
- **Reliability & Safety**: Crisp brake pads and fresh fluid mean your vehicle's ready to handle abrupt stops or long hauls without issues.

Annual Inspection
- **Local Requirements**: Many regions demand yearly check-ups on brakes, emissions, lights, tires, etc.
- **Aced Tests**: If you're proactive about maintenance, you'll save time and stress come inspection day—no last-minute scrambles to fix failing components.

Common Mistake: Waiting for a Problem
Don't adopt the "if it ain't broke..." approach. Regular upkeep prevents issues from ever hitting "broke" status.

BASIC ROUTINE CHECKS

Fluids: The Lifeblood of Your Car
- **Oil**: Check monthly—top up if low, and change at recommended intervals (often 3k-5k miles or as manual dictates).
- **Coolant, Brake Fluid, Power Steering**: A quick peek under the hood can reveal if levels dip too low, which can hamper performance or safety.

Filters & Belts
- **Air Filters (Engine & Cabin)**: Clogged filters strain your engine and worsen interior air quality. Swap them as guided in your manual.
- **Serpentine & Timing Belts**: If they fray or slip, your car could break down unexpectedly—catch wear signs early.

Tires & Pressure
- **Tread Depth**: Bald tires lose grip, especially in wet or snowy weather. Use the penny test or a tread gauge.
- **Inflation**: Proper pressure boosts fuel efficiency and handling, and is often checked during annual inspections.

Pro Tip: Pair It with Fill-Ups
Glance at your oil, coolant, and tire pressure every few gas station visits—it's a quick routine that saves grief later.

TIRE CARE & ALIGNMENT

Rotation & Wear
- **Regular Rotation**: Shifting tire positions (front to back, side to side) ensures even wear and extends tire life.
- **Uneven Patterns**: If one side is wearing faster, you might need an alignment or check for suspension issues.

Alignment & Balance
- **Signs of Misalignment**: Steering wheel pulling left/right, uneven tread, shaky wheel at certain speeds.
- **Fuel Economy**: Misaligned tires create drag, translating to more stops at the pump.

Common Mistake: Skipping Professional Tire Checks
A quick at-home glance doesn't reveal everything. Periodically let pros measure alignment/balance, especially if your manual suggests it.

SCHEDULED MAINTENANCE INTERVALS

Owner's Manual: Your Roadmap
- **Oil Changes & Beyond**: Spark plugs, brake checks, coolant flushes—your manual outlines them at set mileages or time intervals.
- **Milestone Services**: At 30k, 60k, 90k miles, bigger items like transmission fluid or timing belt replacements might come due.

Why Follow the Schedule
- **Maximized Vehicle Life**: Neglecting, say, a timing belt change can lead to catastrophic engine damage.
- **Higher Resale Value**: Well-documented maintenance can make your car more appealing if you sell it later—also helpful during an annual inspection to show it's in shape.

Pro Tip: Set Reminders
Use your phone's calendar or an app to ping you when service is due—no guesswork required.

DIY VS. PROFESSIONAL SERVICE

Simple Tasks at Home
- **Wiper Replacements**: Easy to swap; instantly improves visibility.
- **Top Off Fluids**: Windshield washer fluid, coolant (if you're confident), or power steering fluid (if you've read the manual).

Leave It to the Experts
- **Complex Repairs**: Transmission overhauls, advanced electronics, or anything you can't confidently handle.
- **Routine Inspections**: Mechanics spot leaks or part wear you might overlook, especially beneficial before your annual inspection.

Common Mistake: Tackling Advanced Fixes Blindly
YouTube can help, but be realistic. If you're out of depth, you risk bigger damage and bigger bills.

WHAT AN ANNUAL INSPECTION ENTAILS

Essential Items Checked
- **Brakes & Tires**: Thickness, tread, signs of uneven wear or brake pad life.
- **Lights & Signals**: Headlights (high/low beam), turn signals, brake lights, reverse lights, license plate lights.
- **Emissions & Exhaust**: Ensuring your vehicle meets local environmental standards.
- **Steering & Suspension**: Checking ball joints, shock absorbers, alignment for safety.

Passing with Flying Colors
- **Prep in Advance**: If you notice a worn wiper or out-of-whack alignment, fix it before inspection day.

- **Documentation**: Keep records of recent repairs or fluid changes—some states ask for that proof.

Post-Fix "Readiness" Cycles
- **ECU Markers:** After disconnecting the battery or making major repairs, your car's computer (ECU) may require several driving cycles before all readiness markers show "complete."
- **Avoid Immediate Testing:** Don't head straight for the inspection; give the ECU time to finish its self-checks or you could fail due to incomplete tests.

COMMON PITFALLS & TIPS

Ignoring Warning Lights
- **Dashboard Clues**: If the check engine, ABS, or tire pressure lights pop on, investigate. A small sensor fix might save a bigger issue.
- **Proactive Over Reactive**: The longer you wait, the costlier it could become—particularly if it's something the inspection will flag.

"I'll Do It Later" Mentality
- **Inching Toward Problems**: A squeaky belt or grinding brakes won't magically improve on their own.
- **Set a Schedule**: Whether it's seasonal swaps or every few thousand miles—pick a routine and stick to it.

Record Keeping
- **Maintenance Log**: Note the date, mileage, service done—plus keep receipts. Handy for resale or inspection verification.
- **Digital or Paper**: An app or a small folder in your glove box works fine—just use whichever method you'll actually stick to.

Common Mistake: Assuming "It's Fine"
Odd noises or small leaks are your car's cry for help—address them early before they turn into bigger problems.

Keeping an eye on your car's "figure" isn't about sweating the small stuff—it's about **confidence**, **safety**, and **saving money** in the long run. By following routine check-up schedules, topping off fluids, rotating tires, and documenting it all, you'll sail through annual inspections and daily drives alike. Preventive care stops small problems from bloating into big headaches. So grab that manual, set your reminders, and watch your ride stay in top shape—**because a healthy car is a happy car**, and a happy car makes for a much happier driver.

61. NAILED IT (LITERALLY): HERE'S HOW TO CHANGE A TIRE

You're cruising along when you hear that ominous **flap-flap** noise—uh-oh, a flat tire! It's like discovering a giant hole in your shoe: inconvenient, but fixable with the right know-how. Changing a tire is simpler than you might think, and it spares you from waiting on a tow truck or pleading with strangers for help. In this chapter, we'll cover the ins and outs of **safe tire swapping**, from spotting early signs of trouble to torquing those lug nuts in a star pattern.

SPOTTING A FLAT OR DAMAGED TIRE

Signs of Trouble
- **Dashboard Alert**: Many modern cars have low-pressure warnings—don't ignore that little symbol.
- **Wobbly Handling**: If your steering goes mushy or the ride feels bumpy, check your tires ASAP.
- **Sudden Thumping**: A rhythmic "thud" often signals under-inflation or a slow leak.

Pull Over Safely
- **Hazard Lights**: Let other drivers know you're in distress.
- **Look for Flat, Firm Ground**: Avoid slopes or soft shoulders—jack stability depends on it.

Common Mistake: Stopping in the Middle of Traffic
Limp along slowly (on hazard lights) until you find a safe spot. Don't risk changing a tire where cars whiz by inches away.

SAFETY FIRST & GATHERING TOOLS

Secure the Car
- **Parking Brake**: Prevents rolling while you're tinkering.
- **Wheel Chocks or Bricks**: Place them behind or in front of tires (opposite end of the flat) if you have them.

Essentials
- **Spare Tire (Inflated)**: Check it monthly—no point having a flat spare.

323

- **Jack & Lug Wrench**: Ensure they fit your car's lug nuts—some cars use special locking nuts.
- **Extras**: Gloves (for grime-free hands), flashlight (night-time changes), and a kneeling mat (your jeans will thank you).

Pro Tip: Review Instructions Now
Peek at your owner's manual or watch a quick how-to video beforehand. Confidence kills panic when the real deal hits.

CHANGING THE TIRE: STEP-BY-STEP

Loosen Lug Nuts (Before Jacking)
- **A Quarter to Half Turn**: Breaking them free on the ground is easier. When loosening the lug nuts, the order doesn't matter—but tightening is a different story. Follow the star pattern rule below.
- **Don't Fully Remove Yet**: Just enough so they're no longer stuck.

Jack It Up
- **Proper Placement**: Consult your manual for the recommended lift point—often a metal pinch weld. Placing the jack in the wrong spot can risk damage to your car's subframe.
- **Lift Until Tire Clears Ground**: An inch or so off the pavement is plenty.

Swap Tires
- **Remove Lug Nuts & Flat**: Keep track of nuts—use your pockets or a small container.
- **Mount the Spare**: Align wheel holes with studs, push on gently.

Tighten & Lower
- **Finger-Tight Lug Nuts**: Start threading them by hand first to avoid cross-threading. Then, lightly snug them with a wrench—just not to full torque yet. Tighten in a star pattern to keep the tension even. Ensure the wheel is properly aligned and flush against the hub before lowering the car.
- **Lower the Car**: Gently bring the jack down, then firmly tighten nuts with your wrench. Use a torque wrench and refer to your car's manual for the correct specifications.

Common Mistake: Skipping Final Torque
After lowering the car, give each lug nut a final tighten in a star pattern to ensure even pressure—loose nuts can cause wobbles or serious issues.

AFTER INSTALLATION: WHAT NEXT?

Driving on the Spare
- **Speed Limit**: Many donut spares cap around 50–55 mph. Full-size spares often handle normal speeds, but confirm your manual's guidelines.
- **Short-Term Fix**: A spare tire is a "get-home" or "get-to-shop" solution—repair or replace the damaged tire ASAP.

Seek Professional Help (If Needed)
- **Patch or Replacement**: A mechanic can advise if the old tire's salvageable.
- **Re-Torque**: If you have a torque wrench, double-check after a short drive, or ask a mechanic to confirm proper tightness.

Pro Tip: Practice in Your Driveway
Doing a quick "fake flat" change at home makes the real thing stress-free. Plus, you'll know if any crucial tool is missing.

COMMON MISTAKES & TIPS

Leaving Hazard Lights Off
- **Stay Visible**: Flick them on before you even step out—drivers need the heads-up you're stopped.
- **Reflective Triangles**: If you have them, set one behind your car, especially on highways.

Wrong Jack Placement
- **Plastic Bumpers**: Don't place the jack on fragile spots; find the metal lip or recommended spot from your manual.
- **Unlevel Ground**: Inclines increase the risk of the jack slipping.

Ignoring the Spare's Condition
- **Check Pressure**: Spares deflate over time. Ensure it's up to spec once a month or so.
- **Expired Donut?**: Old spares can degrade. If you've had it for ages, consider replacement.

Common Mistake: Panicking Mid-Process
Breathe. Changing a tire is methodical. Follow the steps, stay calm, and you'll be done in minutes.

Pro Tip: Celebrate the Win
Once you're rolling again, do a quick safety re-check after a few miles, then treat yourself—because fixing a flat single-handedly is a badge of driving honor!

Common Mistake: Postponing Tire Replacement
Driving on a donut is meant to be temporary. Get the damaged tire assessed or replaced soon.

A flat tire might not be on your agenda, but now you're ready to handle it like a pro. With the **right tools**, **a little patience**, and a **solid understanding** of the process, you can swap out that damaged tire and get back on the road safely. Just remember to double-check your work, keep your spare properly inflated, and schedule a permanent fix as soon as possible. A little preparation today can save you from a major headache tomorrow.

62. MANUAL VS. AUTOMATIC: THE GREAT GEARHEAD DEBATE

You're ready to buy or rent a car, or maybe just curious: **manual or automatic?** This topic can open a whole can of worms—especially if you dare bring it up around your friends. Manual transmissions offer a direct connection with the engine, while automatics promise smooth, effortless shifting. In this chapter, we'll pop open the gearbox, explore both worlds, and help you figure out which transmission suits your style. After all, whether you crave a hands-on approach or a laid-back ride, there's a "just right" answer for everyone.

BASIC TRANSMISSION OVERVIEW

What's in the "Box"?
- **Manual Gear Selection**: You press the clutch, pick the gear, and release the clutch to engage power—like being in sync with your engine.
- **Automatic Shifting**: The car's system decides when to shift gears, using fluid pressure or electronics—no clutch pedal required.

Beyond Just "Auto vs. Manual"
- **CVTs (Continuously Variable Transmissions)**: Use belts and pulleys for "infinite" gear ratios. Smooth, but can feel strange to some drivers.
- **Dual-Clutch & Semi-Automatics**: Offer lightning-fast shifts, bridging the gap between a pure manual and a traditional automatic.

Common Mistake: Thinking All Automatics Are the Same
Tech has evolved—some automatics are more efficient than old manuals, while certain CVTs maximize MPG. Know your options!

PROS & CONS OF MANUAL

Driver Engagement
- **Tactile Thrill**: Controlling each gear shift can be deeply satisfying, especially on winding roads.
- **Fuel Efficiency (Sometimes)**: Skilled drivers can eke out better MPG by optimizing shift points.

The Downsides
- **Learning Curve**: Stalling is normal while you master clutch control. And hills? They're a unique challenge!
- **Traffic Headaches**: Stop-and-go congestion means endless shifting—your left foot might beg for mercy.

Pro Tip: Practice in a Calm Area
Get comfy with the clutch on quiet backstreets or empty parking lots— no honks and less pressure.

PROS & CONS OF AUTOMATIC

Ease of Use
- **No Clutch, No Stress**: Automatics handle shifting, letting you focus on steering and traffic.
- **Smooth in Traffic**: Creeping along in a jam is less hassle—no constant shifting or stalling fear.

The Downsides
- **Less Involvement**: Performance enthusiasts may find it less engaging.
- **Maintenance**: Automatic transmissions can be pricier to fix if something goes wrong. And fluid changes are often overlooked by drivers.

Common Mistake: Forgetting Fluid Changes
Automatic gearboxes need their own fluid changed periodically—skip it, and repairs become wallet-busting.

COST & MAINTENANCE CONSIDERATIONS

Manual Clutch Replacements
- **Wear & Tear**: Riding the clutch or poor shifting habits can accelerate clutch wear.
- **Costs**: Clutch replacement can be expensive, but typically less complex than an automatic overhaul.

Automatic Fluid & Repairs
- **Transmission Fluid**: Must be clean and at proper levels—dirty fluid leads to slipping gears.
- **Rebuilds**: Automatic rebuilds can cost a small fortune if major damage occurs. Prevention beats pricey fixes.

Resale Value
- **Market Preferences**: In some places, manuals are hard to resell because fewer people want them. Elsewhere, a sporty manual might command a premium from enthusiasts.

Pro Tip: Drive Gently
Whether manual or automatic, smooth acceleration and careful shifting reduce strain, prolonging transmission life.

GLOBAL POPULARITY & CULTURAL DIFFERENCES

European vs. North American Trends
- **Manual Dominance (Europe)**: Fuel prices and tradition keep manuals common. Many learn on a stick from the start.
- **Automatic Norm (North America)**: City traffic plus convenience means most U.S./Canadian drivers learn auto first.

Changing Tides
- **Advanced Automatics**: Modern technology narrows the MPG and performance gap.
- **Younger Drivers**: Some want manual for the "cool factor," but the convenience of auto transmissions still wins many hearts.

Common Mistake: Assuming Everyone's System Is the Same
Travel overseas? Manual rentals might be the norm, so practice or risk stalling across foreign landscapes.

HOW TO CHOOSE

Lifestyle & Environment
- **City Commutes**: Heavy stop-and-go might make a manual burdensome; an automatic can spare you the repeated clutch drama.
- **Rural Roads & Fun Factor**: If you love twisty drives or you're a car enthusiast, manual offers a direct engine feel that's addictive.

Learning Goals
- **Gaining Skill**: Manual teaches you more about engine behavior—some say it makes you a more attentive driver.
- **Long-Term Ownership**: Factor in potential maintenance (clutch vs. transmission repairs) and local mechanic familiarity.

Feeling is believing—some folks switch sides once they experience the other option's pros.

COMMON MISTAKES & TIPS

Manual Shifting Errors
- **Riding the Clutch**: Constant partial engagement kills the clutch faster than you can say "burnt friction". If you do it, you'll smell it (the smell of burnt clutch is unmistakable).
- **Ignoring Strange Noises**: Grinding gears or squeaking pedal? Time to have the clutch assembly checked.

Automatic Overconfidence
- **Skipping Routine Checks**: Transmission fluid doesn't last forever—neglect it at your peril.
- **Forgetting Engine Braking**: Automatics still let you drop to lower gears on downhill stretches—master this trick to save your brakes! Flip back to the chapter on twisty roads for a refresher on why constant braking on steep inclines can spell trouble.

Final Considerations
- **Your Comfort Zone**: If you dread stalling on hills, maybe an auto is right. If you love a challenge, manual awaits.
- **No Wrong Answer**: Both can be smooth, fun, or efficient—it depends on your preference and environment.

Common Mistake: Locking Into Stereotypes
Manual = "only for racers," Automatic = "for lazy drivers"? Myths. Modern transmissions break these clichés daily.

Pro Tip: Change It Up
If you're used to automatic, try learning manual on a friend's car or a driving course. Expanding your skill set is never a bad move.

Manual or automatic, it's not a battle of good vs. evil—just different ways to engage with your car's heart and soul. **Manual transmissions** offer that intimate connection with the engine, appealing to those who crave control (and don't mind a calf workout in busy traffic). **Automatics** deliver convenience, making city crawls almost serene. Your choice? Weigh lifestyle, environment, and personal taste. Think of it as picking a musical instrument—both can produce beautiful results, but each demands its own rhythm.

63. WHAT'S THAT EXTRA PEDAL: A BEGINNER'S GUIDE TO DRIVING STICK

You sit down in the driver's seat, glance down, and see not two but **three** pedals: gas, brake, and... that mysterious clutch. Panic? Not if you learn the basics of **manual transmission driving**—the world where you orchestrate gear changes instead of letting the car do it. If you've ever wanted to feel more "connected" to your vehicle, this is your chance. In this chapter, we'll break down how to **start, shift, and not stall** while tackling everything from gentle cruising to hill starts, and remind you that manual is just an extra step in the driving adventure.

UNDERSTANDING THE CLUTCH PEDAL & GEAR SHIFTER

Clutch Basics
- **Disconnecting Engine & Transmission**: When you press the clutch, you're temporarily "unhooking" the engine from the wheels, letting you change gears without grinding metal.
- **Gear Patterns**: Most manuals have an "H" layout (1st at top-left, 2nd at bottom-left, etc.). Some cars have 5 gears plus reverse, others 6 or more—consult your car's manual.

The Joy of Engagement
- **Control Freaks Rejoice**: Each shift is your call, from mellow upshifts to rowdy downshifts.
- **Listening to the Engine**: In a manual, engine revs become your guide—shift when it sounds right, not just when a gauge says so.

Common Mistake: Forgetting Reverse Layout
Many cars place reverse differently—lift a collar, push down, or find it near 1st gear. Know yours before you panic, thinking you have no reverse!

BASIC STARTING & SHIFTING TECHNIQUES

Finding the Bite Point
- **Clutch + Gas Combination**: Gently release the clutch while slowly pressing the gas. The spot where the car starts rolling is the "bite point."
- **Smooth Release**: Jerky starts mean you're letting the clutch out too fast or giving too little gas. Patience and practice fix that.

331

Upshifts & Downshifts
- **Upshifting**: Let off the gas, press the clutch, shift up a gear, then smoothly release the clutch while reapplying gas. Voila—new gear!
- **Downshifting**: Similar but might need a slight "blip" of throttle to match engine RPMs for a smoother transition.

Pro Tip: Listen Up
Instead of watching the tachometer religiously, tune in to engine sound. If it's screaming, upshift; if it's chugging, downshift or add gas.

HANDLING HILLS & TRAFFIC

Hill Starts
- **The Fear**: Rolling backward is every new manual driver's nightmare.
- **Techniques**:
  - **Parking Brake Assist**: Engage the handbrake, ease the clutch and gas until bite point, then release brake.
  - **Quick Feet**: Release brake while giving enough gas so you don't roll. Takes practice!
- **The Pro Test**: Feeling confident? Put yourself to the ultimate test with an uphill, reverse lateral parking maneuver starting from a standstill (try not to burn your clutch to a crisp while you're at it).

Stop-and-Go Situations
- **Clutch Wear Warning**: Riding the clutch in bumper-to-bumper traffic kills it quickly.
- **Smooth Creeping**: Move slowly in first gear or find a gap to shift to second if traffic speeds up—just remain vigilant for sudden stops.

Common Mistake: Staying in 1st Gear Too Long
In slow traffic, you can shift to 2nd if there's space. Constantly revving 1st might jerk your car and overwork the clutch.

SHIFTING TIPS & DRIVER ENGAGEMENT

Engine Sound & RPM
- **Know Your Car's Sweet Spot**: Some engines prefer lower RPM shifts, others enjoy revs for better power.
- **Smooth or Sporty?**: Gentle shifts suit daily commutes, higher RPM shifts give pep if you want performance.

Rev-Matching (Advanced Move)
- **Downshifting Without Jerk**: Blip the throttle briefly while clutch is in, so when you re-engage, engine speed matches wheel speed.
- **Feels Pro**: This technique leads to buttery-smooth downshifts and fewer squeaks or jolts.

Pro Tip: Enjoy the Connection
Manual driving turns your car into an instrument—each gear change is a chord change, and you're the maestro.

COMMON MISTAKES & THEIR CONSEQUENCES

Riding the Clutch
- **Partial Pressure**: Keeping your foot on the pedal halfway is a quick route to wearing out the clutch—also known for a burnt smell.
- **The "Stink"**: If you do it, you'll sense that distinct hot, friction odor—time to ease up.

Skipping Gears & Jerky Shifts
- **Is Skipping OK?**: Occasionally skipping from 3rd to 5th is fine if revs align. Just ensure you're not lugging the engine.
- **Jerky Changes**: Typically, from mismatched engine speed. Practice the gas-clutch timing until shifts feel natural.

Common Mistake: Abusing 1st Gear
Holding 1st until high RPM or dragging it out too long. Shift up promptly once you're rolling.

MAINTAINING A MANUAL CAR

Clutch Wear & Replacement
- **Driving Style Impact**: Smooth transitions and minimal "clutch riding" prolong life significantly.
- **Signs of Slippage**: Engine revs rise but speed doesn't keep up—time for inspection or new clutch.

Transmission Fluid
- **Not Just Automatics**: Manuals also have fluid—usually gear oil that might need periodic changes.
- **Cables & Linkages**: If gear engagement feels stiff or notchy, a mechanic can adjust or replace worn components.

If shifts suddenly feel harder or the clutch pedal acts strange, get it checked before it becomes a costlier fix.

MASTERING CONFIDENCE & SAFETY

Practice in Low-Stress Zones
- **Empty Lots**: Get the hang of bite point, hill starts, and shifting with no pressure from honking traffic.
- **Short Errands**: Gradually introduce city streets or mild hills—build skill step by step.

Stalls Are Normal
- **No Shame**: Even pros stall occasionally, especially on awkward slopes. Breathe, restart, and move on.
- **Don't Panic**: If you stall in an intersection, turn hazards on, start calmly, and get going again—nobody died from a quick second of stall-time.

Common Mistake: Throwing in the Towel Too Soon
The first few tries can be frustrating, but muscle memory grows fast. Stick with it, and you'll soon shift with ease.

Pro Tip: Spread the Love
Already comfortable with manual? Pass the knowledge on—friends might be surprised how quickly they "get it" with a patient instructor.

Driving a manual transmission adds an extra pedal and a whole lot of fun (once you get past that initial learning curve). From the careful balance of clutch and gas to the sweet satisfaction of a perfectly rev-matched downshift, **manual driving** offers a unique, engaged relationship with your car's mechanics. Just be patient with hill starts, respect the clutch, and brace for a few stalls early on. Soon enough, you'll be shifting gears like a maestro—enjoying the direct control that automatics can't quite replicate. Ready to make those three pedals a normal part of your driving experience?

64. AFTERMARKET MODS: JUST BECAUSE YOU CAN, DOESN'T MEAN YOU SHOULD

Have you ever seen a sleek, souped-up car and wondered, "How'd they get it to look (and sound) so cool?" Enter the world of **aftermarket parts**—ranging from performance-boosting exhausts and suspensions to stylish rims and interior upgrades. These aren't just for "gearheads" craving speed; they can also enhance handling, comfort, or just give your car a unique flair. But buyer beware: not all modifications are created equal, and some might even be **illegal** depending on local laws. In this chapter, we'll explore the many ways you can **personalize** your car's looks and performance, what each type of mod does, and how to stay on the right side of the law (and your insurance policy).

WHAT ARE AFTERMARKET PARTS?

Definition & Variety
- **Non-OEM Goodies**: These are parts not supplied by your car's original manufacturer. They come from third-party brands catering to different budgets and styles.
- **From Mild to Wild**: Options run the gamut—**performance mods** (engine, exhaust, suspension), **cosmetic tweaks** (body kits, spoilers), and **comfort upgrades** (infotainment systems, seats).

Potential Benefits
- **Cost Savings**: Often cheaper than OEM replacements.
- **Personal Touch**: Customize your car's look, feel, and performance in ways the factory never did.

PROS & CONS OF AFTERMARKET UPGRADES

The Upside
- **Performance Gains**: A better intake, exhaust, or turbo kit can genuinely boost horsepower and torque, or improve fuel economy.
- **Aesthetic Enhancements**: Body kits, spoilers, or new rims can transform a car's personality—leading to those "wow" looks.
- **Cost & Selection**: Aftermarket often means cheaper alternatives than OEM, plus a broad menu of style choices.

The Downside
- **Quality Variance**: Some brands cut corners. A crappy exhaust might rust or rattle, cheap body kits can misalign or crack.
- **Warranty & Legality**: Installing certain mods might void parts of your car's warranty. Plus, some states ban specific mods (like loud exhausts or neon underglow).

Pro Tip: Research, Research, Research
A little online forum digging or YouTube reviews can warn you if certain upgrades fail early or don't deliver on promises.

PERFORMANCE MODS: THE ENGINE & BEYOND

Engine & Exhaust
- **Air Intakes**: Improve airflow to the engine, potentially upping power slightly and giving a throatier sound.
- **Headers & Cat-Back Exhausts**: Reduce exhaust restriction, adding horsepower and often a sporty roar.
- **Turbochargers & Superchargers**: Major horsepower jumps, but require thorough supporting mods (fuel, cooling, tuning).

Suspension & Brakes
- **Lowering Springs & Coilovers**: Enhances handling by dropping the car's center of gravity—less body roll in corners.
- **Performance Brake Kits**: Bigger brake discs and pads withstand heat, offering stronger, consistent stopping power—ideal for spirited driving or track days.

Common Mistake: Forgetting a Proper Tune
Bolt-on upgrades can be worthless without an ECU retune. A mismatch of parts and factory engine mapping might yield poor results or reliability issues.

COSMETIC & STYLE ENHANCEMENTS

Body Kits & Spoilers
- **Aerodynamics & Looks**: Some claim better airflow or downforce; often it's purely visual.
- **Material Matters**: Fiberglass can crack easily, while carbon fiber is light but costly. Polyurethane is a middle ground for durability.

Wheels & Tires
- **Rims & Offsets**: Proper size ensures no rubbing on wheel wells. Wider rims can improve grip but might hamper fuel economy.
- **Tire Upgrades**: Performance tires can drastically improve handling, but watch for faster wear.

Interior Touches
- **Shift Knobs, Seat Upgrades**: A racing seat might hold you snugly in corners, but comfort on long trips might suffer.
- **Infotainment**: Aftermarket head units, sound systems, or custom gauge clusters can modernize older cars.

Pro Tip: Subtle Over Gaudy
A cohesive look often beats piling on random flashy bits. Consistency ensures your car doesn't scream "Frankenstein mods."

LEGAL & SAFETY CONSIDERATIONS

Street Legality
- **Noise & Emissions**: Loud exhausts or removed catalytic converters can breach local laws. Some states have decibel limits or strict smog tests.
- **Lighting Mods**: Neon underglow, strobe brake lights—cool in some places, illegal in others.

Insurance Impact
- **Premium Hikes**: Big engine mods or custom bodywork might boost your insurance rates.
- **Specialized Coverage**: If your car is heavily modified, you might need a policy that recognizes those upgrades.

Safety Inspections
- **Install Quality**: A poorly fitted spoiler can become airborne at high speed. Shaky wheels or untested brake kits can fail under stress.
- **Crucial Checks**: Some states require annual inspections—subpar or illegal mods could fail you instantly.

Common Mistake: Ignoring Local Laws
Always check your state's stance on tinted windows, exhaust volume, or ride height. Avoid fines (or forced removal) after investing in pricey mods.

CHOOSING QUALITY PARTS

Brand Reputation
- **Known Manufacturers**: Companies with proven track records cost more but often guarantee fitment and reliability.
- **Research & Reviews**: Car forums, YouTube channels, and social media groups are treasure troves of user experiences.

Professional Installation vs. DIY
- **Complex Mods**: Turbo kits, coilovers, or big-brake conversions might need advanced mechanical expertise.
- **DIY Simplicity**: Simple bolt-ons, intakes, shift knobs, or cosmetic bits are often easy for novices with basic tools.

BUDGETING & MAINTENANCE

Cost vs. Benefit
- **Performance Gains**: An upgraded intake and exhaust can provide a slight power increase, but a full engine rebuild comes with a hefty price tag. Weigh the performance benefits against the investment.
- **Aesthetics ROI**: Wheels, spoilers, or custom paint can look awesome. Just remember you might not recoup that expense on resale.

Ongoing Care
- **Frequent Checks**: Performance brake pads can wear faster. Custom suspensions might need periodic alignments.
- **Document Everything**: If you love modifying your car, keep receipts and maintenance records—they'll come in handy if you ever decide to sell.

Common Mistake: Overloading Mods
Stacking mismatched mods can hurt performance—think a high-powered engine with weak brakes or oversized rims that wreck ride quality.

COMMON MISTAKES & TIPS

Over-Modification
- **Clashing Mods**: A huge spoiler on a low-powered sedan might look out of place; giant wheels with stock suspension can hamper performance.
- **Daily Drivability**: Extreme lowering can scrape speed bumps or hamper turning in daily routines.

Ignoring Compatibility
- **ECU Tuning**: Many engine mods only work well if your engine's computer adjusts fueling/ignition accordingly.
- **Suspension Geometry**: Lowering or stiffer springs can throw off alignment angles, leading to uneven tire wear or poor handling.

Slow & Steady
- **Start Small**: Try a mild exhaust or upgraded brake pads before going all-in with turbos and ECU custom tuning.
- **Ask the Community**: Car clubs and forums love discussing mods—learn from others' successes and fails.

Pro Tip: Have a Vision
Decide early: Do you want a sleek cruiser, a track-day warrior, or a unique show car? A clear plan prevents random, mismatched additions.

Pro Tip: Test It Out
After installing new mods, go on a gentle drive to feel any changes in handling, sound, or power—don't just gun it on the highway untested.

Aftermarket mods can elevate your car's style, power, or comfort—but they demand **research, caution, and a realistic budget**. Fitting the wrong part or ignoring local laws can land you in hot water (or with a car that drives like a clown show). Whether you're aiming for a **subtle sporty edge** or **full-throttle transformation**, approach upgrades step by step. Buy reputable brands, consider professional installation for complex mods, and keep safety (and the law) at the forefront. In the end, **driving in style** can be fun—but only if it's done responsibly.

65. NEED FOR SPEED: EXPLORE RACING WITHOUT BREAKING THE LAW

So you've realized that simply commuting from A to B isn't enough. You crave **adrenaline, strategy, and the roar of an engine** under pressure. Welcome to the world of **racing**, where drivers of all backgrounds come together to test their limits (and their cars). From weekend autocross sessions to full-blown circuit battles, there's a motorsport niche for everyone. In this chapter, we'll introduce you to the **types of racing**, the **safety gear and licenses** you might need, and how to dip your toe (or entire foot) into organized competitions. Get ready to fuel that passion—legally and responsibly!

DIFFERENT TYPES OF RACING

Circuit & Track Days
- **Lap-Based Fun**: Circle around professional or amateur tracks. Speeds can be high, but the environment is controlled—guard rails, run-off areas, corner marshals.
- **From Casual to Pro**: Some local clubs host track days open to novices. You can show up with your daily driver (within reason!) and learn track lines, braking points, and apexes.

Autocross & Time Attack
- **Short & Technical**: Usually set in large parking lots or small closed courses. Drivers navigate a coned path aiming for the best time.
- **Precision Over Power**: You won't always need big horsepower. Skillful handling and smooth lines often trump raw speed.

Common Mistake: Confusing Speed with Skill
Especially in autocross, a well-driven low-power car can outrun a high-horsepower beast that's sliding all over the place.

SAFETY & LICENSING

Protective Gear
- **Helmet & Suit**: Most organized events require at least a certified helmet. More advanced series want fire-resistant suits, gloves, and shoes.

- **Roll Cages & Harnesses**: At higher levels, or for track cars, steel cages and racing harnesses protect you during high-speed collisions.

Driver Training & Certification
- **Basic Course**: Many organizations or schools teach race fundamentals—like corner entry, threshold braking (braking as hard as possible just before the tires lose traction and lock up), and track etiquette.
- **Racing Licenses**: If you aim for competition (club or pro), you'll often need a special license. Different tiers let you enter different race classes.

Pro Tip: Take a Class
Even if you've clocked thousands of street miles, track driving is different. A short training course can pay huge dividends in skill and safety.

GETTING STARTED & LOCAL CLUBS

Beginner-Friendly Events
- **Track Days**: Also called "open lapping" or "HPDE (High-Performance Driver Education)." Usually instructor-led, you learn to handle your car at speed.
- **Autocross**: A low-cost, low-risk introduction, with speeds rarely exceeding highway norms but focusing on technique.

Community & Mentoring
- **Car Clubs**: Groups like the SCCA (Sports Car Club of America) or local rally clubs connect novices with veterans who love to share tips.
- **Rentals & Ride-Alongs**: Some tracks let you rent or do "arrive-and-drive" deals, or you can ride passenger with an instructor to see how it's done before gripping the wheel.

Common Mistake: Jumping Straight to Pro Gear
Don't blow your savings on a dedicated race car right away. Start small, see if you truly love it, then invest further.

BUDGET & COSTS

Entry Fees & Equipment
- **Range of Expense**: An autocross day might cost you tens of dollars, while a full track weekend can run hundreds or more. Pro-level events go way higher.

- **Gear Investments**: Helmets, suits, and gloves have certification periods—expect replacements as rules update (roughly every few years).

Tires, Fuel & Consumables
- **Wear & Tear**: Spirited driving chews through brake pads, tires, and even engine oil faster.
- **Planning for Replacements**: Factor these into your racing budget—shredded tires or overheated brakes can cut a day short if you're unprepared.

Pro Tip: Sponsorship Isn't Just for TV
At higher levels, local shops or businesses might sponsor you. But building skill and exposure first is key to attracting them.

PROGRESSION & COMPETITIONS

Amateur to Pro
- **Racing Ladder**: Clubs feed into regional championships, then national levels if you climb the ranks.
- **Points & Seasons**: In many series, you accumulate points each race, culminating in a season champion.

Finding Your Specialty
- **Drifting**: Focus on style and angle control.
- **Endurance**: Testing reliability over hours or even days.
- **Touring & GT Cars**: Door-to-door circuit battles with production-based car models.

Common Mistake: Skipping Experience Building
Jumping classes too quickly can be overwhelming. Master each level's challenge before moving up.

CULTURE & COMMUNITY

Motorsport Atmosphere
- **Pit Lane Camaraderie**: Sharing tools, jokes, and occasional band-aid fixes. Racers bond over mechanical heartbreaks and triumphs.
- **Spectator Fun**: Many events are like festivals—barbecues, live music, and families cheering from stands.

Team vs. Solo
- **Crews & Setups**: Rally or endurance events require co-drivers, pit crews, or advanced logistical planning.
- **Solo Efforts**: Autocross is typically just you and your car—simple, direct, minimal fuss.

Pro Tip: Embrace the Social Side
Chat with fellow drivers—many are eager to share advice, tools, or even ride-alongs to help you learn.

RESPONSIBLE DRIVING & TRACK ETIQUETTE

Respect for Rules
- **Flag Signals**: Colors and patterns mean caution, debris on track, or a need to pit. Missing these leads to accidents or penalties.
- **Clean Overtaking**: Deliberate contact is frowned upon in most series—rubbing might be "racing," but full-on banging is not.

Keep Racing on the Track
- **Public Roads Aren't Raceways**: Street racing is illegal and dangerous. Save that adrenaline for sanctioned events.
- **Apply Skills Wisely**: Better awareness from track experience can improve your daily driving, but always obey speed limits off-track.

Common Mistake: Transferring Track Ego to Streets
Don't let your newfound skills tempt you to show off on highways. Speed belongs in the right environment.

COMMON MISTAKES & TIPS

Overestimating Skill
- **Crash Risk**: Attempting pro-level speeds too soon can cause spin-outs or collisions.
- **Ramp Up Gradually**: Master fundamentals of braking, cornering, and track awareness at moderate pace.

Ignoring Car Maintenance
- **Stressing Parts**: Racing puts extra load on brakes, tires, and engine. Pre- and post-race inspections are essential.
- **Fluid Checks**: Coolant and oil matter more under track stress. Overheating is a common rookie pitfall.

Start with Instruction
- **Mentor Advantage**: Trackside tips or in-car coaching from an instructor can accelerate your driving skills dramatically.
- **Confidence Builder**: Knowing you're not alone at your first event calms nerves and raises enjoyment.

Pro Tip: Enjoy the Journey

The best part of racing is the **process**—improving lap times, meeting fellow enthusiasts, and conquering new track layouts. Embrace every twist and turn.

Pro Tip: Gradual Progress

Dive in step by step: attend a track day, do a few ride-alongs, maybe volunteer as a marshal to learn from the inside out.

Common Mistake: Expecting Instant Stardom

Rarely do amateurs jump straight to podiums. Racing is about learning curves—pun intended! Enjoy each incremental improvement.

If your heart races every time you see a checkered flag, it might be time to scratch that motorsport itch. Whether you choose an **autocross weekend** or dream of **circuit racing**, the track world welcomes newbies with open arms. Just remember: safety gear, patience, and plenty of practice (plus a healthy respect for budgets and mechanical upkeep) keep your newfound passion both exhilarating and safe. Buckle up, chase that apex, and find your perfect racing lane—**the finish line** might be just the start of your next big adventure.

PART V:

STAYING SAFE WHEN YOU'RE NOT DRIVING

66. PEDESTRIAN SMARTS
SO YOU DON'T BECOME A HEADLINE

Walking is as old as humanity—yet modern roads are full of fast-moving cars, hurried drivers, and a hundred distractions. You might be traveling on foot for exercise, to run errands, or simply because it's an eco-friendly choice. But stepping out among traffic demands awareness and strategy. In this chapter, we'll learn how to **stand out**, **avoid hazards**, and **remain vigilant** so you can stay out of trouble. Ready to give your "pedestrian game" a power-up?

VISIBILITY & AWARENESS

Bright or Reflective Clothing
- **Dress to Be Seen**: In low-light or nighttime conditions, a reflective band or light-colored jacket can alert drivers earlier to your presence.
- **Flashlights or Phone Lights**: If walking at night, shining a small light when crossing helps ensure drivers see you.

Maintain Eye Contact
- **Spot the Driver**: Before stepping off a curb, look at the driver's face or headlights. If they're not looking your way, they might not realize you're crossing.
- **Never Assume**: Just because it's a marked crosswalk or the "Walk" signal is on doesn't guarantee drivers will stop or yield.

Common Mistake: Invisible Mode
Wearing all-black at night with headphones blaring can make you practically vanish to drivers. Stand out, not blend in!

CROSSWALK & INTERSECTION ETIQUETTE

Use Marked Crosswalks
- **Predictability**: Drivers expect pedestrians at corners and crosswalks. Jaywalking in the middle of a block raises the risk they won't see you.
- **Wait for Signals**: "Walk/Don't Walk" or traffic lights control flow. Rushing on a stale yellow is tempting, but cars might also speed through.

Look Left-Right-Left
- **Double Check**: Even if you have the right-of-way, scanning for turning vehicles or speeding cars prevents surprises.
- **Turning Lanes**: Cars turning right may be laser-focused on other cars, not you. Be ready to pause if they don't brake.

Pro Tip: Be an Active Walker
Think like a driver—notice who's signaling for a turn, who's speeding, or if the cross street has a blind corner. That awareness is your shield.

AVOIDING DISTRACTIONS

"Zombie Walking"
- **Phones Off the Sidewalk**: Texting or gaming while walking can lead to collisions with poles, other pedestrians, or stepping off a curb at the wrong time.
- **Headphones Volume**: Keep it low enough to hear car horns or engine noise, giving you an audio cue if something's amiss.

Eyes on the Environment
- **Look Up, Not Down**: The more you see, the more time you have to react.
- **Conversing Cautiously**: Chatting with friends is fun, but if you're crossing a busy road, give the moment full attention.

Common Mistake: Tunnel-Vision on Screens
If you must use your phone, step aside into a safe spot—don't drift across traffic with your nose buried in a text.

NIGHTTIME & POOR VISIBILITY TIPS

Reflective Accessories
- **Light Up**: A reflective armband, a bright hat, or clip-on LED helps cars spot you from afar.
- **Carry a Small Light**: A flashlight or phone light can also show drivers your presence when crossing.

Stay in Lit Areas
- **Choose Streetlights**: Well-lit streets reduce the chance of hidden obstacles and help drivers see you sooner.
- **Darker Routes**: If you must walk through a dim area, proceed slowly, sticking to the edge of the path.

Pro Tip: Plan Your Walk
If your route at night has a safer, well-lit alternative, take it—even if it's a minute longer. Safety first.

RIGHT-OF-WAY VS. REALITY

Not All Drivers Yield
- **Legal ≠ Reality**: You might have the right-of-way, but a distracted or speeding driver could ignore it.
- **Stay Alert**: Remain ready to jump back if a car doesn't stop or turns without signaling.

Oncoming Turns
- **Turning Vehicles**: Especially left-turners might be scanning oncoming traffic, not looking for a walker in the crosswalk.
- **Make Eye Contact**: A brief glance to ensure they see you could save you from a near-miss.

Common Mistake: Blind Trust
The law says drivers should stop for pedestrians—but some drivers miss or ignore the rules. Keep your guard up!

ADDITIONAL SAFETY PRACTICES

Walk Facing Traffic (If No Sidewalk)
- **Better Visibility**: If forced onto the roadside, walk on the left so you can see cars coming at you, not behind you.
- **Swerve Space**: You can move aside quickly if a car drifts your way.

Children's Safety
- **Adult Supervision**: Teach kids to cross at corners, press the crosswalk button, and never dash between parked cars.
- **Set the Example**: If you run through a "Don't Walk," kids might think that's okay. Show them safe habits.

Alcohol & Drugs
- **Impaired Walking**: You can be a hazard to yourself if your reflexes or judgment are dulled.
- **Plan a Safe Stroll**: If you've been partying, walk with a buddy or arrange safer transport.

Common Mistake: Ignoring Driveways and Alleys
Cars can pop out of hidden spots quickly—don't assume a parked car won't suddenly reverse or pull forward.

COMMON MISTAKES & TIPS

Ignoring Driveways & Alleys
- **360-Degree Awareness**: Keep an eye on tail lights or engine noise as signs a car might emerge.
- **Slow Step**: Approaching an alley or driveway, glance left-right-left again.

Overconfidence
- **Headphones & Hoodies**: They reduce your peripheral vision and hearing. Fine for a lazy park stroll, but risky near busy roads.
- **Waiting a Second**: If uncertain, pause an extra second or two—nobody gets ticketed for crossing "too slowly."

If Unsure, Don't Rush
- **Better Late**: A few seconds' wait can spare an accident. You can't always trust others to do the right thing.
- **Walk Predictably**: Sudden mid-block dashes confuse drivers—avoid playing frogger on multi-lane roads.

Pro Tip: Use Your Ears
Cars can sneak up from behind or a side street. Be aware of engine revs, squealing tires, or honking—it all helps you react faster.

Common Mistake: Zoning Out
Whether daydreaming or diving into your phone, losing situational awareness can lead to close calls or worse. Keep those eyes up and ears open!

Walking might be the simplest form of transportation, but modern streets are busy, and not every driver is on top of their game. By **staying visible, avoiding distractions**, and **anticipating drivers' blind spots**, you keep your footsteps safe—morning walk, lunch break errands, or late-night stroll included. Remember: **the right-of-way** doesn't stop a careless driver from ignoring you, so stay engaged and cautious. Enjoy your walks with confidence and peace of mind… and maybe a reflective strip or two after sunset.

67. HOW CYCLISTS
CAN STAY SAFE AROUND CARS

Pedaling past rush-hour traffic, feeling the breeze against your face—biking can be a fantastic way to get around and stay healthy. But roads built with cars in mind demand **extra awareness** from cyclists. Whether you're commuting to work or enjoying a weekend ride, a few straightforward tips can help you stay upright, visible, and safe. In this chapter, we'll cover everything from bright clothing to route selection, ensuring you conquer each ride with a grin (and maybe a little sweat).

VISIBILITY & PROTECTIVE GEAR

Bright Clothing & Reflectors
- **Stand Out**: Vibrant jerseys or reflective accents catch a driver's eye before it's too late—especially at dawn, dusk, or night.
- **Reflectors & Lights**: At night, a front white light and rear red light aren't just helpful—they're often required by law.

Helmet Up
- **Proper Fit**: A helmet that wiggles around or perches too high won't protect well. Strap it snugly so it stays in place.
- **Life Saver**: A quality helmet can reduce serious head injuries. If it's done its job once in a crash, replace it.

Common Mistake: Wearing Black at Night
Dressing in dark colors while riding after sunset can turn you invisible to drivers. A reflective vest or armbands can be an easy fix.

PROPER ROAD POSITION & SIGNALING

Taking the Lane
- **Don't Hug the Gutter**: Riding too close to the curb can lead to hitting potholes, drain grates, or opening car doors.
- **Legal in Many Places**: Often, it's safer to be a bit more centered, so cars pass only when they can truly see you.

Hand Signals
- **Clear Communication**: Extend your left arm straight out to signal a left turn; bend it upward for a right turn (or use your right arm).

- **Stopping Alert**: An arm bent down with the palm facing back is a universal "I'm stopping" cue.

Pro Tip: Think Like a Driver
If you were driving, how would you want a cyclist to behave so you could predict their moves? That's how you want to ride.

FOLLOW TRAFFIC LAWS

Obey Lights & Signs
- **No Running Reds**: Blowing through a light or stop sign might save seconds but can lead to collisions.
- **Right-of-Way**: If it's your turn, take it—but keep scanning for drivers who might cut you off.

Predictability
- **Act Like a Vehicle**: Ride with traffic (not against it, like a pedestrian would), use the correct side of the street, and merge or switch lanes cautiously.

Common Mistake: Assuming Cars Will Always Yield
Even if you have priority, some drivers might be distracted or ignorant. Plan for them not to stop, just in case.

BEWARE OF BLIND SPOTS & CAR DOORS

Parked Cars & "Dooring"
- **Door Zone**: A suddenly opened door can throw you off balance. Keep a buffer if the street layout allows.
- **Scan Ahead**: Look for brake lights or heads in the driver's seat—signs a door might swing open.

Large Vehicles
- **Avoid Side-Hugging**: Trucks and buses have massive blind spots. If you must pass, do so confidently and quickly when safe—don't linger beside them.

Pro Tip: Eyes Front, Eyes Side
Flick your gaze at windows or side mirrors to see if someone's about to exit a parked car.

NIGHT RIDING & POOR VISIBILITY

Lights Are Essential
- **Front & Rear**: A bright white headlight helps oncoming traffic see you, while a red tail light or reflector warns cars behind.
- **Recharge or Replace**: Keep them fresh—dim lights are almost as bad as no lights.

Route Choices
- **Well-Lit Streets**: Skip that dark shortcut. Better to add a few minutes in exchange for streetlights and more drivers seeing you.
- **Reflective Extras**: A reflective ankle band or helmet sticker further boosts your presence in car headlights.

Common Mistake: Forgetting to Check Battery Levels
If your front light dies mid-ride, you're nearly invisible from the front. Top off that charge before every night ride.

BIKE MAINTENANCE

Brakes & Tires
- **Brake Pads**: Worn pads reduce stopping power; replace them promptly. Check cables for fraying.
- **Tire Pressure**: Correct inflation = better control and fewer flats. Pinch test or use a gauge.

Chain & Gears
- **Lubricate Regularly**: A squeaky chain can seize up or snap. A little chain lube goes a long way.
- **Gear Shifts**: If shifting feels clunky or delayed, a simple tune-up or derailleur adjustment might fix it.

Pro Tip: Pre-Ride Scan
A quick "ABC" check—Air (tires), Brakes, Chain—makes sure your ride's ready before you roll.

STAYING ALERT & AVOIDING DISTRACTIONS

Headphones & Phones
- **One Earbud Rule**: In some places it's legal if one ear is free, but ideally, keep both ears open to hear traffic.
- **Pull Over to Text**: If you must check your phone, find a safe spot—texting on the move is a recipe for crashes.

Road Scanning
- **Constant Vigilance**: Look up the road, check side streets, glance behind occasionally. Your environment changes quickly in traffic.
- **Potential Surprises**: Loose pets, potholes, or a sudden leftover construction cone—be ready to adjust.

Common Mistake: Zoning Out
Long rides can become routine, but losing focus can lead to missing a hazard. Stay mentally present.

AVOID AGGRESSIVE MANEUVERS

Ride Predictably
- **No Zigzagging**: Quick lane switches or weaving between parked cars can confuse drivers. A steady path is safer.
- **Slow for Intersections**: Even if you think it's clear, a quick glance can prevent a nasty T-bone with an unexpected driver.

Intersection Etiquette
- **Claim Your Space**: If turning left, move into the left turn lane properly—drivers are used to vehicles occupying that space.
- **Don't Surprise**: Signal intentions early. Drivers need time to register you're not going straight.

Pro Tip: Respect for Others
You want drivers to treat you safely—return the favor by following the rules and being courteous on the road.

Pro Tip: Community Rides
Join local biking clubs or group rides. You'll learn from seasoned riders, discover safer routes, and never have to tackle unfamiliar roads alone.

Common Mistake: Assuming a Car Sees You
No eye contact or wheels angled toward you? Be ready for evasive action.

Cycling isn't just good for your health or the planet—it can be downright fun. But roads built with cars in mind mean **you** must ride proactively, staying visible, obeying traffic laws, and anticipating potential risks like stray doors or blind-spot merges. With the right gear (think helmet, lights, reflectors) and a heads-up attitude, you'll navigate city streets or country roads with ease. Embrace the freedom of two wheels, pedal confidently, and let the wind in your hair (under that helmet, of course) remind you of the simple joy of riding safe.

WHERE DO YOU GO FROM HERE?

Well, look at you go! Congratulations, you've made it to the finish line! But here's the thing about driving: the real lessons don't end when this book does. Every merge, parking job, missed turn, or "Oops, that was my exit" moment is part of your growth behind the wheel. You don't need to be perfect. You just need to keep learning.

Your Learning Doesn't End Here

You've picked up the fundamentals, the weird rules, the stuff nobody tells you, and the kind of wisdom that comes from both close calls and laugh-out-loud mistakes. Now it's time to take all that knowledge and actually use it out there—on highways, side streets, and twisty roads.

Keep the Good Stuff Coming

Want more tips? Need a refresher on something you forgot by Tuesday? Head over to **www.notadummy.com** for bonus goodies:
- Behind-the-scenes updates on future projects
- Fresh driving tips and seasonal checklists
- Printables for your glovebox (yes, actual checklists!)
- Links to recommended gear, safety gadgets, and more

Let's Connect!

I share bite-sized tips, relatable fails, and the occasional "what NOT to do" moments on social media. Follow me for:
- Polls, mini-quizzes, and funny observations from the road
- Encouragement from a fellow learner (yes, I'm still learning too)

Find me **@notadummydriver** on TikTok, Instagram, X, and YouTube.

If you picked up a new tip—or think I got something totally wrong—hit me up on my socials and let me know!

 If this book made you laugh, think, or check your blind spot twice, I'd love to hear from you. Your review helps other readers find the book and keeps projects like this in the fast lane. **Scan the QR code with your phone, or simply tap it if you're reading on Kindle.**

ONE MORE THING...

If you feel like you're the only one figuring this out as you go—you're not!

Every confident driver you see was once a nervous mess who forgot where the wipers were.

So give yourself some grace. You're learning, and that means you're already ahead of the curve.

Keep showing up. Keep driving forward.

And for the love of your bumper—use your turn signal!

See you out there,
my friend.